Second T

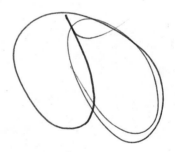

Second Takes

Remaking Film, Remaking America

ANDREW REPASKY MCELHINNEY

McFarland & Company, Inc., Publishers

Jefferson, North Carolina, and London

Frontispiece: John Gielgud in *Prospero's Books* (Peter Greenaway, 1992)—this adaptation of Shakespeare's *Tempest* is perhaps the first masterpiece of the media era (Photofest).

LIBRARY OF CONGRESS CATALOGUING-IN-PUBLICATION DATA

McElhinney, Andrew Repasky, 1978–
    Second takes : remaking film, remaking America / Andrew
Repasky McElhinney.
        p.   cm.
    Includes bibliographical references and index.

    ISBN 978-0-7864-7761-6
    softcover : acid free paper ∞

    1. Film remakes—United States—History and criticism.
2. Motion picture industry—United States—Technological
innovations.   3. Mass media—United States.   I. Title.

PN1995.9.R45M34 2013
791.43'6—dc23   2013030861

BRITISH LIBRARY CATALOGUING DATA ARE AVAILABLE

On the cover: Art Holiday Theater in Philadelphia (Photograph
by the author)

Manufactured in the United States of America

McFarland & Company, Inc., Publishers
  Box 611, Jefferson, North Carolina 28640
  www.mcfarlandpub.com

This work is dedicated
to three wonderful movie mentors:

RALPH HIRSHORN
who told me "a good projectionist fills the screen,"
and then loaned me his mint-condition Arri 16 mm camera with pistol grip

JACE GAFFNEY
who gave me a great cinematic education — introducing me to
Edgar G. Ulmer, Budd Boetticher, *Point Blank*, Douglas Sirk,
Rouben Mamoulian, *Le Soulier de Satin*, *The Night of the Hunter*,
Peter Ibbetson, *The Beguiled*, *Vivre Sa Vie*, Max Ophüls,
Reflections in a Golden Eye, Abraham Polonsky, *Ulzana's Raid*,
I Am Cuba, *Kiss Me Deadly*, *What Price Hollywood?*,
Jean-Pierre Melville, *A Cold Wind in August*, *Murder by Contract*
and, most of all, Robert Bresson

RON KALISH
picture and sound editor extraordinaire and master of self-discipline,
who knows cinema is made in the recutting

Table of Contents

Acknowledgments

First and foremost, my mother, Suzanne B. Repasky, and father, George S. McElhinney, must be applauded for their strong commitment to education and for always providing me with the best educational opportunities possible.

Second, I must extend deep thanks to my partner, Nicole Elizabeth Cook for her affection as well as unfailing support of—and critical eye on—this project and its various drafts and revisions.

Third, my grandfather, George McElhinney, who had the good sense to take me to "questionable" movies during my formative years of 1988 to 1995, including *A Cry in the Dark*, *The Music Teacher*, *Stealing Home*, *A Taxing Woman Returns*, *The Wizard of Loneliness*, *Dead Calm*, *Major League*, *Monsieur Heir*, *Shirley Valentine*, *May Fools*, *The Miracle*, *Thelma and Louise*, *Bitter Moon*, *The Crying Game*, *Damage*, *Farewell My Concubine*, *Kika*, *M. Butterfly*, *The Music of Chance*, *The Piano*, *Schindler's List* and *The Bridges of Madison County*, whom I took to see *The Baby of Macon* in 2002, and who always wanted to watch the film run out of the gate at the end too.

Fourth, my sister, Sara Josette Repasky McElhinney, for her warmth, friendship and support.

Fifth, The Honorable Susan Devlin Scott for her meticulous read and feedback on this manuscript.

Sixth, I'd like to remember the colleagues, friends and family who did not live to see the completion of this book—Callie Angel, Jamie Gillis, Roberta Hill, David Mallery, my grandmother Genevieve McElhinney, Archie Perlmutter, Kitty Quinn, my grandparents Mike and Mary Repasky, Carl Andrew Spicer, and especially my dearest friend, David "Speedy" Semonin.

The gestation and completion of this project would be unimaginable without the resources, support and encouragement of the faculty, staff and students of EGS—the European Graduate School. The brainchild of visionary founder Dr. Wolfgang Schirmacher—who is a true, modern-day philosopher king—EGS is an extraordinary institution on the cutting edge of advanced education

Acknowledgments

where it has been my supreme privilege to earn a doctorate of philosophy. Personally, Dr. Schirmacher's advice to reorganize this project away from genre theory toward a theory of remakes was an invaluable intellectual focusing and typical of his astute, strong and highly nurturing guidance.

I wish to personally thank Dr. Peter Price and Megan Bridge of Philadelphia for first bringing me into the EGS "fold." In addition to Peter, the students of EGS must be acknowledged for how well they complement the faculty and have participated in the course works that nurtured this project. I would like to recognize Caitlin Biskup, Paul Boshears, Stuart Candy, Hannes Charen, Meredith Forbes, Barbara Fornssler, Tim Gilman, Christian Hänggi, Andrej Jachimczyk, Nico Jenkins, Ryan King, Lori Martindale, Marina Masic, Anthony Metivier, Matthew Mitchem, Chuck Pettebone, Jake Reeder, Ben Segal, Zak Sharif, Sean Smith, Berit Soli-Holt, Andrea Stanislav, James Teems, Jason Wagner, the delightful Benedîkt Wahner and, most of all, Alejandro Cerda Rueda for his exceptionally nuanced feedback throughout the writing process.

This project is also especially grateful to EGS' select group of instructors whose influence resonates far outside their seminars and writings, namely Giorgio Agamben, Pierre Alferi, Hubertus von Amelunxen, Alain Badiou, Catherine Breillat, Victor Burgin, Judith Butler, Simon Critchley, Manuel Delanda, Claire Denis, DJ Spooky (Paul D. Miller), Atom Egoyan, Heinz Emigholz, Bracha Ettinger, Mike Figgis, Chris Fynsk, Heiner Goebbels, Antony Gormley, Peter Greenaway, Tom Kalin, Geert Lovink, Erin Manning, Brian Massumi, Jean-Luc Nancy, Jacques Ranciere, Laurence A. Rickels, Michael J. Shapiro, Hendrik Speck, Sam Webber, Friedrich Ulfers, Gregory Ulmer, Siegfried Zielinski, Slavoj Žižek and Tom Zummer.

Most especially and profoundly at EGS, Avital Ronell, celebrator of misprision and Jacques Derrida Chair, must be credited for bringing Melanie Klein's life and work to my detailed attention in her fascinating August 2008 seminar, "Finitude in Philosophy, Literature and Art."

Finally at EGS, enough gratitude cannot be expressed to Virginia Cutrufelli, whose administration of the summer sessions in Saas-fee are warm, wise and unparalleled.

Penultimately, I'd like to express gratitude to the following individuals and organizations for their help: *Abington Friends School*, Fred Adelman, Brian Albright, *Amazon.com*, *The Ambler Theater*, *The American Museum of the Moving Image* Astoria, *Amoeba Records*, Bill & Amy Anderson, Alan Andres, Jack Angstreich, the *Animal Husbandry* cast (Anne Bailis, Charlotte Ford, Konya Hood, Jeb Kreager, James Laster, Christian Pedersen, Tobias Segal, Kristina Valada-Viars and Frank X), *Another Story Bookstore* Allentown, *Anthology Film Archives*, David Stanley Aponte, Rita Apsan (*Freud Museum*), Margaret Barton-Fumo, *Benchmark School* (Irene W. Gaskins, Thorne Elliot, Carol Flatau who got me a copy of *A Clockwork Orange* in 1992, Eric MacDonald, Joyce Ostertag,

Sharon Rauch), *Big Jar Books*, Judy Binus, Louis Bluver, *The Book Trader*, Mark Bowen, Mike Brand, *Brat Productions*, *Brickbat Books*, Carrie Brownell, Mary Chris Brownell, Dan Buskirk, Robert Cargni, Donald F. Carter, Michael Chaiken, Glenn Chartrand, *The Chestnut Hill Film Group* (Margaret Brunton, David and Judith Buten, Rosemary Collins, Marianne and Paul Dodge, John and Carolyn Friedman, Jace Gaffney, Natalie and Jack and Ralph Hirshorn, Judith Mallery, Martha Repman, Paul Sofian, Harold and Emmy Starr, Ella Torrey, George and Diana Woodward), *The Chestnut Hill Local*, Arianne Ulmer Cipes, Jerry Clark, Renae Clark, Gretjen Clausing, *Cleveland Institute of Art*, Bernie Cohen, Philip Cohen, Rachael Cohen, Scott Cole, *The Colonial Theater* Phoenixville, Jess Conda, Consulat général de France à New York, Heather Cook, Isabelle Cook, Rick and Jen Cook, Sherri Cook, *The County Theater* Doylestown, Travis Crawford, Alain D'Elbreil, Mike Dennis and *Reel Black Cinema*, Mark Desman, Joanne Dhody (who let me leave her credit card as deposit while I rented VHS of *Eraserhead*, *El Topo* and *Pink Flamingos* one afternoon in 1994), *Diabolik DVD*, Susan and Andy DiMichele, Michael DiPaolo, John and Sue Draus, Drexel University, "Cousin" Sean Dundon, Ray Duval, Edward J. Eberwine III, *Eugene Lang College / New School University* (Colette Brooks, Steven Cahil, Dare Clubb, Kathleen Dimmick, John Freitas, Michelle Handelman, J. Hoberman, Kai Jackson, Branden W. Joseph, Stefania de Kenessey, William Lurres, Chris Packard, Amit Rai, Cecilia Rubino, MM Serra, Jonathan Veitch, Peter Wallace), *Exhumed Films*, Keri Farrow, *Film Forum* NYC, *Film Forum* Philadelphia, *Filmtech-Philadelphia's Independent Film School*, Flicker Alley (Jeff Masino, Josh Morrison), Gene and Nancy Foehl, Crestina Forcina (Wellcome Library, London), Melissa Elizabeth Forgione, Janet Frazer (movie fan and gracious faculty sponsor of "Art Films" at Abington Friends School 1993–7), Sam Fulginiti, Skylar Gahagan, Kean and Janice Ganan, Meredith Gatschet, *The George Eastman House* Rochester, Debbie Gerbec, Joseph A. Gervasi, Greg Giovanni, Cory Goetz, Mary and Patrick Richardson Graham, Walter Granger, Harry and Jamie Guerro and the rest of the "Garagehouse" Gang, Steve Gutin, Howard B. Haas, Lauren Hallden-Abbeton, Jim Healy, Dale Herrick, Bernd Herzogenrath, James Hollenbaugh, Abe Holtz, The Hotel Allalin, *House of Our Own Books*, Eric Bond Hutton, *International House* Philadelphia, Dagon James, Adrienne Jenkins, *Jerry Ohlinger's Movie Material* (Dollie), Mark Johnson and *Shocking Videos/Revenge Is My Destiny*, Beth Johnston, Steve Kaplan and *Alpha Classics*, Ted Knighton, Kristine Krueger (National Film Information Service: Margaret Herrick Library), Jayson Lamb, James and Madlon Laster, Kim Lenny, David Litofsky, Hope and Paul Makler, Kevin Mitchell Martin and Bina Sharif, Missy Mazzaferro, Amanda and Jordan McClain, Mary McCool, Jimmy McDonough, Jean McGinn, Layla Milholen, Roberta Mitchell and *Darker Image Video*, MoMA NY Film Study Center, Glen Muschio, *The Museum of Modern Art* NYC, Billy Name, Monique Naton,

Netflix, Barbara Noska, Silvia Hortelano Peláez, Ruth Perlmutter, *The Philadel-phia Shakespeare Theater*—Carmen Kahn artistic director, Cathy Quinn, Michael Rapp, Kate Reinke, Gina Renzi and *The Rotunda*, The *Rutgers-Camden* English Department (Shanyn Fiske, Dee Jonczak, Howard Marchitello, Geoffrey Sill and Carol J. Singley), *Rutgers* Library System (Jeris Cassel, Melissa Gasparotto, Theo Haynes, Kimberly Kaiser, Priscilla Lee, Barry Lipinski, Megan Lotts, Jill Nathanson, Bethany O'Shea, Jan Reinhart, Glenn Sandberg, Paul Young), *The Rutgers–New Brunswick* Writing Program (Tisha Bender, Debbie Borie-Holtz, Tracy Budd, Donna Cantor, Darcy Gioia, Judy Karwowski, Grace Kincaid, Elizabeth Madden-Zibman, Trinyan Mariano, Rosemary Moore, Emily Renaud, Emma Rumen, George Schroepfer, Peter Sorrell, Alessandra Sperling and Kurt Spellmeyer), Carolyn Schlecker, Harvey Schwartz, Jay Schwartz, Bill Scott, Paul Semonin, Maureen Sestito, Mark Simonson, my darling cat Desiree Skiperdee, Chris Slater, Eric Spilker, Mel Staffin, Richard Stoddard, Chris Strompolos, Rajeev Tanwar, Susannah Thomer, Frank Thornton, *TLA Video*, *The Two Books Pioneer Theater*, *Video Library*—West Philly & Mt. Airy, Wagner Society of New York (Neil Friedman), *Walk a Crooked Mile Bookstore*, Ryan Walker and Lauren-Alice Lamanna, WHYY TV, WYBE TV, *Xploited Cinema*, Eric Zala, and Mike Zaleski.

Finally, I'd like to acknowledge the cinema writers whose work (and sometimes conversations) have enriched cinema culture and my own thinking about movies — Sam Adams, Emily Atkinson, Dan Buskirk, Vincent Canby, Carol J. Clover, Rick Currnutte, Manohla Dargis, Roger Ebert, Howard Gensler, Anthony Glassman, Phil Hall, Leslie Halliwell, Ed Halter, Dennis Harvey, Molly Haskell, J. Hoberman, Stephen Holden, Johnny Ray Huston, Noah Isenberg, Pauline Kael, Dave Kehr, Jeremiah Kipp, Gary M. Kramer, Bill Krohn, Dennis Lim, Leonard Maltin, Janet Maslin, Todd McCarthy, Maitland McDonagh, Elvis Mitchell, V.A. Musetto, Joyce Nishioka, John Petkovic, Matt Prigge, Steven Rea, Rex Reed, Carrie Rickey, David Rooney, Jonathan Rossenbaum, Andrew Sarris, A.O. Scott, Matt Zoeller Seitz, Steven Shaviro, Irv Slifkin, Bob Stephens, Amy Taubin, David Thomson, Carrie Tobey, Peter Travers, Bruce Walsh, Elizabeth Weitzman, Armond White, Robin Wood, and the indispensible *Time Out (London) Film Guide*.

Thank you.

Introduction: Remakes, from Shakespeare to the Post-Literate Problem

Movies are a compulsive dream state that reflect viewers' phantasies and dreams while espousing both mainstream and underground political ideologies. Part history of cinema, part cultural examination, and part media theory, *Second Takes: Remaking Film, Remaking America* examines twentieth-century English-language movie remakes. Cinema can be perceived in two distinct, closed eras — silent and sound — which overlap at the advent of talkies. The popularization of video in the 1980s, the advent of digital video, computer generated images (CGI), and the proliferation of "infotainment" resulted in a galvanizing deconstruction of the feature film format by the late 1990s. It heralded cinema's end state and total transformation into the new format of media. Remade cinema exists in an especially privileged sphere, as these "doubled" films are not only variations on preexisting themes but are a meta-cinema, wherein the difference between editions becomes the subject itself, revealing unexpected social constructions. To critically read a remake is to be aware of the content being commentary. Remakes heighten the indications of both cultural psychological pleasures and trauma, resulting in a greater understanding of the psychology of the United States of America and the directions that have shaped it.

From 1931 to 1998, the sound era, this text explores the meaning of cinema's increasing influence in the shaping of the greater popular culture of the United States. This analysis uses Melanie Klein's psychoanalytic theories as a fulcrum for interpretation. It postulates that Klein's play technique is synonymous with the art and act of theater, and that movies made between 1931 and 1998 are an extension — or hybrid of— theater in the tradition of Shakespeare. This introduction traces the line from Shakespeare's plays to nineteenth-century domestic drama and Richard Wagner's operas, to arrive at Sigmund Freud's applied psy-

1

choanalytic theory in the early twentieth century. Klein is chosen as the reader's prism because her lucid writing advances, essentializes and complicates early psychoanalytic theory, while removing its problematic gender stereotypes. Far ahead of her time, and still underappreciated today, Klein should be venerated as a thinker more important than her successors, Donald Winnicott, J. Huizinga and Jacques Lacan. Cinema creates and displays American myths, and doing so illuminates cultural trends whose study is of the utmost importance for future scholarship and cultural choices.

The Concept of the Cinema

Literary critic Harold Bloom proposes that "the invention of the human" sprang out of William Shakespeare's nearly paranormal ability to create individuals uniquely and expressively themselves. For the first time, these individuals overhear themselves speaking aloud, both to other individuals and in soliloquy, allowing Bloom to read Shakespeare as "the original psychologist."[1]

Using this Shakespearean "talking cure"—a nickname for psychoanalysis—Bloom argues that Western humans have thus employed the Bard of Avon since his time as a guide to self-remaking and self-evolution. In short, "Shakespeare teaches us how and what to perceive, and he also instructs us how and what to sense and then to experience as sensation."[2] The dominance of Shakespeare in the current English-speaking vernacular is undeniable both in production of the plays and appropriation of poetry snippets—a sort of shorthand—in common conversation. The English-language-speaking world uses Shakespeare's drama as an unchanging, but adaptable, filter for human experience, which crystallized with, among others, Freud's method of psychoanalysis.

Freud's applied psychoanalysis is often considered his most currently significant contribution, and this reading, along with Bloom's, firmly places Freud as a disciple of Shakespeare and,

William Shakespeare (April 26, 1564 [baptized]–April 23, 1616). Movies made between 1931 and 1998 are an extension — or hybrid of — theater in the tradition of Shakespeare.

therefore, of the theater at large. Since the Ancient Greeks, theater has been a form of therapy. As Helmut Käutner's title would suggest, individuals owe *Gratitude toward the Theater*: "Play is the core of the theater. Originally an end in itself, it gradually becomes a purposeful, common activity under influences that are partially cultic, partially erotic, and partially political."[3] Theater makes individuals — both with projection of character and imitation of character.

Friedrich Hebbel helps to bring Shakespearean drama into the middle-class house and hearth, and toward cinema, because his characters and their problems are, for the first time on the stage, more common than royal. More than an advent of bourgeois stagecraft, Hebbel sees drama as "in every way a product of all preceding ages, the connecting link between a series of centuries about to close, and a new series about to begin."[4] In his 1844 *Preface to "Maria Magdalena*," he writes, "The function of drama, as the summit of all art, is to clarify the existing state of the world and man in their relationship to the Idea, that is, to that moral center which conditions all things, and which we must accept as existing, if only for the sake of the self-preservation of those things."[5] Hebbel's goal of analysis is the most sophisticated remake of Plato's cave possible without the availability of inexpensive, stable electric current. The manufacture of this current made the mechanization of theater, that is cinema, possible.

In the mid–nineteenth century, Richard Wagner again transfers the domestic scene into the (Shakespearean) realm of gods, giants, dwarfs and mermaids. However, he adds to it underscoring and leitmotif, making and naming this production *Gesamtkunstwerk*— a total event with sound, light, painting, actors, etc. Conceptualized for a state-of-the-art theater, Wagner's musical dramas, from *Der Ring des Nibelungen* on, realize this total environment — truly a cinema before its era.

Richard Wagner (May 22, 1813–February 13, 1883). Conceptualized for a state-of-the-art theater, Wagner's musical dramas from *Der Ring des Nibelungen* on realize a total theatrical environment — truly a cinema before its era.

Cinema's Late Nineteenth-Century Antecedents

Roughly two decades later, motion pictures emerge and begin their journey to become the mass-reproduced form of Wagner's *Gesamtkunstwerk*, and with this appropriation, cinema removes the living process of musical drama. In the sound era, the adoption of Wagner's system of leitmotifs by twentieth-century movie composers becomes the predominant way of conveying meaning for Hollywood movies. Furthermore, the theory of cinematic montage can be traced back to Wagner, understood as springing out of the *Ring*'s transitions and most especially *Parsifal*'s Act 1 transformation scene where space and time become one.

Post-Wagner writers, including Henrik Ibsen, Frank Wedekind and Bertolt Brecht progress Hebbel's psychological and social impulse with works that are increasingly difficult to stage because they ask of the stage what only anonymous viewership and prerecorded, manipulated moving-sound image can provide. This links the director-less, set-less, "original practice" of Shakespeare's model of theater — and its resulting psychoanalysis — to the new medium of cinema, already understood as inherently undead, or perhaps embalmed, *Gesamtkunstwerk*.

Twentieth-Century Cinema: Fantasy, Psychology and the Kuleshov Effect

Along with the two great libretto scribes Wagner and Béla Balázs, Hugo von Hofmannsthal connects opera to psychoanalysis and so imprints opera's impulses into cinema's binary of fantasy and psychology while again linking it up with the Shakespearean tradition. Writing of the photo-play medium in 1921 as *The Substitute for Dreams*, Hofmannsthal first points out the fantasy involved in cinema, suggesting, "what all the working people are looking for in the movie theater is a substitute for dreams. They want to fill their imagination with pictures, strong images in which the essence of life is summarized and that at the same time are constructed out of the viewer's inner being and go to his heart. For life owes them such images.... Their heads are empty, not by nature, but rather because of the life that society forces them to lead."[6] Importantly, motion pictures are here dramaturgically separated from theater (but not opera) by audience experience. Hofmannsthal does not comment on the "how," and it is disappointing that so clever a mind would not comment on the obvious issues of spectator transference clearly at stake — especially when his libretto for *Der Rosenkavalier* (1911) focuses on these numerous issues of psychoanalytic transference. While Hofmannsthal deals with the issues of class somewhat clumsily in *The Substitute for Dreams*, he keenly zeros in on the fact that society — what is called culture — deprives individuals via cinema/media.

That which is absent is supplied by the Kuleshov effect, where montage always results in more meaning, as when given fragments of cinema it is in an individual's nature to project or imagine the connections. The Kuleshov effect also produces a placebo result in cinema, when the connections of two independent images edited together inherently imply connections that may not be intentional.

So cinema is given a partially synonymous definition with the theater/musical-drama, while also — and just as importantly — illustrating how the drama of theater was guided to an increasingly psychological, if not psychoanalytic, methodology, more scientifically studied (if less poetic) than Shakespeare.

Lev Kuleshov (January 13, 1899–March 29, 1970). That which is absent is supplied by the Kuleshov effect, where montage always results in more meaning, as when viewers are given fragments of cinema and it is in an individual's nature to project or imagine the connections.

The Introjection of the Political Into Cinema

Silent and sound are the two obviously distinct, if overlapping, eras of cinema. The silent era lasts roughly from the 1880s to the early 1930s where movies evolve from *being*, and being attractions — loops and illusions — to documents, then edited narratives, and finally, with early sound, to "features"— an indissoluble marriage of document and fantasy, which can be manipulated so as to discourse ideology. The second and last era of cinema, 1931 to 1998, encompasses the body of sound cinema. Here the visual lessons of silent cinema are largely unlearned. The medium of cinema remakes itself with theater, largely because of its new ability to reproduce the human voice, reaffirming Shakespeare's paramount psycho-cultural dominance.

Shaped as an artist-theoretician by the twentieth century's world wars, Walter Benjamin categorizes cinema not as psychoanalytic, but as inherently political in nature. The forces of the political morph cinema into media as much as the introjection and advancement of technology. Benjamin states in *The Work of Art in the Age of Mechanical Reproduction* that "mechanical reproduction emancipates the work of art from its parasitical dependence on ritual."[7] Benjamin anticipates how media is a home medium — portable, if not individual — whereas cinema is based in the relationship of community, and therefore has a special extraterritoriality because it is at once solitary and deeply collaborative. The ritual that remains after mechanical reproduction is the individual's compulsion to cinema. Born out of mechanic technology, Benjamin accurately anticipates the largely digital media era and how "entertainment" becomes "infotainment," dispensing ideology. "To an ever greater degree the work of art reproduced becomes the work of art designed for reproducibility," he says. "Instead of being based on ritual, it begins to be based on another practice — politics."[8] To be shared, politics must be reproducible as well as able to be remade. By the mid–1980s, where politics starts to fully dominate the English-language sound film by harnessing the tool of nostalgia, the change has taken place between viewers seeking a psychoanalytic exchange causing gratification and viewers receiving an analysis based not in the self but in the political.

The Cinema of Remakes

Cinema is the first time where the psychoanalytic double is made inescapably manifest because in cinema the double inherently recurs. Movies exist as doubles themselves, present an actual double of individuals, and these actor-doubles are doubles themselves for the audience. Examining these tensions can reveal the facets of cultural history, especially when the cinema studied has been redoubled — that is remade. "Remakes," with their innate plurality, offer the most substance for concentrated cultural analysis and take on significant, extra psychoanalytic value.

Remakes in *Second Takes: Remaking Film, Remaking America* are conceived as films that are based on earlier films or, more abstractly, as a movie that harnesses genre and/or archetype, remaking the "rules," or postures, of specific stereotypes. All cinema is inherently remade, as it is an inherently collaborative process. A process between crew and actor, spectator and image, distributor and consumer, with deliberately obscure boundaries very much like the dream state of viewing. In *The Visible Human*, Balázs writes that film is "the *folk art* of our century. Not in the sense, unfortunately, that it arises from the spirit of the people, but that the spirit of the people arises from it."[9] Just as Shakespeare and theater created humans, cinema continues in this line but is yoked to technology and reproducibility that accelerates its influence.

Cinema provides the motives for human behavior vis-à-vis easy and pervasive imitation and imitability. The technology of cinema has also directly altered the course of the world. Cinema editing condenses time and so has sped along human development in a way that drama, musical or otherwise, has not. Cinema has accomplished this feat first by sharing ideas with and without aural capability — creating a language of either impressions or codes — and then by providing familiar patterns, and patterns to imitate and/or eschew. The magic of cinema is how these illusions are constructed, the (cross-)purposes to which movies are often assembled, and the myriad of intentions that go into the collaborative human creation of drama — performance being an act which in and of itself, more often than not, radiates positively for the physical reasons elucidated by Hebbel and his peers.

This construction, however, is undone by cinema's negative and long-lasting cultural harm, born of its focalized nature, wherein the medium becomes a substitute for dreams. It is an empty, but temporarily fulfilling, ritual for those unable to relate to their fellow man or woman with actual physicality. Even more unfortunately, cinema can fulfill an emotional response absent in "real life" with moving pictures and the agency of watching. The birth of cinema is also the birth of "fast-food" culture, and the discrepancy between what is, what is represented, and what could be is clarified as the central tension of all theater, cinema, and media no matter what the content. It is this that is also inherently remade in each work the culture produces.

Melanie Klein and Cinema as Therapy

Melanie Klein's link to Freud, and therefore Shakespeare, makes her work applicable to not only medicine, but to the theater/cinema. Among her many practical

Sigmund Freud (May 6, 1856–September 23, 1939). The English-language-speaking world uses Shakespeare's drama as an unchanging, but adaptable, filter for human experience, which crystallized with, among others, Freud's method of psychoanalysis. (©Freud Museum, London.)

contributions to child rearing, Klein advanced the use of "play technique" for analyzing, elevating and/or curing neurotic symptoms in her patients. Upon comparison, Klein's play technique is the method of acting in cinema; and, as well, viewers "play" with a movie, as Klein would with a willing patient, seeking transference and offering analysis.

Klein pioneered the application of Freudian psychoanalysis to infants and children. Klein essentializes the psychoanalytic subject to the individual, reducing problematic Freudian and pseudo–Freudian male centricity, real or projected. In *On the Theory of Anxiety and Guilt* (1948), Klein reaches two conclusions: "(a) in young children it is unsatisfied libidinal excitation which turns into anxiety; (b) the earliest *content* of anxiety is the infant's feeling of danger lest his need should not be satisfied because the mother is 'absent.'"[10] The twin anxieties of unsatisfied libidinal desire and the fear of the needs being denied remain with the child into adulthood and are the two agents of cinema which entice and frustrate viewers in equal measure. It is this frustration that makes cinema a compulsive behavior.

In *Love, Guilt and Reparation* (1937), Klein writes that the "capacity for identification with another person is a most important element in human relationships in general, and is also a condition for real and strong feelings of love."[11] What cinema offers is a mechanical substitution for that human relationship — the automation of desire in a false dream state that is both sterile and intimate.

Cinema offers viewers a chance to identify and love represented persons so that the Kleinian social drives are satisfied by a placebo effect, akin to the "regaining" Klein addresses in her work. In connection with this, Klein writes, "Since in being identified with other people we share, as it were, the help or satisfaction afforded to them by ourselves, we regain in one way what we have sacrificed in another."[12] There is an emotional transference at work in Klein and cinema. Identifying becomes "acting" in a way that viewing also triggers these same psychological results. On screen or off, the impulse and conception of love in the individual allows that person to,

> play the part of a good parent, and behave toward this person as we felt at times the parents did to us — or as we wanted them to do. At the same time, we also play the part of the good child toward his parents, which we wished to do in the past and are now acting out in the present. Thus, by reversing a situation, namely in acting toward another person as a good parent, in phantasy we re-create and enjoy the wished-for love and goodness of our parents. But to act as good parents toward other people may also be a way of dealing with the frustrations and sufferings of the past. Our grievances against our parents for having frustrated us, together with the feelings of hate and revenge to which these have given rise in us, and again, the feelings of guilt and despair arising out of this hate and revenge because we have injured the parents who at the same time we loved — all these, in phantasy, we may undo in retrospect (taking away some of the grounds for hatred), by playing at the same time parts of loving parents and loving children. At the same time, in

our unconscious phantasy we make good the injuries which we did in phantasy, and for which we still unconsciously feel very guilty.[13]

Klein here identifies how it is the act of play or pretend that triggers emotional response. Whether it is "playing the part," "acting out," "acting toward," it is all an "act" wherein the individual recreates the dynamic of their parents' relationships. Gilles Deleuze identifies this acting of the parents in *Cinema 2: The Time-Image*, stating that psychoanalysis has "only ever given cinema one sole object, one single refrain, the so-called primitive scene."[14] Klein suggests that when the primal scene is remade successfully, gratification experienced and guilt channeled, the individual alleviates anxiety. Cinema does remake individuals' primal scenes, but the problem of cinema is that its relief is, more often than not, temporary and largely illusionary because of its lack of interactive physicality and lack of reality.

Melanie Klein (March 30, 1882–September 22, 1960). Klein is chosen as the reader's prism because her lucid writing advances, essentializes and complicates early psychoanalytic theory, while removing its problematic gender stereotypes. (Wellcome Library, London.)

The Phenomenology of Cinema: A Method

Cinema has been proposed as the seventh great art form; however, viewing motion pictures from the perspective of art is a fallacy. Cinema is not art but a medium, and what is appreciated as art in cinema is applied psychoanalysis. It is not the images, words or audio that give movies of the sound era their power, but rather their offer of multilayered cultural therapy.

In cinema, the viewer's willing suspension of disbelief between what is happening with the end product (viewed light with coordinated sounds) and what *could* be happening (the content proposed by the sound and the light) bonds cinema to the uncanny, the unconscious, dreams, fantasy and phantasy. According to Klein, "phantasy" is subconscious, while "fantasy" is conscious dreaming. It is movies' special nature that they straddle both prefixes. In a note to *Notes on Some Schizoid Mechanisms*, Klein remarks further on this doubling —

not in the context of cinema — but as a result of feedback from Dr. W.C.M. Scott on "splitting" in her work. "He," she writes, "stressed the importance of the breaks in continuity of experiences, which imply a splitting in time rather than in space. He referred as an instance to the alternation between states of being asleep and states of being awake. I fully agree with his point of view."[15] First, "splitting in time rather than in space" links this method of thinking back to *Parsifal* and Wagner's innovations on the Shakespearean, as it denotes how cinema, like music — that great crutch of English-language sound cinema — is about the capturing of time. Second, because of the way the celluloid moves through a projector's gate, there are numerous imperceptible blackouts, "breaks," every minute, which split the medium in two at what can be considered its "primal scene." Via persistence of vision, these breaks are subconscious and therefore repressed. When, in this text, Klein is applied to read the era of sound cinema through its representative genres, the social problems of cinema become clear as do the reasons for mutations or evolutions in the medium.

Sound cinema is schizoid in conception as fragments of moving images juxtaposed. One image is "cut" and replaced by another — breaks and reflection, seemingly randomly repeated, remaking the content and creating atmosphere where there was previously emptiness. This is what of course happens in the media era — however the unit of the frame/cut is no longer a microcosm but the actual content of media's point-and-shoot visual style. Yet, in the sound era, thousands of frame/cuts created a surrogate world, initially an escape from the political. Benjamin writes, "The feeling of strangeness that overcomes the actor before the camera, as Pirandello describes it, is basically of the same kind as the estrangement felt before one's own image in the mirror. But now the reflected image has become separable, transportable."[16] The "transportable," that is, doubled, image is interpretable and empowered by its unreality and therefore cloaked in phantastic/fantastic safety until there is the anxiety created by the intrusion of the political into the world of dreams. Before the intrusion of the political, cinema could be seen as allowing a mastery of reality. The political brings along the bedfellows of withdrawal from reality, unreality, and the need for punishment. Individuals find their doubles in cinema, as cinematic creations find their doubles, alerting even the most timid imagination to the inherent coded messages illuminated in remaking.

Cinema's therapy is universal because, to return to Balázs, "memory lies in words; one can refer and allude with them to that which is not present. The image, though, speaks only for itself."[17] Cinema is fantastic. Susan Sontag remarks that fantasy can "normalize what is psychologically unbearable, thereby inuring us to it. In one case, fantasy beautifies the world. In the other, it neutralizes it."[18] In both cases, fantasy is another reality, linked to dream and the unconscious wherein the inexpressible and expressible may both find a voice, if not agency. Seeking cultural absolution, and pointing out how cinema cannot be art, V.F. Perkins asks the reader to see *Film as Film*: "The camera neither lies nor tells the truth, because the camera does not make statements. It is we who convert images into assertions."[19] The "art" of cinema — what is really psycho-analytic transference — thus lies within ourselves.

Coupled with the science of persistence of vision, the Kuleshov effect gives every viewer at least a slightly different perception of a cinematic experience. This phenomenon must no doubt tap the individual's latent or otherwise creative-fantasy resources which, germane and unique to every human, are crucial in remaking. Given the semi-anonymous, confessional-like nature of the cinema experience, this remaking may perhaps also afford access to those parts of the viewer's self that are otherwise unavailable. Just as therapy and punishment depend on repetition, so an individual's attraction to movies and possible fetishization of this illusion can be a result of this constant stimulation and perhaps unconscious provocation inherent in remaking.

Because movies are extraordinary, born of fantasy and dreams, they offer much the same, if not more, opportunities for transference than psychoanalysis because there is not only the relation between subject (analysis) and viewer (patient), but between the ideas/impulses presented and ideas received. Movies are such effective therapy because they are not grounded in reality — and therefore they are not hindered by ethics — yet they have the same privileges as a session of psychoanalysis. It is appropriate to take the analysis of children and apply it to adults and adult functions because cinema is primal, post-literate, infantile, and, as Klein reminds her readers, "I also believe that the infant's intellectual capacities are often underrated and that in fact he understands more than he is credited with."[20] Cinema offers viewers metaphoric analysis and transference, essentialized so that the act of understanding is interpretation for the viewer. In *The Psychological Principles of Infant Analysis*, Klein writes about what may as well be the popularity of cinema and media when she observes, "The pleasure in play, which visibly ensues after an interpretation has been given, is also due to the fact that the expenditure necessitated by a repression is no longer required after the interpretation."[21] It comes as no surprise that both Kleinian analysis and cinema viewing result in that oldest of dramaturgical concepts — catharsis.

Picture and blackness, alertness and unconsciousness, waking and sleeping — life and dreams; life and cinema. As cinema mutated toward media, the central tension of the sound era became between cinema as dream or cinema as politics. This briefly flourished as a specific life-dream-political ménage à trois with the on-screen cinematic tensions of the 1960s and early 1970s. However, it was a short-lived nexus as the rise of the blockbuster from *The Exorcist* (1973) on increasingly gave all away to the political. Certainly, silent cinema was very close to dreams, fantastic in nature and unencumbered with physical reality (realism); but with sound cinema, movies are remade as representative of the stage and proscenium, making the form more directly psychoanalytic. In addition, sound cinema's return to the stage traces how the true individual is removed from the process by cinema's move from dream to politics — a shift in the twentieth century that results in the media era. Voyeurism and fetishism plus technology equals media, and media is so reconfigured to obliterate cinema so that its product may be less specific and more readily available.

Cinema as Mythmaker

Cinema creates myth and represents the state of marriage as the greatest myth of all. Mythmaking is how cinema grows in power ever more seductive and never so seductive as with twenty-first-century media, where format is content and content is essential and a product. Politics enters the sphere of cinema as soon as the mythos on screen cannot be related to individuals' tangible realities because it points out specific class/wealth disparities that change the viewer from *relating to* the movie to being *informed by* the movie. The dream most usually depicted in cinema is one of ph/fantastic desire, and for Americans desire in the sound era is usually linked to concept and to avoidance, escapism and commodity. Patrons buy the concept, and so catharsis has retreated from the climax of the drama to the act of (ticket) purchase. In the cinema of the sound era, individuals are increasingly subjugated as receiver, finding out how they need to be to themselves and to the world, from the medium and their remaking (i.e., understanding) of the medium. Uncertain impulses are repressed, while conformity is rewarded, and cinema so harms its viewers. The credo of the spectacle might as well be — *"If we act as we see our equivalents do in movies, then we can remake our lives after that, so that I am ever more so the star of my life."* From this point of departure, it is a simple leap from late sound cinema to Second Life via computers and the Internet to the media era where there are no dreams, only the politics of consumerism.

One of the other great, explicit desires in American sound cinema is marriage, which is often a euphemism for commerce, or a sort of advantageous breeding of family lines — all political. So often in this fantasy of marriage it is the union which will magically resolve things into an unquestionably "happy end," perhaps granting social-class movement that is of the highest fantastic nature. Part of movies' power is their running commentary on themselves. As the media era approached, it became harder and harder for cinema to not acknowledge itself. Cinema's own propaganda thus supplied its own importance while underlining capital's ideology of commerce all the while diverting the psychoanalytic to the political. Ergo, viewers are told the myth of Cinderella in everything from Clara Bow in *It* to Sarah Jessica Parker in *Sex and the City*. Yet, rather than a rags-to-riches journey, it is a subterfuge of cinema's psychoanalytic transference. Siegfried Kracauer examines this in the aptly named piece,

The Little Shopgirls Go to the Movies (1927), writing the counter-reading of the dominant paradigm. "In reality it may not often happen that a scullery maid marries the owner of a Rolls Royce. But doesn't every Rolls Royce owner dream that scullery maid's dream of rising to his stature? Stupid and unreal film fantasies are the *daydreams of society*, in which its actual reality comes to the fore and its otherwise repressed wishes take on form."[22] This repression then recurs in many multiplicities, with subsequent movie experiences adding to individual's maladies rather than relieving them.

In *The Uncanny*, Freud states this very basic tenet of psychoanalysis, which is "correct in maintaining that every emotional affect, whatever its quality, is transformed by repression into morbid anxiety, then among such cases of anxiety there must be a class in which the anxiety can be shown to come from something repressed which *recurs*."[23] Kracauer understands that society is wealth and that cinema is an illustration and the proposed imitation of wealth. Morbid anxiety is exacerbated by cinema, as it fuels the individual with surrogacy which at first slakes the anxiety — however, when the individual is confronted with the end of the fantasy, or its unsatisfactory outcome, the resulting trauma increases the preexisting void of the lost object within, and cinema so harms the viewer.

Since Kracauer's *From Caligari to Hitler: A Psychological History of the German Film*, it has been indisputable, as he puts it, that the "films of a nation reflect its mentality in a more direct way than other artistic media for two reasons: First, films are never the product of an individual.... [and] Second, films address themselves, and appeal, to the anonymous multitude.... What films reflect are not so much explicit credos as psychological disposition — those deep layers of collective mentality which extend more or less below the dimension of consciousness."[24] Below consciousness is the repressed and the unknown — the two great causes of cultural anxiety, spoken and unspoken.

Cinema's Journey to Media

At the start of the sound era, the medium lurches largely backward from fluid silent film craftsmanship to static talkies. After some technological growing pains, and technological advancements as a by-product of (world) warfare, cinema moves forward again to the golden years of the studio system. This moment ends in the 1950s and 1960s with the disbursal of that talent concentration because of more location shooting as well as the rise of independent film out of Hollywood (Maya Daren), New York (Ron Rice, Jack Smith) and the drive-in/grindhouse circuit (Herschell Gordon Lewis, Russ Meyer). Hollywood returns to market dominance in the 1970s by embracing figures of the "New Hollywood" — like Robert Altman, Jack Nicholson, and Diane Keaton — and even more so in the 1980s by Steven Spielberg and George Lucas' solidification of the blockbuster and sequels as a genre and means of production. The popularity of home video, the proliferation of "infotainment" (synthesized during the O.J. Simpson trial), and the birth of digital video resulted in a dismantling of the feature film format by the late 1990s and very early naughts.

Director Gus Van Sant's remake of *Psycho*, released in the United States December 4, 1998, by Universal Pictures, represents one of the most indelible markers of the sound cinema era's end. First, in an act whose symbolic self-devourment cannot be denied, the Van Sant *Psycho* is nearly an identical remake — but in color — of the Alfred Hitchcock original. Second, Van Sant's additions to Hitchcock's mise-en-scène are largely of the CGI variety, denoting not only the triumph of the digital revolution, but how digital media robs bodies of themselves by rendering them technologically obsolete, thus making product and possession even more alluring as identity.

The current media era was fully cemented into being with the New York–set events of September 11, 2001. Not only did international policies and concepts of freedom change that day, but viewing habits were irrevocably altered. Advance sales at theaters plummeted, while home entertainment blossomed with Xbox and Netflix, aided by digital technology being less physically cumbersome than analog technology. Post-modernity is a blurring, as Theodor Adorno elucidates in *Transparencies on Film*. "One will have observed that it is difficult, initially, to distinguish the preview of a 'coming attraction' from the main film for which one is waiting. This may tell us something about the main attractions. Like the previews and like the pop hits, they are advertisements for themselves, bearing the commodity character like a mark of Cain on their foreheads. Every commercial film is actually only the preview of that which it promises and will never deliver."[25]

Media's Propensity for Problematic Spectacle

To surf YouTube is to witness that "cinema" has become "media," and that "media" is now "spectacle" in the Debordian sense. Current media remains not fully formed because of its reliance on technology, which is largely designed with planned obsolescence in mind — ensuring that a remake-replacement may be sold to consumers. Secondly, media's culture must be ever changing, ever "evolving," for nearly the same reason — even when that "evolution" may, in greater accuracy, be standing still or regressing to achieve the desired simulation of "new" commodity. Third, the act of media interfacing is predicated on "remaking" and remixing by consumers. Media's dominance of the early twenty-first century — and its possible longevity of cultural influence in the decades to come — is that format is now content, content is the individual, and everyone is the star of their own reality TV show. Of course, this precept exists purely conceptually, aided by the illusion of twenty-first century media, which is constantly reinvented because these elements are always able to — and thought of

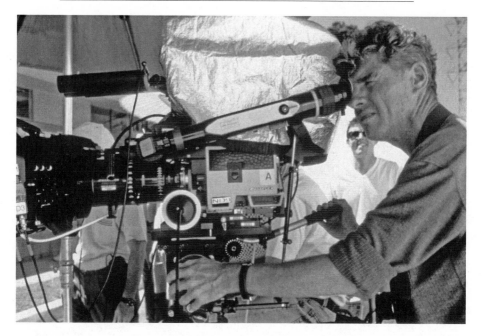

Cinematographer Christopher Doyle on the set of *Psycho* (Gus Van Sant, 1998), which represents one of the most indelible markers of the sound cinema era's end. (Photofest.)

as being able to — be remade. If "spectacle" is replaced with "media," Guy Debord gives an apt description of this moment; "The spectacle is the ruling order's non-stop discourse about itself, its never-ending monologue of self-praise, its self-portrait at the stage of totalitarian domination of all aspects of life. The fetishistic appearance of pure objectivity in spectacular relations conceals their true character as relations between people and between classes: a second Nature, with its own inescapable laws, seems to dominate our environment."[26]

American culture, that is, the culture of the United States at the start of the second decade of the twenty-first century, is post-literate due to the proliferation and dominance of moving images in the twentieth century and their more accessible/obvious tactile value over the written word. Media has no need for text, because unlike cinema, it is not of the theater and the Shakespeare-Wagner-Freud psychoanalytic line that constantly remakes the individual. Media feeds on itself. Rather than a fusion of mediums, as with Wagner's *Gesamtkunstwerk*, a layering of meanings as with Freud, or the great surrogate for dreams that is cinema, media is without tradition and without greater dramatic structure, so individual meaning is diminished and juxtaposition rules. If individuals in America are to shape this themselves, they must understand the problems that cinema caused and work to turn media back into an intellectual literature.

The twin towers of the world trade center on September 11, 2001. The current media era was fully cemented into being with the New York–set events of 9–11, as not only did international policies and concepts of freedom change that day, but viewing habits were irrevocably altered. (Michael Foran Flickr.)

Forward!—An Outline of This Text

To define the current era of media better, and perhaps shape it in positive, literate directions, its manifest anxieties past and present need to be decoded and relieved or exploited. Twentieth-century cinema provides many examples of America's cultural baggage. However, hope lies in that media may be the continuing, best path toward a universal, visual language where difference is not actual but only interpreted.

Chapter 1, "Edible Wrecks," analyzes the trajectory from *The Black Cat* (1934), to *Peeping Tom* (1960), to *Crash* (1996), demonstrating how technology remakes the body, eventually turning it into a subordinate vehicle for its own commodity. This takeover of the body by technology sets the stage for the media era where community gives way to communication, and the emphasis is shifted away from literacy toward sensation.

Chapter 2, "The Birth of Neo-Conservatism through Violence," traces capital's relationship to crime and violence from *The Public Enemy* (1931), to

Point Blank (1967), through to *Bad Lieutenant* (1992). Gangster movies here remake the idea of capital for the public. They help content the public with empowering wish-fulfillment fantasies, while facilitating the co-option of the dream state by the political.

Chapter 3, "'In the grimace of intense desire,'" uses the 1933 novel *Imitation of Life*, along with its 1934 and 1959 movie adaptations, to examine women's emerging liberation in the twentieth century up to the birth of the second wave of the feminist movement in the early 1960s. Exploring the changes made to the central narrative with each successive remaking of *Imitation of Life* stresses the damaging interplay between gender construction and women's agency in society.

Chapter 4, "The Bequests of Shadows," illustrates how parental relationships in sound cinema are based in how Shakespeare's *Hamlet* remakes Sophocles' *Oedipus*. Renegade 1940s film noirs *The Magnificent Ambersons* (1942), *One More Tomorrow* (filmed 1942; released 1946) and *Strange Illusion* (1945) together illustrate how the father shapes the child — especially the son. These movies each reveal marriage as a state of falsehood, which inherently corrupts the relationship of parent and child. Collectively, the three movies illustrate the growing ailment of the nuclear family and a national psyche whose dreams are uneasy and increasingly shaped by — yet left wanting by — cinema.

Chapter 5, "'It's all very realistic!,'" reads two "pop" and popular Anthony Burgess adaptations of the same novel, Andy Warhol's *Vinyl* (1965) and Stanley Kubrick's *A Clockwork Orange* (1971). These twined works raise the question of what image itself means, what it suggests, and how it is both made and unmade. The cultural departure from singular sensation is revealed to be a trend of cinema's move toward media.

Chapter 6, "Self-Deliverance," exposes how, after the Second World War, cultural anxieties born out of the nuclear family afford *Psycho* (1960/1998) and *The Parent Trap* (1961/1998) to be read dually as family comedies and horror films. They are family comedies, as *Psycho* is the essentialized and exaggerated American ur-narrative of how parents warp their progeny, while *The Parent Trap* is a more fantastical-than-actual comedy of errors in the classical Greek tradition. This oft-imitated, bifurcated narrative purpose results in the promiscuous imprinting of impossible familiar expectations onto child viewers.

Chapter 7, "Chapter Six, Part 2!: Remaking Hollywood," unpacks *Forced Entry* (1973 and 1981), *Despair* (1978), *Raiders of the Lost Ark* (1981) and *Raiders of the Lost Ark: The Adaptation* (1989). All five movies are self-aware and self-conscious acts of filmmaking deliberately patterned after a preestablished Hollywood model. Over the course of a decade and a half, they dramatize America's shift toward a place of permanent cultural cynicism.

Chapter 8, "I Know Who Killed Me," moves from genre theory to auteurist theory to look at how Orson Welles and David Lynch take cinema as far as it can go in terms of object and art. Welles and Lynch independently refashion themselves as creative artists with *The Immortal Story* (1968) and *Twin Peaks: Fire Walk with Me* (1992). Analysis of these two movies, linked with the observation of late twentieth century cultural changes, illuminates two unique and personal perspectives on cinema's mutation into media.

"Conclusion: For a Remaking" summarizes how during the sound era, 1931–1998, the forces of technology, capital and the pornological, coupled with an increasingly self-aware Hollywood, remade cinema into a new form, with new properties, called media. The reader is challenged to reboot the cycle of the current era, which is at ebb tide as the result of cinema's cannibalization of itself and the emerging dominance of anti-intellectual media. Attempted rebirth must begin with the individual — the performer — but resonate out to re-encompass literacy and critical thinking, privileging responsible intellectual curiosity above all else.

CHAPTER 1

Edible Wrecks

Charting Technology Remaking the Body in The Black Cat *(1934),* Peeping Tom *(1960) and* Crash *(1996)*

To analyze the sound era's relationship with technology is to observe a culture where community gives way to communication, shifting the emphasis from literacy toward sensation. Language becomes meaningless, while feelings further numb with each repetition, and the limited number of natural resources — pleasure, oil, forest — are consumed further. Cinema's link to the pornographic escalates in the sound era, for as politics enter and assume the dream state, the desire for an even greater reality of image dominates as the whole medium becomes less tangible. Silent cinema is erotic with possibility because it is a poetic representation of life, whereas all sound cinema is pornographic as it cannot escape the actual penetration of the body by technology.

In 1931, on the cusp of the change from silent to sound, Brecht writes, "The intellectuals are uncertain about technology; its crude, but powerful interference in intellectual concerns fills them with a mixture of contempt and amazement; it is becoming a fetish to them. In art, this relationship to technology is expressed thus: one can forgive anything if it is 'masterful.'"[1] Media represents that it is impossible to communicate without technology, and so to pursue social activity is to submit. The "masterful" is the link between Wagner and cinema. The "fetish" is the part of ritual that remains in Benjamin — that which cannot be emancipated from mechanical reproduction itself, even if mechanical reproduction can remove ritual from art. The faster the cycle becomes, the less "masterful" it has to be to maintain a persistence of audience vision, and so the cinema is able to forget Wagner and become post–Wagnerian in its conception of totality. A physical example of the cycle consuming more is the change from

Hjalmar Poelzig (Karloff) with his concubine Karen (Lucille Lund), who is the daughter of rival Dr. Vitus Werdegast (Bela Lugosi, not pictured) in *The Black Cat* (Edgar G. Ulmer, 1934). (Courtesy the Chestnut Hill Film Group.)

sync sound standardized at twenty-four frames per second in the sound era to thirty frames per second in the media era. The current thirty frames per second is itself a remaking of the actual drop-frame rate, 29.97, again underlining the unreality at play.

    The Black Cat is science fiction phantasy — or what Laurence A. Rickels coins "psy-fi." Susan Sontag outlines the science fiction genre in 1965 and brings it into the post–World War II era, making influential movies like *2001: A Space Odyssey* (1968) and *Star Wars* (1977) possible. "Science fiction films are not about science," she writes. "They are about disaster, which is one of the oldest subjects of art. In science fiction films disaster is rarely viewed intensively; it is always extensive. It is a matter of quantity and ingenuity. If you will, it is a question of scale."[2] Disaster appeals to the Kleinian frame, as disaster has to be remade, corrected, reparated and/or healed. To experience the representation of disaster is to play at disaster, where the neurosis of the individual is given the cosmic state of exception. In footnote 18 to her essential paper, *Mourning and Its Relation to Manic-Depressive States*, Klein suggests that, "by means of the well-known principle of representation by the contrary, an external happening can stand for an internal one. Whether the emphasis lies on the internal or the external situation becomes clear from the whole context — from the details of associations and the nature and intensity of affects."[3] The large science fiction cum disaster spectacle represents mythically, in varying balances, viewers' inner disasters — their anxieties, or reflected sociological fears.

Klein's use of the term "mourning" connects to not only death-related sadness, but the small losses and disappointments which often complement daily life, and which must be grieved by the individual for a healthy psyche, no matter how small the actual event or loss. When mourning does not happen, a repression takes place, and Klein suggests that "some people who fail to experience mourning may escape from an outbreak of manic-depressive illness or paranoia only by a severe restriction of their emotional life which impoverishes their whole personality."[4] On a national scale, this impoverishment reflects on the devaluation of literacy and the appeal of— if not need for — escapism through media that predominates in today's era.

Klein adds, "Certain manifestations of very acute anxiety and the specific defense mechanisms against this anxiety (particularly an increase in denial of psychic reality) indicate that an internal situation predominates at the time."[5] With the advent of the digital age, the science fiction genre has become more realistically representational. It is a surrogate psychic reality that allows repression of real — that is, noncinematic — psychic reality. From the late 1970s onward this culturally manifests itself in the United States with the emergence of the new cultural identity, that of "film geek," which has become a type of person, a faux-outsider label to identify oneself, rather than a manifestation of personal enthusiasm for the medium. Something akin to the compulsive masturbator, it is he or she that cinema harms most. One sees that technology and cinema here further removes the individual from the equation. Those drawn to the movies do not have to dream, because their dreams are illustrated before them, and they can sleep on pillows of ignorance having found English-language cinema's surrogacy.

The Black Cat culls images of twentieth-century atrocity with primal enactments of taboo interpersonal relationships, while suggesting that these impulses course in the veins of viewers themselves. The movie's stance is ambivalent — certainly knowing — perhaps anarchist. It is made all the more uncertain by Universal Pictures' post-production redaction of the movie. Like that other famous *film maudit*, *The Magnificent Ambersons*, *The Black Cat* is more (and, weirdly, more all-of-a-piece) because of its recut nature. It is the next level of cinema — cinema that elicits a higher level of literacy from viewers.

Another excellent science fiction film, though one that is not often categorized as such, *Peeping Tom* extends *The Black Cat*'s prophetic interpolation of technology and repressed urges. The titular figure, Mark Lewis, needs a camera to complete him. The movie itself, reviled upon first release, now attracts viewers because culturally Mark's damage is not the sad story of a lone pervert, but the represented baggage of the entire era — the era that leads to the dawn of the media age.

Finally, at the sound era's *fin de siècle*, *Crash* playfully and disinterestedly links sex with auto accidents as technology has lead the psyche beyond flesh. Ultimately, the film delivers a treatise on how the death urge is the primary compulsion of modern society and forwards the concept that media desires viewers to actualize their (our) disasters as quickly as possible. Benjamin observes that mankind's "self-alienation has reached such a degree that it can experience its own destruction as an aesthetic pleasure of the first order."[6] Self-alienation, self-elimination, self-deliverance becomes the ideal, as it both represents a retardation and an action, but really grants no personal development, as the quicker the system exhausts itself, the sooner it can reboot (as in versions of *Psycho* and *The Parent Trap* discussed in Chapter 6). In the media era, success is largely a matter of scale, of mass production. Reconnecting to Sontag, science fiction scale and the scale of media's success have interchangeable core elements and trajectories. This interchangeability illustrates that reality is now platformed on unachievable or unrealistic fictions. Friedrich Dürrenmatt in "Problems of the Theatre" writes about this from a specific, early Cold War moment: "The state has lost its physical reality, and just as physics can now only cope with the world in mathematical formulas, so the state can only be expressed in statistics. Power today becomes visible, material only when it explodes as in the atom bomb, in this marvelous mushroom which rises and spreads immaculate as the sun and in which mass murder and beauty have become one. The atom bomb can not be reproduced artistically since it is mass-produced."[7] The confusion of mass murder and beauty is the confusion of the media era, a confusion that ethically tears society apart.

The postwar culture of the United States is a progressive assault to literate culture because it favors the infrastructure of society at the expense of the society itself. If thinking happens, it does not move beyond comprehension to evaluation. The citizenry sees itself as it believes it presents itself, what Debord writes of as the *Society of the Spectacle*: "The reigning economic system is a *vicious circle of isolation*. Its technologies are based on isolation, and they contribute to that same isolation. From automobiles to television, the goods that the spectacular system *chooses to produce* also serve them as weapons for constantly reinforcing the condition that engender 'lonely crowds.' With ever-increasing concreteness the spectacle recreates its own presuppositions."[8] The sound era offered viewers in movie theaters a type of isolation, which the media era accelerates so that technology isolates the individual within the home, removing the theater — and therefore the theatrical — via the promise of information but with the delivery of infotainment.

The Black Cat (1934)

The Black Cat, directed by Edgar G. Ulmer and released by Universal in 1934, came on the successful heels of the first sound versions of *Dracula* and

Frankenstein, both initially unspooled to the public in 1931. *The Black Cat* features Béla Lugosi (Count Dracula) and Boris Karloff (Frankenstein's monster) together for the first time, and this original "monster mash" remade genre archetypes firmly set in place by the aforementioned Stoker/Shelly literary adaptations, their successors and immediate imitators.

Primarily shot in a studio, *The Black Cat* remakes reality first in that the movie is set in a world both clearly "now" (i.e., 1934) and clearly in the future. The milieu is rife with superhuman forces pivoting between the potentially theological and inhumanly technological. To support its fantasy rooted in reality, *The Black Cat* often recontextualizes stock footage to bridge the extravagant set pieces of the movie "suggested by the immortal Edgar Alan Poe classic." In truth, Ulmer and Peter Ruric's screenplay is an appropriation of Poe, where most of the actual details are reconfigured according to a highly individual reading of the source story's impressions. The discontinuity of story links *The Black Cat* with *The Magnificent Ambersons* where technology is firstly represented by the automobile and second by the huge city, "spreading incredibly." The discontinuity of story in both *The Black Cat* and *Ambersons* is mostly a result of a somewhat radical remaking by the studio prior to release. As sound cinema evolved to media, discontinuity of story, initially a filmic refraction of the modernist movement in literature, became an editorial-aesthetic style. The height of this fashion was the mid–1960s, and the English-language films that best personify this technique are *Blow-Up* (1966) and *Point Blank* (1967). It seems as if Ulmer was not unaware of the discontinuity of *The Black Cat*'s story because the tone is so consistent. Clearly a metaphoric or allegorical movie, *The Black Cat* suggests an early illustration, one before the Second World War, of how the narrative of the future — the future which is now the media era — is designed along a theory of planned obsolescence. Thus, everything needs to be consumed again, remade, both for the sake of coherence and for the sake of the impression of progress, which provides emotional stability by offering up an interpretation for viewers "uncompleted" on their own.

What is so horrific about *The Black Cat* is that the action transpires in a world that is clearly presented as the near future, and that future has ceased to make any logical sense. This intent makes *The Black Cat* closer to dreams or nightmares than other movies. Today, this makes the movie a highly apt choice for cultural psychoanalysis. Klein writes in *Early Stages of the Oedipus Conflict* that "the early feeling of *not knowing* has manifold connections. It unites with the feeling of being incapable, impotent, which soon results from the Oedipus situation. The child also feels this frustration the more acutely because he *knows nothing* definite about sexual processes. In both sexes the castration complex is accentuated by this feeling of ignorance."[9] Ulmer compounds Oedipal trauma with technological domination, linking the state of *not knowing* from the sexual to the scientific, thereby creating a nightmare which has the same central trauma applied to very different things — science and the body. This of course alludes to science and body's mid-century collision in the Nazi death camps, which most often iconically represents the height of the machinery of murder.

Beginning with the Universal logo at the start, *The Black Cat* offers the continual premise of modernity — of science above everything — which not so incidentally is the ideology of National Socialism and a very modern, and still possibly advantageous, position in 1934. However, *The Black Cat* is even more fraught with the dangers of such a rationale. In many ways, the movie is weirdly playful as it is trying to elicit interpretation out of viewers, and this carelessness adds a real danger and ambiguity to viewer remaking because it provides no certain answers.

The lovers at the center of *The Black Cat* are Peter Alison (David Manners) and his wife, Joan (Jacqueline Wells). He is a pulp mystery writer, and they are on their European honeymoon when they are stranded with psychiatrist Dr. Vitus Werdegast (Lugosi) and avant-garde architect Hjalmar Poelzig (Karloff). From the start, Werdegast and Poelzig are mortal enemies, Poelzig apparently having sold Werdegast out during the First World War and having taken both his wife, and later his daughter Karen, as concubines. Werdegast, meanwhile, was sent to prison where his soul was "killed slowly" as Poelzig fled to America to wait out the conflict. The exposition is a lurid reminder of cinema's history as expose-posing-as-education, of movies' dueling inception as journalism and the titillation meant to appeal to those with unfulfilled sexual relations. It is also a parable of the great Germany-to-Hollywood migration of the 1930s.

The sensation of necrophilic impulse — most specifically the Bluebeardian crypt of lost women under Poelzig's house — ignites the sexual energy of *The Black Cat*, one of the last films to make it through to release before the Motion Picture Producers and Distributors of America (MPPDA) disemboweled the frank content of early talkies with its production code. Early in *The Black Cat*, when Joan is asleep in the train, Werdegast fondles her with sexual interest married to scientific impulse, as if he is the doctor and she his patient — or he Dracula and she Mina Harker. After the crash, drugs render Joan, like Mina, "mediumistic" — "a conduit for all intangible forces around her" — and from this point on, Joan becomes the audience's most sympathetic surrogate and a metaphor for viewing cinema herself.

The quartet is indefinitely lodged/held captive in Poelzig's fortress house — a Valhalla he designed on top of a ghastly war prison. Werdegast calls the house "the masterpiece of construction built upon the ruins of the masterpiece of destruction — masterpiece of murder." Peter more deliberately understates the dwelling as "a very tricky house." This uneasy aesthetic represented by Poelzig's modern house echoes the uneasy task — flirting with absurdity — of restating ethics after war. What developed in America during the sound era's cinema restating of ethics after World War II (and later after conflicts like Korea, Vietnam and

Iraq) is a highly selective individual/national perspective and un-interdependent, selective memory aided and abetted by cancerous technology.

Most of all in *The Black Cat* there is the reliance on technology for function, and later — certainly from *Peeping Tom* onward — for identity. The Alisons' honeymoon excursion is based on the advancements that define the modern age — planes, trains, cars, printing press and radio. The Alisons are also the victims of technology, as when technology fails, it places them — more than anything else — in mortal danger. The most specific harbinger of doom is wryly spoken by Poelzig as the Alisons seek to politely escape his house: "The phone is dead, even the phone is dead." The threat that technology will be, or has already been, unknowingly harnessed for deliberate destructive purposes is the key anxiety of *The Black Cat* — the key threat terrifying the audience. The film is so foreign both in its ethnicity and psychoanalytic perspective that it travels full circle from nonsense to total sense, especially when read as an allegory.

Automobiles and the changes they bring contribute to the ruin of the Ambersons and the Alisons. Roughly perfected around the same time, car and cinema share a long history before they are co-eulogized in *Crash*. A crash figures in *The Black Cat*, sending the honeymooning lovers to Poelzig's dwelling where they face death more closely than ever before. The crash is both fate's interjection and the revolt of the technological in the face of nature (represented in *The Black Cat* by a storm and certain nonscientific, spiritual elements). In the tradition of Wagner, of whom Ulmer was a great admirer, *The Black Cat* places technology within the imagined world. *The Black Cat's* characters destructively disregard its domination as they seek to summon a spiritual force in a universe perhaps without god or devil. Ulmer taps the Marquis de Sade, along the lines of Octavio Paz who explains in his tract on Sade, *An Erotic Beyond* (1961), that, "with the same insistence with which theologians refer to God, Sade invokes nature: the supreme engine, the cause of all causes. A cause that destroys itself because everything is in perpetual change."[10] In this regard, then, the Satanists who hold a black mass at *The Black Cat's* climax are the only true individuals in the movie, a sort of neo–Luddite cult, whose sympathies — if they may be called that — are in tandem with Ulmer's deeply humanist bent (admittedly more predominantly on display in works of his like *Damaged Lives*, *The Light Ahead* and *St. Benny the Dip*). The fact that the Satanists are more or less anonymous illustrates that identity is not identity, but a posture wherein the human becomes part of the (ever-growing) technological rational.

In *The Black Cat* it is said that "evil is deathless" and that some things are as "eternal as evil." But the movie is also inconclusive, so that the viewer has to wonder, "What is evil?" and "Who is evil?" Ulmer takes the audience back to a view of Satan as rebel, as the angel who defies an uptight Old Testament God. Given Werdegast's crazed creepiness, Poelzig's rationality and civility (read: efficiency of murder) suggests Satan as the sane, logical choice in the mad, mod world of *The Black Cat*. Poelzig reads *The Rites of Lucifer* before he goes to sleep, and the old adage that "the best people are in hell" comes to mind, as does Brecht writing in 1930s' *Rise and Fall of the City of Mahagonny* that "we're living in a hell already."[11] Along these Satanic/Sadeian lines, Paz states that society is being "governed by beasts disguised as philanthropists. Our religion is a hoax in which fear is allied with ferocity: an unrealistic god and a hell that would be ridiculous if it were not a waking nightmare."[12] Ulmer, a displaced Jew in America, here suggests that Poelzig's Satanic cult, which seeks to sacrifice Joan, is no greater or less than the sacrifices codified into the (confused) Christian tradition.

Ulmer's whole inception of *The Black Cat* is otherworldly and steeped in the Other. He uses classical music to underscore the drama, causing the whole movie to nearly buckle under a wealth of allusion and shearing of actual apparent meaning. When Werdegast kills Poelzig's black cat and Joan immediately enters, Franz Schubert's "Unfinished Symphony" (1822–1828) underscores the scene. It is a screen action linking the cat and Joan, making Joan's sacrifice as much of a revenge killing as Werdegast's homicidal, hypomanic return for Poelzig. The Schubert music cue is also a quite sophisticated and avant-garde appropriation of Lugosi's *Dracula* baggage — an elaboration of the use of *Swan Lake* in the 1931 Universal Bram Stoker adaptation directed by Tod Browning — and an anticipation of the use of preexisting music in those doubled Anthony Burgess adaptations, *Vinyl* and *A Clockwork Orange*.

Ulmer uses imaginary geography based in reality and foreign locals much like Brecht created an imaginary United States in *Mahagonny* where the Alaska Gold Coast; Chicago, Illinois; and Pensacola, Florida exist in the same hemisphere. Ulmer further breaks down meaning in *The Black Cat*, encouraging remakes of his outsider perspective, by playing with language subterranean to any literal meaning. The name "Werdegast" means nothing as an English-language word, but conjures "weird-aghast" when uttered, which is pretty much the most common reaction to Lugosi's character. "Poelzig," incidentally the name of the art director on 1920's *The Golem*, on which Ulmer worked, also suggests "Poe-zigzag," endemic of the movie's treatment of the short story that is the movie's source material.

Here (and many other places in his oeuvre), Ulmer lavishes screen time upon ethnic character roles, often to provide comic relief, but also skillfully using what are nearly ethnic stereotypes, to illustrate the cultural difference of Old World Europe and modern America. The use of foreign names, like Werdegast and Poelzig, allow Ulmer to comment on the xenophobia and ethnophobia rife within America, despite the nation being a melting pot — or as revision would have it, a "tossed salad" — of immigrants. American's lack of ethnic-cultural identity — that which is always shed for whiteness — results in the removal of tradition and learned behaviors, thus flaming the cultural need for cinema's remaking. When Joan says to Peter, "I don't like Mr. Pigslow or whatever his name is," it is an example of the American tendency to fear the Other and thus mock it, absolving the self of any empathy — empathy of course being the usually most healthy way to regard fellow humans. No wonder that Poelzig finds Joan such an apt choice for Luciferian sacrifice.

Finally, any semblance of normalcy ruptures in *The Black Cat* when the servant Thamal (Harry Cording), who at various times has appeared, mercenary-like, to be on both Werdegast's and/or Poelzig's side, knocks Peter Alison unconscious as he tries to escape the death house. Joan faints at the violence, and Thamal takes her upstairs in a fashion remaking King Kong absconding with Ann Darrow, but without the romance or sexual desire. It is essential to note that work has desexualized Thamal and that his servitude has robbed him of any individual

Work has desexualized Thamal (Harry Cording), and his servitude has robbed him of any individual meaning in *The Black Cat* (Edgar G. Ulmer, 1934). (Courtesy the Chestnut Hill Film Group.)

meaning. In the future, this prototype of the servant will allow for characters like Verbena in *The Parent Trap* (1961) or Martin in *The Parent Trap* (1998), who will become part of the family, not out of affection but duty and vocation. For Peter in *The Black Cat,* this moment is his literal trip into the unconscious, into his fear (where he is most vulnerable). The cat is, so to speak, out of the bag, and the entire movie must be understood as the nightmare of the future — the nightmare of now.

At the very end of the motion picture, Thamal returns — seemingly from the dead (as he has been shot) — to help capture Poelzig so that Werdegast may torture him. This is Ulmer's commentary on the impossibility of buying people's minds, as it is the reality of any era of only being able to indenture not own. Furthermore, individuals are susceptible to whatever influence — usually financial, but sometimes also psychological, spiritual or cinematic — is offered them because modern culture cannot allow individual completion and conformity to coexist. Whatever the case, the servant Thamal dies with his arms outstretched like Christ on the cross.

The Black Cat ends with a bang (more "documentary" stock footage) and the lovers amazingly resilient despite what they have been through. Safe on a train, they read a newspaper review of Peter's newest book and chuckle over its complaint that his freshly issued novel "stretches credibility." Apparently poking fun at itself, *The Black Cat* may also be illustrating how all movies are contrived and "strain credibility," yet this acknowledgment only leaves the poetic truth of *The Black Cat*—its images of sadism and its theory of holocaust. Black cats are spoken of as the "living embodiment of evil," and it appears that this embodiment is what Poelzig, like Sade, seeks and so motivates his actions during the movie. What is so unsettling in *The Black Cat*, and the fission that propels the work, is that Ulmer suggests there is not a true, living embodiment of evil — that there are no absolutes — just relative states all leading to a path of doom exacerbated by technology.

Peeping Tom (1960)

To Paz, Sade is the philosopher who represents that "there is nothing more natural than sexual desire; there is nothing less natural than the forms in which it is made manifest and satisfied.... Eroticism and sexuality are independent kingdoms belonging to the same vital universe."[13] The pull between eroticism and sexuality is made deeper by technology's encroachment on American lives, and this tension regarding the "forms in which it is made manifest" is the very split between what is represented on screen and what is actual, thus introducing sadism into the cinema. In many ways, individual viewing is a search, if not an attack; for what is perceived as inside the screen is — in actuality — intangible and nonexistent. Klein finds these impulses codified in childhood: "I have already mentioned that phantasies and feelings of an aggressive and of a gratifying, erotic nature, which are to a large extent fused together (a fusion which is called sadism), play a dominant part in the child's early life. They are first of all focused on the breasts of his mother, but gradually extend to her whole body. Greedy, erotic and destructive phantasies and feelings have for their object the inside of the mother's body. In his imagination the child attacks it, robbing it of everything it contains and eating it up."[14] Hence, "eating up the cinema" displaces individuals from their actuality, leaving them hungrier and puzzled. If individuals do feel satiated by motion pictures it is an untruthful sensation caused by cinema's illusions being so majestic.

Paz remakes Sade for the twentieth century noting that "eroticism is sexual desire and something more, and that something is what makes up its essence. That something feeds on sexuality; it is nature. And yet, at the same time, it is unnatural."[15] This unnaturalness is never more concrete than in the act of cinematic sexual gratification, which is the most seductive of all illusions because it appears to be what is missing from real life. It abstracts the body, removing it — through the lenses — from all tangible, actual connections. Paz surmises that "eroticism is a form of the social domination of instinct, and in this sense it can equip a technology" as "society subjects sexual instinct to regulations, and thus confiscates and exploits its energy.... Eroticism presents a set of prohibitions — magical, moral, legal, economic, and more — intended to prevent the sexual tide from submerging the social edifice, leveling hierarchies and divisions, washing away society."[16] It "evaporates, and all that remains in our hands, with a few dates and hypotheses (the so-called 'historical conditions'), is a shadow, a gesture of pleasure or of death."[17] When there are no surrogates for dreams — no attainable dreams — then it is natural for the death instinct to kick in and for sexuality to be transformed by sadism, and then both be remade by the political, so that destructive impulses replace constructive images in the sound era.

Death is the key pleasure of the second half of twentieth-century English-language cinema, and *Peeping Tom* is the first film of this second half. It is the story of the self-realization of cameraman Mark Lewis — a traumatized son — who, despite much castration anxiety and many deep feelings of inadequacy, winds up making a greater impact on the world than his greatly feared psychologist father. As Mark remarks of his paternal torturer, "I think he learned a lot from me."

Peeping Tom marks the beginning of its director Michael Powell's second act as he transferred from co-productions with Emeric Pressburger to more psychologically galvanizing fare like *Herzog Blaubarts Burg* (1963) and *Age of Consent* (1969). A movie of doubles beginning with its dual-faced distributor — Janus Films — offering art at a price, *Peeping Tom* is a movie of London remaking itself after the blitz, as written by a man, Leo Marks, who was a war hero skilled in cryptography.

Post–World War II America was so resplendent that Hitchcock had to photograph his *Psycho* in black and white, whereas Powell's new world in *Peeping Tom* so quivers with construction and collision that only garish color will suffice to capture all the nuance. Powell and cinematographer Otto Heller's use of Technicolor makes the movie unreal, while elements like point-of-view shots make the movie an extremely first-person experience at the same time. *Peeping Tom* has continuity of story, but the discontinuity between visuals and subject presents the work as needing viewer interpretation. *Peeping Tom* is a movie about moviemaking, its commentary on cinema never more total than when Mark and his love interest Helen Stephens (Anna Massey) have an increasingly tense conversation in his darkroom, and this tension is paralleled by the physical tension of developing film. *Peeping Tom* ripples outwards from this point — a Wagnerian transformation scene — forward and back, where time and space are one. Medium is here synonymous with material, and this is an example of cinema's movement toward media.

Peeping Tom is a movie full of free associations which confirm Balázs'

Carl Boehm as "Mark Lewis" in *Peeping Tom* (Michael Powell, 1960). Himself, Mark is two — the "camera" and the "man" — his body only completed by his camera-knife-penis-mirror, a mirror which reminds that cinema itself is a mirror, just as *Peeping Tom* is a mirror of cinema. (The Museum of Modern Art/Film Stills Archive.)

assumption that "the filmmaker is a machine that, in its way, is creating living and concrete internationalism: *the single, common psyche of the white man.*"[18] Mark's pathology is that of the modern neurotic. His faintly German accent suggests the uneasy tensions in German and English reintegration after the Second World War. Himself, Mark is two — the "camera" and the "man" — his body only completed by his camera-knife-penis-mirror, a mirror which reminds us that cinema itself is a mirror, just as *Peeping Tom* is a mirror of cinema, for as Paz states, "Without the Other there is no eroticism, for there is no mirror."[19] It comes as no surprise that *Peeping Tom* is a huge favorite among filmmakers.

Mark's downstairs neighbor and Helen's mother, Mrs. Stephens' (Maxine Audley), remarks, "All this filming isn't healthy." It is a comment made more ironic by Mrs. Stephens' lack of sight, yet her ability to conjure a "second sight" out of herself. By escaping cinema — if not the visual entirely — greater, higher truth is apparent. Mrs. Stephens is privileged by her lack of sight in a way that returns her into cinema where technology defines movie people and, as with Mark, is their identity. Filmmaking is a "state of exception"—first, for Mark's father A.N. Lewis' behavior toward him as a child, and second, for Mark himself when the sanctity of the studio's red light ensures that he will be able to photograph-murder Vivian uninterrupted.

Moral ambiguity permeates the post–World War II London air in *Peeping Tom*. A man in a news shop dickers with the owner over the price of pornographic "views," and this act returns them to the everyday world of political commerce from the stimulation of the erotic photographs. It is an illustration of how war first loosens moral codes when the threat of imminent, allegedly noble death hangs in the air, and second, how the act of war — that is, violence fused with technology — has a desexualizing effect, and how erotic concerns must grow outside of the body. In his study of Sade and Leopold von Sacher-Masoch, *Coldness and Cruelty*, Gilles Deleuze suggests that "desexualization has two possible effects on the workings of the pleasure principle: either it introduces functional disturbances which affect the application of the principle, or else it promotes a sublimation of the instincts whereby pleasure is transcended in favor of gratifications of a different kind."[20]

Scopophilia, voyeurism — the morbid desire to watch — is the primary agent of cinema and media as it adds the technology of camera to impulse, thereby transforming physical identity into nonidentity, so making identity only possible with technology. The cinema remakes the gratification of the scopophiliac impulse and does so moving this desire from body to screen in a type of psychoanalytic transference. Mark's orgasms do not come during the murder-penetration, but afterward, in the moment in the screening room just before he knows whether he has achieved his cinematic aim. This displaced orgasm reflects viewers' catharsis moving during the sound era from the movie's climax to the act of ticket purchase before the screening.

Peeping Tom is extremely self-referential to itself and the process of feature filmmaking. Furthermore, it blatantly equates cinema with the pornographic, which is the most honest use of the technology of sound cinema, because it is actual, that is, "true." The link between the reality of pornography and the escalation of the political in sound-era cinema underlines the link between pornography and sports, media's co-option of both and the twenty-first century's eschewing of structure and the feature film format.

Peeping Tom concretely acknowledges cinema's greatest historical opponent — televised sports — in a way that few mid–twentieth-century movies do. In fact, Chief Police Inspector Gregg (Jack Watson) is at home watching the game at the climax of *Peeping Tom* when Helen journeys alone into Mark's darkroom, into Mark's forbidden psychic reality where all anxieties are still vulnerable with childhood Oedipal trauma. Inspector Gregg's technological surrogacy is still rooted in the (sporting) body, whereas Mark's semi-mechanism is an instrument of murderous bodily harm, causing a conflation of sports and pornography in a world where technology — the television, the camera — define the human. Sex is a sport, cinema is an escape. To add narrative — that is, to collaborate with technology to create meaning — is to remove the body from centricity. This conflation is wryly illustrated when Inspector Gregg visits the studio and the director hurries him along, bemoaning, "If you only knew what a single day wasted would cost," and the officer replies gravely, "We do." The irony is that the inspector speaks of human life, whereas the director speaks of the economic-artistic problems, which in cinema are removed from physical reality. Humanity and the value of real life are lost on the filmmaker as the technology of cinema removes humans from themselves.

Peeping Tom is clearly a horror movie, though it is more upsetting and unnerving than scary or gory. When any seemingly random murderer is afoot, the meaning of life must be evaluated more closely by individuals — as any action could be a costly, fatal misstep. In the best horror movies, this tension escalates so that it is not quite clear if outside influence, or the nature of human-ity itself, is the enemy. The police inspector — perhaps a victim of postwar trauma himself— tells the movie people at the studio that he "suspects them all." This paranoia — exacerbated by World War II espionage — is new to the cinema of the late 1950s and 1960s and further removes the individual from the actual, as he or she can no longer trust what is unprocessed by cinema and, later, its successor, media.

It is often remarked that gallows humor is what got the English through the 1940s blitz, and true to its nation of origin, *Peeping Tom* is loaded with per-versity, which often suggests the entire project as an exceptionally cruel joke — a Sadian tract — rather than a horror film. Paz links Sade to the Satanists at Poelzig's Black Mass, and as Paz quotes Sade from *Juliette* he absolves Mark and Poelzig, stating, "Crime has no reality: that is, the possibility of crime does not exist because there is no way to outrage nature." Paz quantifies what might be called Sadian comedy, writing that the divine Marquis' "greatest originality con-sists in having thought of eroticism as a total, cosmic reality, that is, *as reality*."[21] False reality bleeds for Mark from the studio to the home. He seeks to remake himself and capture a new perspective — a new angle for his movie — when he visits the crime scene of a murder he committed the night before. Asked by a police officer to verify what newspaper he is from, Mark facetiously replies, "*The Observer*." Other cruel ironies abound as well: An actress is only able to deliver the scream the director wants by seeing an actual atrocity; mannequins are dismembered in shop windows, alluding to the grisliness of Mark's crimes (which the viewer never sees); pornography is readily displayed, such as the whore at sunset whom Mark murders before the movie's opening credits.

The prostitute Dora (Brenda Bruce) and the "views" model Milly (Pamela Green) are doubles. Milly is such a detached sex worker that she is able to imagine the banality of her mirror self Dora, but unable to find any real empathy in her murder, save for the remark that "she won't be doing the crossword tonight." Milly knows that shooting pornography is Mark's spare-time gig, perhaps some sort of sexual lark, or justification of sexuality — sexuality without murder. For her, the job seems to be the former, as well as her sole livelihood. Paz states, "We want to see something. That something is erotic fascination, that which takes me from myself and brings me to you: that which makes me go beyond you,"[22] and he might almost be describing the tragic, nearly nonexistent romance between Milly and Mark. It is a tragedy because, as cameraman and model, they have the potential to complete each other, and thereby through cinema find life outside of cinema. However, in and of herself without Dora, Milly is schizoid as a result of her era — she explains a facial bruise to Mark saying that she went out with her boyfriend but got beat up by her fiancé because of it. "Fix it so the bruises don't show," she commands to Mark — like a Dietrich or a Garbo seeking soft focus. Yet, as interested in her representation as she is one moment, the next moment she chides Mark for dithering too long under the camera blanket making a technical adjustment. "What have you got under there, a girlfriend?" she asks Mark like a belligerent mother. Millie is a mother figure to Mark, and this makes *Peeping Tom* into *Sunset Blvd.*'s successor in black comedy as much as *Psycho* (1960) is.

Helen, another mother figure, says to Mark, "You walk around like you haven't paid the rent." Mark — having inherited the house from his father — admits he has not. Of course, the house is wired for sound and is therefore its own studio, complete with cinematographic lab, screening room and multiple soundstages. Mark's house is another uncanny house like the Ambersons', or Poelzig's in *The Black Cat*, what Carol J. Clover traces from *Psycho* (1960) onward as the horror genre's "terrible place." In *Psycho* (1960), the terrible place is the sphere of the mother, however, because as Gertrud Koch writes, "the historical differentiation of voyeurism and exhibitionism along the lines of gender roles, which makes the woman the object and the man the active bearer of the look, consequentially predicated the aesthetics of narrative cinema on the patriarchal orchestration of the look."[23] Mark's house is always the house of the father, and the argument can be made that the house is always in the domain of the patriarchy, be it authoritarian, emasculated, or absent. Tangible examples of this, apart from *Peeping Tom*, include Poelzig's self-designed house in *The Black Cat* and that it was Mrs. Bates' paramour who urged her to build the roadside motel in *Psycho*. Klein confirms this viewpoint and then illustrates how this element can be viewed most clearly by removing genders. "The analyses of boys and men fully confirmed Freud's view that castration fear is the leading anxiety of the male, but I recognized that owing to the early identification with the mother (that feminine position which ushers in the early stages of the Oedipus complex) the anxiety about attacks on the inside of the body is of great importance in men as well as women, and in various ways influences and moulds their castration fears."[24] These "terrible place" houses represent an internal absence and are the anxieties that predominantly motivate adult behavior of the sound era.

When Mark watches the footage of his killing, it is different than the footage viewers "witnessed" firsthand being shot through the viewfinder in the pre-credit sequence. Like any dream, there is a disparity in *Peeping Tom* between memory and reality. Mark wants to remake his father's home movies and the home movies have become his "documentary." Documentary cinema is usually mistakenly perceived as truer than fantasy, and it is this urge to make the perfect, real film (of trauma) that spurs Mark to kill and kill again as much as his Oedipal anxieties do. Mark is the focus puller at the movie studio; here his career remakes his father (played in *Peeping Tom* by director Powell), whom viewers saw adjust focus in a crucially formative home movie that Mark shares with Helen. Mark's psychological baggage evokes noir–Hamletian obsessions — the son who is the father, while not being the father — which creates a disparity of purpose and emotional paralysis. Culturally, there is no past until Oedipus, which is the drama that gives Western culture a past. Like the Hamlet of Act 5, Mark wants to die, because if he were to change, the uprooting of his neurosis would remove Mark's technology surrogacy and force him to remake an identity without technology, without the past and with his body. As Klein laments in *Early Stages of the Oedipus Conflict*, "one of the most bitter grievances which we come upon in the unconscious is that this tremendous questioning impulse, which is apparently only partly conscious and even so far as it is cannot yet be expressed in words, remains unanswered."[25] Mark, like the twentieth century which contains him, is a terminal case.

Crash (1996)

The most original Hollywood movie production company of the 1980s and 1990s was New Line Cinema. Between 1991 (*My Own Private Idaho*) and 2004 (*Vera Drake*), New Line sought to answer the market's demand — brought about by the branding "independent film" care of the Sundance Film Festival — by remaking themselves as "Fine Line Features." The 1996 David Cronenberg adaptation of J.G. Ballard's 1973 novel, *Crash*, was one of Fine Line's most striking products and met with controversy, but also somewhat universal praise, or at least acceptance, including a Cannes Jury Prize for "audacity," on its first release. It is a cinematic bow more deserved by *Peeping Tom*, but nonetheless illustrative of how the viewing public in the sound era was by 1996 desensitized to atrocity because atrocity could be fully understood cinematically. Jurij Lotman notes this tendency at the inception of cinema: "It was just this feeling of the genuineness of the picture that activated in the first cinema audience those unquestionably base emotions which are typical of the passive observer of genuine catastrophes, auto accidents, and which appeased the quasi-aesthetic and quasi-sporting emotions of audiences at Roman circuses — not unlike the reactions of the present-day fans of Western automobile racing."[26] What the twentieth century adds to the spectacle of live Roman circuses is a potential for reproducibility and rewrites. It is what author Robert Bloch touches on in his sequel novel *Psycho II* (1982), when the reproducibility of incident is how events are remade to be familiar and therefore more alluring.

> "I don't mean pictures." Post finished off his beer. "But think about this. Some politician gets up and reads a speech. His opponent reads a rebuttal. Then a TV commentator reads a report explaining what the two men read. All of it — the speech, the rebuttal, the explanation — is the work of some anonymous writers in the back room. And we call it 'news.'"[27]

Bloch's construction of media illustrates its inherent fragmentation and untruth while linking this to the technology of television, something Cronenberg explores in his "video circus" masterpiece, *Videodrome* (1983), wherein — presciently — video is evolution.

The opening titles of *Crash* drive toward viewers in the glare of headlights — an assembly line of credits reflective of too many cars on the road and how, for the first time, largely because of personal computers and the Internet, there was an information onslaught in the United States. Content could be directly interfaced, and therefore the social organizations that had previously guarded knowledge were rendered, like the body, more obsolete because of technology. Without the organization of education to structure literacy in the 1990s, the very possibilities and value of information diminished, and the post-literate trend further took hold.

Sontag writes that "perversity is the muse of modern literature."[28] More than willing suspension of disbelief, real absurdity is perversely mangled into a logic in cinema — the motion of the film in the gate forces the viewer to keep up and leap over applying true logic. The concept of crashing as a true accident becomes absurd. *Crash* is an endpoint, where cinema, automobile and the repressed desires of audiences collide. Eisenstein saw "montage as a *collision*. A view that from the collision of two given factors *arises* a concept. From my point of view, linkage is merely a possible *special* case."[29] *Crash* takes this at a literal level where concept arises from action, not the juxtaposition that gives illusion its veracity. Crashing is therefore necessary as it represents and redoubles the random nature of society — it provides agency as well as impact. Sensation is further dulled by repetitious modernity and its suggestion of a cure to a problem that is false and created as a means of domination. In *Crash*, even the local hospital keeps beds waiting for airplane casualties — the hospital's identity predicated not on an actual reality, but a proposed reaction to a possible reality.

Crashing is a necessity for connection, meaning, metaphor. In *Crash*, the hero, James Ballard (James Spader), is a producer of commercials, one step removed from Mark whose interaction with the materials of the medium gave his surrogacy a tangible reality. Like *The Black Cat* and *Peeping Tom*, *Crash* is a movie about movies, one that exists in a state where the anxieties of the previous two have been accepted as the cultural norm. For the final assault on the body by cinema-becoming-media, the nature of pleasure and the sexual urge is requantified, abstracted, so that what becomes desirable is not an exchange of human fluid between live flesh, but the seeking of the sensations of gratification through technology.

James Ballard is everyman — J.G. Ballard the novel's author, as well as James Spader the actor. Fused into one, the viewer understands that "James Ballard" is not a character but a stand-in for him- or herself. It is a remaking that allows hiding in plain sight — the "perfect" twenty-first-century placement. Spader's participation in *Crash* echoes his role of Graham Dalton in *sex, lies, and videotape* (1989). In that movie, Spader was impotent unless watching a movie — in *Crash* the sex act itself has become impotent, a dead-end because culture and commodity have carefully created false cultural goals to abet their own manifestations, so leaving true erotics obsolete. Mark makes an impact not with his camera's images but by using it as a device of torture — Ballard's social impact is not in the advertising he creates but in the crashes that upset patterns with their inherently semi-random nature. Unlike Mark, Ballard indulges in camera-room fucking because the medium is not able to offer a surrogacy for him as content has been neutralized by capital. Later Ballard lies to his wife Catherine (Deborah Kara Unger) about the Camera Girl (Alice Poon) not orgasming during their studio tryst. Catherine offers a type of solace, remarking, "Poor darling. Maybe the next one." Ironically, this dialogue will also serve as *Crash*'s closing line after Ballard and Catherine's most life-threatening — but not life-extinguishing — collision in the movie. Anything is permissible when there is hope for a different future.

For Ballard and Catherine, sex talk remakes — if not replaces — sex acts. Catherine's airplane hangar intercourse begins the movie in fantasy awoken out of the phantasy of twentieth century "jet age" culture. The mid–twentieth-century moment of *Peeping Tom* and *Psycho* is the beginning of the decline of the sound era where planes remake trains and the 1960s reinvent the 1950s. Actual coitus between Ballard and Catherine "feels like traffic accidents." Conversation removes the element of reality as their modernity has led to a destruction of the tangible and the alluring position of dreams. Fantasy therefore becomes a greater truth at an end state, such as at the beginning of the new, post-literate age.

Ballard has a sense of relief about having had the accident with Helen Remington (Holly Hunter) and her husband. The dread and anxiety of the late 1990s wasn't millennial panic as it was then often explained; rather this epoch of *nervous splendor's* ailment was the repression of the evidence that the

"Maybe the next one"— Catherine Ballard (Deborah Kara Unger) and James Ballard (James Spader) achieve a new type of intimacy in *Crash* (David Cronenberg, 1996). (Courtesy Andrew's Video Vault at the Rotunda.)

infrastructure — or, more dangerously problematic, what might be called "values," — of North American civilization were crumbling. President Clinton's affair with Monica Lewinsky was culturally upsetting specifically because it was a symbolic transgression like Oedipus'. The lack of clarity of fate, the schism between what cinema offers versus what it is, resulted in a wave of nihilism that permeated the *fin de siècle*. Catherine milks hospitalized Ballard's cock with her hand, but he stops her from making him cum, however. She replaces his member with a cigarette, cementing that the pleasure of orgasm has been rendered false, perhaps because it is so undeniably true.

To experience orgasm's communion results in degraded psychic space, a remaking of Catholicism/Christianity with its guilt attached to sex, where pleasure is dangerous because of how out of place the experience has become with modernity. This denial of pleasure is also apparent in *Crash*, which, for a movie that is rather sexually explicit, lacks the photography of any penises and of any representation of actual intercourse. At most, pubic hair is glimpsed, but genitals are always obscured — frustrating in terms of prurience, but symbolic of the removal of the body for modernity that *Crash* is perceptively about.

Crashes represent an intellectualization or technologicazation of sex into pathology and fetish. In *Crash*, the death dive quite literally replaces libido. The only real ejaculation in the movie is the car wash. It is at once the erupting phallus and an all-encompassing womb-wound. Sex is removed from the physical body into psychology and its surrogates. Catherine's sex bruises made by Ballard's hands and mouth in the car wash are badges of experience rather than a token of an actual event. A film about witnessing, *Crash*'s attitude toward sex is also its relation to itself and to the cinema.

Like that other great movie of society's end, Jean-Luc Godard's *Week-End* (1967), *Crash* is absurd and playful. A nonsmoker, Helen starts to smoke cigarettes in the hospital as the insane world gives way into her paranoia: "The day I left the hospital, I had the extraordinary feeling that, all these cars where gathering for some special reason I didn't understand. There seemed to be ten times as much traffic," she says. Ballard asks her, "Are we imagining it?" and her elusive reply is, "You've bought yourself exactly the same car again." In true screwball-comedy fashion, Helen is crazier than Ballard! They have several "meet-cutes" before their affair begins in earnest — Helen's breast is revealed to him at their first meeting in the aftermath of the crash, they next coincidentally meet in the hospital hallway, and finally conjoin at the junkyard where Ballard remarks to her, "I never should have come here. I'm surprised the police don't make it more difficult." Ballard is not oblivious to romance; he just understands that in the 1990s — as the sound era gives way to media — negation is what is going to get him laid. Like Poelzig and his humanist–Satanic cult, Ballard can only live with the imagination of higher authority. If Ballard can defy something, then he himself gains value and perhaps sexual adoration — his denial of self is a result of technology and capital forcing identity through jobs. Or, as the Nazis told the world at Auschwitz, "Work produces Freedom."

Crash's anti-hero, and another double for Ballard, is Vaughn (Elias Koteas), whose motives and modus operandi are never clear, except perhaps in his worship of celebrities who have died before their time and thereby achieve a symbolic meaning. His actions are an attempt at fulfilling the death drive, as well as an anthropological teaching of the meaning of the web that attaches sexuality to the occurrence or sensation of death in a meaningless world.

After Vaughn's reenactment of James Dean's fatal car crash — hilariously broken up by the arrival of a squad from the Department of Transportation — Vaughan smokes a joint and brings up his notion of remaking Jayne Mansfield's deadly car crash of June 29, 1967. Like Beethoven in *A Clockwork Orange*, the crash is a signifier of commodity as well as the sex act — the car, the crash, the car crash. Like a media-era computer surfer, Vaughn pauses after crashes, but then jumps to the next thing — the momentum itself continuingly driving events faster. Like Mark's camera, cars are necessary to Vaughan's sexuality. Right before he seduces Ballard, Vaughn's car is referred to as a "bed on wheels." In *Crash*, the transgression is not the man-on-man action of Vaughn making love to Ballard, but the transgressive foreplay of Vaughn calling Ballard at work,

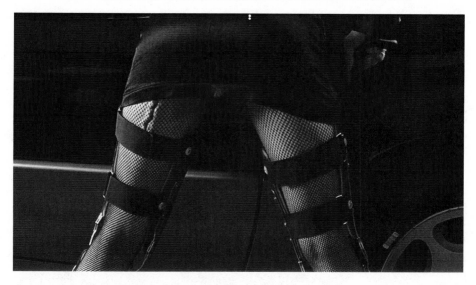

The new, fourth orifice of Gabrielle (Rosanna Arquette)—a semi-healed leg wound found in *Crash* (David Cronenberg, 1996). (Courtesy Andrew's Video Vault at the Rotunda.)

interrupting him at his job — his identity — and breaching the "red light seal" that is the code of noninterruption of both Ballard's and Mark's movie studios.

Vaughn states *Crash*'s thesis: "the reshaping of the body by technology"; and in lieu of actual sex — meat shots and cum shots — viewers have explicit new orifices first introduced by the "wound" in Helen's car door. Later Gabrielle (Rosanna Arquette), ostensibly Vaughn's girlfriend, leans over a car in an automobile dealership — her skirt raises — yet viewers don't snatch a glimpse of vagina, but her new, fourth orifice which is a semi-healed leg wound. This new orifice gives Gabrielle extra agency — because of technology she not only has a new hole, but she is now able to penetrate via her leg brace while still being female and absent of an actual penis. The body is remade by law and ideas — technology remakes the body superseding it, as *Crash* wavers on whether this path is the one to self-destruction or to self-realization. Perhaps what is interpreted here is amoral evolution, neither good nor bad, but the future, the "new flesh" as Cronenberg termed it in a movie made prior to *Crash*. From *Videodrome* (1983) to *eXistenZ* (1999), Cronenberg charts not only the future of the body in the face of technology but the future of cinema and its evolution into media. The slimy, melting cassettes of *Videodrome* give way to the second lives and rabbit holes in *eXistenZ* (1999) and so propose sound cinema's evolution to media, and then suggest media's rebirth wherein new cinema is the video game.

Crash is a film about class. The viewer is never unaware that James and Helen are privileged and more or less slumming it with Vaughn and Gabrielle, whom they erotize. What is ironic commentary on rich people's ailments in the Cronenberg movie is made treacle in the *Crash* from 2005 (not based on J.G. Ballard's novel) where the "agency" of car accidents is given a humanist perfume that masks technology superseding the body. There is no true connection in crashes — just the ricochet and wreckage in its wake.

As with Sade, murder and accident become works of art. Art, as Koch says, "is the wound that breaks open in the margins where nature and society collide."[30] Cinema is not an art but a representation of subconscious desires. In *Crash*, the execution of the death urge becomes the work of art, and the art itself not art but media's illusion of the meaning of meaningless events. In one

The *Zapruder Film* (Abraham Zapruder, November 22, 1963) ushered in the end of cinema and the beginning of reality television — a benchmark of the media era.

of his last texts, *War Porn* (2004), Jean Baudrillard observes, "The worst is that it all becomes a parody of violence, a parody of the war itself, pornography becoming the ultimate form of the abjection of war which is unable to be simply war, to be simply about killing, and instead turns itself into a grotesque infantile reality-show, in a desperate simulacrum of power."[31]

Vaughn asks if Kennedy's assassination is a special type of car crash. It is J.G. Ballard's way of noting that November 22, 1963, and *The Zapruder Film* ushered in the end of cinema and the beginning of reality television — a benchmark of the media era. After Zapruder, the bar of representation in cinema is moved to its end place. Firstly, "home format" (i.e., 8 mm) replaces "professional format" (35 mm), (just as YouTube will usurp cinema in the media era); and secondly, the artifice of any movie not containing actual penetration and/or death is reduced by the total reality of Zapruder's work to mere aesthetic evaluation rather than cultural importance. From *Crash* (1996) onward, simulation will no longer be surrogate, as simulation must become reality. Ballard, the movie character, exhorts that "it's all very satisfying. I'm not sure I understand why." Vaughn's answer is, "That's the future, Ballard, and you're already a part of it."

CHAPTER 2

The Birth of Neo-Conservatism through Violence

Gangsters Remaking Capital in The Public Enemy (1931), Point Blank (1967) and Bad Lieutenant (1992)

The tension of English-language sound-era cinema vacillates between cinema as a dream state and cinema as a political tool of propaganda. The 1930s gangster movie — born out of prohibition and resulting in the vigilante movie popularized by Vietnam-era trauma and the success of *Dirty Harry*, *Taxi Driver* and *Death Wish* in the 1970s — presents an anti-hero archetype often closely related to, if not codified into the mythos of, the American Individual, along the lines of an "urban cowboy." In *The Concept of the Political*, Carl Schmitt writes, "Were it possible to group all mankind in the proletarian and bourgeois antithesis, as friend and enemy in proletarian and capitalist states, and if, in the process, all other friend-and-enemy groupings were to disappear, the total reality of the political would then be revealed, insofar as concepts, which at first glance had appeared to be purely economic, turn into political ones."[1] Using Schmitt, the connection in cinema between money and politics and how the principles of capital are really the institutionalized practices of capital is understood. Gangster films begin being about male friendships, transform around *The Godfather* (1972) to being about family, but end the century with the gangster once again having been made Other. Gangsters reassume an extra-social position at the millennium, running the gamut from Hype Williams to Takeshi

42

Kitano, from *Belly* (1996) to *Brother* (2000). What remains consistent in gangster films from the 1930s to the 1990s is the greed that both inspires or necessitates the initial criminality and at the same time dramatizes how legitimacy is the greatest con of all. This is both an obvious example of the ills that result from motion pictures and an illustration of how cinema perpetuates the American desire for negative attention. However, for cinema to be truly threatening, as it became to America in the 1930s, it had to be coupled with a real-life disparity, creating a need — and greed — that would make the playing of the gangster "cool" and a subversion which could be acceptably culturally adopted. The urge toward the gangster would never be so desirable if the role did not allow extra agency among viewers. Never in a genre have "happy ends" been so suspect, for the final minutes of most gangster movies undo the anti-hero in a way that reasserts the moral order but leaves open the possible necessity of "taking action into your own hands."

In *Our Adult World and Its Roots in Infancy*, Melanie Klein points to the greed that is inherent in humans and their cinema and which is the impetus to gangsterism. "The very greedy infant may enjoy whatever he receives for the time being; but as soon as the gratification has gone, he becomes dissatisfied and is driven to exploit first of all the mother and soon everybody in the family who can give him attention, food, or any other gratification. There is no doubt that greed is increased by anxiety — the anxiety of being deprived, of being robbed, and of not being good enough to be loved. The infant who is so greedy for love and attention is also insecure about his own capacity to love: and all these anxieties reinforce greed. This situation remains in fundamentals unchanged in the greed of the older child and of the adult."[2] With greed being equally rooted in infancy and adulthood — and in a cycle with anxiety — desire for what is not present becomes paramount. Seeking gratification becomes meaning. The exquisite corpse of cinema offers the chance to love without risk for viewers, but it is not a social or emotional outlet, since movies exacerbate anxieties because what is possible on screen is not always so possible in real life. All this reinforces greed rather than love as spiritual nourishment — the act of feeding over the act of digestion.

In *A Study of Envy and Gratitude*, Klein focuses on the nature of greed, using "robbery" as a metaphor, while also examining envy's role in greed. The childlike nature of the cinematic gangster and children's natural criminal impulses here overlap, so that the cinematic gangster becomes the psychologically arrested child or arrested adolescent par excellence. Klein notes these aggressive impulses that the cinematic gangster does not outgrow and which feed the viewer with unrealistic desire. "At the unconscious level, greed aims primarily at completely scooping out, sucking dry and devouring the breast, that is to say, its aim is destructive introjections; whereas envy not only aims at robbing in this way, but also at putting badness, primarily bad excrements and bad parts of the self, into the mother—first of all into her breast—in order to spoil and destroy her; in the deepest sense this means destroying her creativeness."[3] Capital must destroy the creative for its own dominance. Klein's view of greed originating with the mother and needing to destroy creativeness reaffirms the Oedipal threads common to most gangster movies as well the misogyny with which most female figures are treated therein. This presents for the cinema the idea of (male) gender being focused on envy, where the gangster seeks to be his own mother and therefore feed himself what society does not provide, or allow him to enact. The resulting isolation and self-cannibalism crescendos in Abel Ferrara's gangster film, *Bad Lieutenant*, where the office of the law— the very office of the political—is perversely criminal and so self-seeks to both remake and destroy the Mother within the "confines" of the law. From Klein, criminality can be understood from cop or robber, to be "destructive introjections to society," and so that destruction reveals itself to be not completely a matter of nature but a protest over the political being grafted on top of nature. Gangster films promote the fantasy that it is really only through violence that an individual's voice is heard, thus proposing violence as the language of the post-literate, post-intellectual media era. Clearly attractive to a disenfranchised audience, the genre is also motivated by the political taking advantage of under-education. It presents not the fantasy of enlightened success, but a warning of infamy punished so as to make viewers' complacency with the political seem most prudent. If Klein's sense of envy is not only a reflection of desire but also a chance to remake the self and expunge the "bad parts," it presents a source motive for criminality that rests not with the criminal but within the society that produces the criminal. It is this thesis of criminality in America that is advanced by the early, pre-code gangster films of the 1930s. Klein suggests that greed and envy destroy creativeness, but she does not entertain how the urge to destroy is, in and of itself, creative. This contributes to the sensation of charismatic cinematic gangsters who are "rebels without causes" and points to the problem of sound cinema where the dream state is co-opted by the political co-opted by capital.

In *Revolt Against Realism in the Films* (1968), William Earle illustrates the importance of cinematic remaking, arguing that "nothing can become familiar unless previously encountered originally; and a moral order can not be reconfirmed unless it has been threatened."[4] From this the social function of the gangster movie can be understood, where, unlike horror movies concerning technology, viewers are treated to aberrance and then brought back to a reconfirmed moral order—that is, brought back into the system of politics and its relation to currency. From the inception of the sound-era gangster film, there is rarely left the unpunished gangster who avoids reclaiming by this political moral order. In effect, gangster films illustrate how much may be cheated and how far the law may be interpreted, giving a popular example of political original intent/literalism versus modernism/instrumentalism that has confounded the United States in the interpretation of its own bylaws. The flexibility of gangster film morality entices the audience, who incorrectly feel that they have experienced something outside the preexisting moral order. *The Public Enemy, Point Blank* and *Bad Lieutenant* are an examination of American capitalism's constant state of devouring itself to remake its image and concepts of justice and ensure its continued dominance. All three movies appropriate the Christ myth through a reframing of the Passion as a revenge drama, and so the legend is remade where becoming an instrument of vengeance (revenge) is an identity.

This returns to the Greek-Roman tradition of the personification of "Revenge." What Shakespeare added to this dramatic line starting with *Titus Andronicus* (one of his first plays) is the idea — the Kleinian idea, it may be argued — of the individual playing the part of (or becoming) Revenge. *The Public Enemy, Point Blank* and *Bad Lieutenant* can be categorized as successors to

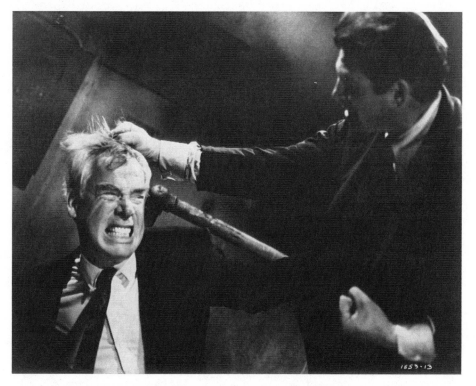

Walker (Lee Marvin), here pictured with Rico Cattani throwing the punch, is a cipher running on the steam of vengeance alone. He loses track of the meaning of his quest as the tangible reality of capital disappears around him in a haze of syndicates, pills and plastic credit cards in *Point Blank* (John Boorman, 1967). (Jerry Ohlinger's Movie Material Store.)

Shakespeare's *Hamlet*, the great modern ur-revenge tragedy of the Western tradition — itself a remake or rewrite of an earlier play (only perhaps by Shakespeare). Tom Powers in *The Public Enemy* is the youthful, brooding individual — the prince as dazzling as he is spastic or perhaps dangerous. Similarly, Walker in *Point Blank* is a cipher running on the steam of vengeance alone, who eventually loses track of the meaning of his quest as the tangible reality of capital disappears around him in a haze of syndicates, pills and plastic credit cards. The titular bad Lieutenant consists of little else than his "sins," so much so that his name and humanity are largely absent and his "sacrificial" actions are ultimately an empty gesture. What is never clear in a gangster film is what grants moral superiority, or if indeed it can be granted rather than just assumed or taken by force. This provides the audience with the comfort of failure as gratification, as well as the opportunity for the expression of an empowered revenge. It is important that the gangster film be remade so that, as in the Tom Powers–Walker–Lieutenant line of this chapter, the gangster can be stripped of the individual (most specifically his gang) and therefore greater social responsibility, and second, maintain the spectacle of false revolution — that one man's violence is able to speak above the fray, which media does not honestly allow as it would too directly challenge itself and capital.

In *Expanded Cinema* (1970), Gene Youngblood builds the argument of how post–World War II movie remaking dulls the senses, "perpetuating a destructive habit of unthinking response to formulas, by forcing us to rely ever more frequently on memory, the commercial entertainer encourages an unthinking response to daily life, inhibiting self-awareness."[5] Noting the link to memory that corresponds from *Point Blank* onward, cinema robs the individual of self-awareness because the viewer is only aware of that which is perceived. It is a state very close to remembering and a move of the medium away from actual dream (i.e., the silent era) to the symbols and stimuli that lead to dreams. Cinema becomes the noise that obliterates the talking cure because pure motion picture making, even in the sound era, relies on the visual as manipulated by the optical. In the cinema, the individual is not heard but received. Siegfried Kracauer comments on this phenomenon in *The Little Shopgirls Go to the Movies* (1927), espousing, "They will risk depicting a successful revolution in historical costumes in order to induce people to forget modern revolutions, and they are happy to satisfy the theoretical sense of justice by filming struggles for freedom that are long past."[6] What makes *Point Blank* and *Bad Lieutenant* such a radical remaking of *The Public Enemy* is that the former takes all vengeance and places it within memory, and in the case of the latter, freedom has been long since removed (or never was) but the struggle itself remains.

The gangster film has remade America by presenting a code of behavior extra to the law and a posturing of, predominantly (though often sexually ambivalent) male identity, sanctioning male gender performance with figures as "questioning" as Prince Hamlet. Tom Powers is clearly bisexual, Walker post-sexual and the Lieutenant asexual. Even the names are reduced in this trajectory. Søren Kierkegaard writes that "in ancient tragedy the sorrow is deeper, the pain less; in modern, the pain is greater, the sorrow less. Sorrow always contains something more substantial than pain. Pain always implies a reflection over suffering which sorrow does not know."[7] In *The Public Enemy*, Tom Powers expresses only some regret that he learned how to steal as a boy from the Fagin-like Putty Nose, but in *Point Blank*, Walker is beyond regret because it is he who has been betrayed and possibly murdered, and with the *Bad Lieutenant*, "pain reflecting over sorrow" is all that remains in the 1980s/1990s zeitgeist because the Lieutenant lives in the reflection of an (a)moral order held up by the self-interest of the political. Sound cinema moves the viewer toward the viscera of pain because of its great reflective powers but does not remove the context from the individual into the community the way tragic sorrow does. With gangster films, viewers are not asked to consider if these figures are them but are presented with figures who are clearly not them and who offer an escapism without consequence. This removes the possibility of the radical from the genre and further delineates how sound cinema moved culture from dream state to political tool.

The Public Enemy (1931)

Warner Brothers' April 23, 1931, release, *The Public Enemy*, directed by William A. Wellman, remakes and embellishes the success of *Little Caesar* six months prior, where the advent of sound added a vitality and imitability of performance that silent-era gangster movies did not possess. *The Public Enemy* introduces the cast — in reality the *posturing* of the cast — to the audience at the very start of the movie, and it is the posture of the characters that the audience will themselves remake, already separating the characters from the plot. After this alluring beginning, a title crawl announces

> It is the ambition of the authors of "The Public Enemy" to honestly depict an environment that exists today in a certain strata of American Life, rather than glorify the hoodlum or the criminal.
> While the story of "The Public Enemy" is essentially a true story, all names and characters appearing herein, are purely fictional.— Warner Bros. Pictures Inc

The language of this notice reveals *The Public Enemy*'s schism, like the schism between the posturing of the characters and the fate of the characters — for instance, how can crime be "honestly" depicted, and is "essentially a true story" anything close to "essentially a true story"? The pull between a movie's dream state and political goals is so reflected in the gangster film as the tension between environment and individual impulse. Criminals are, however, Other, and the "certain strata" they belong to reflects not only their criminality but especially their economic situation. A film of the Depression, *The Public Enemy* identifies itself as a class allegory and cements the allure of cinema's gangsters as being those who remain and triumph in the economic strata (class) of birth by adopting the "unnatural" posture of another in the pursuit of the Kleinian breast. Guy Debord writes:

> The ruling totalitarian-ideological class is the ruler of a world turned upside down. The more powerful the class, the more it claims not to exist, and its power is employed above all to enforce this claim. It is modest only on this one point, however, because this officially nonexistent bureaucracy simultaneously attributes the crowning achievements of history to its own infallible leadership. Though its existence is everywhere in evidence, the bureaucracy must be *invisible as a class*. As a result, all social life becomes insane. The social organization of total falsehood stems from this fundamental contradiction.[8]

Debord illustrates the political's role in co-opting sound-era cinema, replacing the dream state with propaganda supporting its nonexistence — that is, the systematic guiding of the public from individual thinking toward the illusion of purchasing said originality. The insanity of social life is represented in *The Public Enemy* by Tom's ability to advance, his character becoming a decoy of the real subversion of dreams-transforming-to-politics actually occurring.

The end screen title of *The Public Enemy*, however, returns the onus of the gangster to the audience: "The END of Tom Powers is the end of every hoodlum. 'The Public Enemy' is not a man, nor is it a character — it is a problem that sooner or later WE the public, must solve." By the time of *Point Blank*, the idea of the gangster as a problem of society has vanished, as gangsters provide the structure of their (self-constituted) society as a reaction to the failure of actual society. Uniquely, at the point of the release of *The Public Enemy*, society is failing but has not yet failed. Therefore, to indentify "the public enemy" as a problem rather than a character is an ethical charge to the audience representative of early sound cinema's link to the culture it feeds and provides the context for. When movies become an isolated reality unto themselves, they are unable to express anything as being outside their edifice for fear of the political revealing its actual hand. "The public enemy" in *The Public Enemy* is proposed at various times as poverty, Tom Powers, and/or alcohol, and it is this multiplicity of remaking that offers the audience their own individual way into the drama.

The Public Enemy opens in its recent past — 1909 — before the world wars and before Prohibition, with a blend of stock footage and carefully shot studio inserts of streets bustling with automobiles, trolleys and people. This blend of documentary and fantasy is still a radical synthesis of the real and the unreal that only cinema can conjure. Importantly, the role of the automobile is unmistakable and central. It is cars that allow the sound era to be remade into the media era because of the way they alter person-to-person interaction. Specifically, in *The Public Enemy* automotives reflects Tom's status (the Rolls Royce) and work occupation (the getaway cars and tankard trucks).

A "1909" factory whistle from a brewing company blows, linking automobiles, commerce and entertainment to beer. The role of alcohol is remade during *The Public Enemy*, at first as the children's introduction to the adult world and then as a source of income to survive in the adult world. The Salvation Army outside the brewery remakes Brecht's *Happy End*—perhaps the first great synthesis of the gangster idiom — and foreshadows the move to temperance that will occur eleven years from the date of the opening scene of *The Public Enemy*. Shot and released prior to the repeal of Prohibition, the film's relationship between illegal sprits and gangsters is suggested politically to the public in a pointed way by the Warner Bros. movie, which supports the consumption of alcohol while casting an ambivalent gaze on the black market its outlawing creates.

Viewers are introduced to the aggressive young Tom Powers (Frank Coghlan, Jr.) and his best friend Matt Doyle (Frankie Darro) holding a pail of foamy beer, from which Tom desires to take a drink. In the second vignette of *The Public Enemy*, the boys run through a department store pursued, with no context for the chase other than the movie's celebration of anarchy in a social setting. Tom and Matt have an extremely close friendship that continues into their adulthood — the beginning of a surrogate family or perhaps partnership, which recalls Klein writing in *Love, Guilt and Reparation* that "sexual desires are, as we already know, closely linked up with aggressive impulses and phantasies, with guilt and the fear of the death of the loved people, all of which drive the child to lessen his attachments to his parents."[9] Aggression is already a part of Tom's character, and viewers soon witness that he and Matt lack loving parents. Tom's mother seemingly dotes on her "baby" but remains also hesitant and withdrawn, becoming more so when confronted with Tom's adult anger symbolized by his "affectionate punches" (first demonstrated by James Cagney onto the viewer in the opening credits). Tom's father figure — the man's relationship to his mother is never clearly explained — is a policeman who is largely absent other than to administer physical punishments. This sets up Tom as understanding the law as having removed a parent from him, and having made that parent's love tyrannical and obedient to an extra-familiar force. Tom already sees the hypocrisy of meeting cruelty with violence. The close-up of his face during a thrashing reveals adulthood having already set into his face in an unambiguous way, and so viewers understand Tom as having been remade as a man before his time. Tom couples his innate sadism (or "greed" as Klein would term it) with ritual, and thereby he seems to "enjoy" his corporal punishment. The constant remaking of Tom's beating — obviously often repeated — may tax his body, but his mind remains defiant, as when he asks his father figure churlishly of his trousers, "How do you want 'em this time? Up or down?" As viewers watch Tom take the whupping in a facial close-up that reveals his premature aging, he grimaces, and as the harrowing scene fades out, Tom lets loose a defiant fart at his father figure. Childish scatology play is mixed with adolescent rebellion, and the sequence has a homoerotic quality consistent with how abuse victims erotize trauma as a means of survival.

Tom's home life contributes to his sadism/greed, and Tom acts out, giving Matt's sister Molly stolen roller skates and then delighting in her falls. He finds gratification in hurting Molly as a replacement for the normative pleasures he has been denied. Money here is also established — as it will be in *Imitation of Life* — as separating the genders. In a world where men must provide, it is a choice whether to do so legally or illegally. Tom faces the challenge of how to be a man before his time and what the parameters of that manhood are. It is natural to the nuclear family unit that adolescent aggression against the parents becomes sexually wrapped up and focused along homosocial/homosexual inclinations, and, true to this, Tom's first definition of himself is in his partnering with Matt in reaction to his family. Klein addresses these intense adolescent relationships, writing, "Unconscious homosexual tendencies and feelings underlie these relationships and very often lead to actual homosexual activities. Such relationships are partly an escape from the drive towards the other sex, which is often too unmanageable at this stage, for various internal and external reasons."[10] Tom wishes to escape the drive toward his mother for the aforementioned "various internal and external reasons," and as a result his sadism/greed, misogynist and homosexual impulses blossom. Tom so schools young Matt, admonishing, "That's what you get for foolin' with women," when the latter is hit by a door following lustily after a pretty girl. As with Tom's ritualized corporal punishments, his link between sex and pain is again underlined. By the time of adult Tom smashing a grapefruit into his girlfriend Kitty's face, the viewer comes to understand that Tom can only express his sexuality sadistically and that violence has become a language.

Fleeing their family, Tom and Matt's initiation to the adult world is Putty Nose (Murray Kinnell), a piano player in a saloon who fences things the boys steal for him, all the while cheating the kids. The insidious role Putty Nose plays in their young lives will not be fully revealed until the boys remember it years later. It is unlikely that the boys remake the truth of the relationship in their heads, but rather that the remaking is a readjustment actualizing the reality of past events.

By 1915, Tom and Matt are young men and played for the rest of the movie by James Cagney and Edward Woods. Cagney electrifies and propels the movie with his unique swagger, insolent spitting, and unconscious (uncontrolled?) sexual magnetism. His eyelids are swabbed in makeup, his eyeballs unblinking but always moving — an image that Malcolm McDowell and Stanley Kubrick will remake with Anthony Burgess' Alex in *A Clockwork Orange*.

Here with girlfriend Kitty (Mae Clarke), violence has become Tom Powers' (James Cagney) language in *The Public Enemy* (William A. Wellman, 1931). (Courtesy the Chestnut Hill Film Group.)

The Public Enemy is careful to build viewers' knowledge of Tom so that he does not emerge, like Rico in *Little Caesar*, already a criminal, but is remade into a criminal before the audience's very eyes. This reaffirms two things—first the myth (to the 1931 audience) that every great man started small (when in fact many great men come from great fortunes), and second, it is a clear reminder that there is always a primal scene—a first crime. Putty Nose sets up the boy's "big break," a fur warehouse robbery, and gives Tom and Matt the gift of guns, phallic substitutes from the neo–Fagin representing the (homo)sexual initiation of the boys in terms of a criminal initiation. The guns here are also transitional objects in the Winnicott sense. The first robbery is a total failure as Tom is spooked by a stuffed polar bear and starts shooting prematurely and without thinking. As a result, the police are immediately alerted of the attempted robbery, and Tom and Matt's getaway driver, Larry, is shot and killed by a cop. Tom and Matt kill the patrolman in retaliation and flee themselves, expecting to be taken care of by Putty Nose. However, Putty Nose disappears from town, leaving Tom and Matt to their own devices — again betrayed by family and the mother surrogate.

At Larry's funeral, his mother and the women mourn a "good boy" who got into "bad company," while the men drink and ruefully shake their heads at the "bad boy" who got what he deserved. Again, the genders are represented as unreconcilable, and this schism between male and female performance is not lost on Tom and Matt as they pay their last respects to their comrade Larry. The funeral sequence ends with Tom and Matt exchanging incredulous looks in thrillingly economic use of screen acting — technique remade by countless movie tough guys in subsequent decades like Lee Marvin and Harvey Keitel, just as "the first crime" primal scene becomes the center of director Abel Ferrara's first post–*Bad Lieutenant* gangster movie, *The Funeral* (1996).

Tom and Matt are, more or less, one single unit throughout the movie. The real good-boy/bad-boy split of *The Public Enemy* is between Tom and his strait-laced brother, Mike (Donald Cook). Mike does not hang around Putty Nose, for as Tom remarks, Mike's "too busy going to school ... learning how to be poor." The economic factors of *The Public Enemy* are again stressed and the Janus head doubling of Tom and Mike continues for the remainder of the movie.

With the advent of World War I, Mike enlists and, as he leaves home, he confronts Tom about gossip he has heard, as Tom is now, as he says, "the man of the house." Tom humors his brother, but it is clear from Cagney's expression that Tom has considered himself to be a man long before his older brother dispenses his would-be sage advice.

> MIKE: You don't need these rats you're running around with.
> TOM: I suppose you want me to go to night school and read poems. (*Tom sneers at Mike, and moves to leave the room.*) I've been hearing a few things myself—
> MIKE: There's nothing to hear about me!
> TOM: Ahhgh. That's all you know — You ain't so smart. Books and smart stuff don't hide everything —
> MIKE: You're a liar, Tom. You're covering up —

Both men are "covering up," but the extent to which is not clear. The homosexual antagonism that runs beneath both males' accusations presents how these doubles are both trying to pass in a world where — like abused children — they need to hide. Rather than the frontier homosexuality of Ballard and Vaughn in *Crash*, in *The Public Enemy* homosexuality is a result of environment, and it can be so concluded that the impulses that cause Queerness are the very same ones that lead to criminality. Tom's reactions to his brother are the adoption of Mike's accusations, a remaking of his brother, wherein Tom can drag Mike to the same level and thereby place him within the same socio-sexual context. Clearly, Mike is hiding something with night school and poetry reading—

Tom's accusations are not projections, as it is indicated that Mike may very well be stealing from the streetcar company for which he works. Furthermore, throughout the time span of the movie, Mike has no relationships with the opposite sex save for family, which leads viewers to understand that in the above-quoted scene the brothers are hurting each other with truths.

Tom and Matt's descent into the underworld continues as the duo engage in further larceny and gain something of a reputation. Wary of another Putty Nose, Tom and Matt are skeptical of the advances of saloon keeper Paddy Ryan (Robert Emmett O'Connor); however, Paddy tells them what to do with stolen cigars and explains his benevolence to them with the maxim, "You've got to have friends." New Year's Eve of 1920 is a madhouse of alcohol enthusiasts trying to stock up before Prohibition takes effect. Here, *The Public Enemy* fades up on a window sign reading, "Family Liquor Store: Owing to prohibition our entire stock must be sold before midnight," illustrating the harm that is done to the family (and therefore small business) by the Eighteenth Amendment. As Paddy messily eats potato chips, he tells Tom and Matt of liquor's new black-market value. The young men do not understand the implication for organized crime as they are still creatures of impulse and emotion, but not yet thought. Paddy's chips are an indication of the start of fast and junk food undermining true nutrition in America. In many ways, *The Public Enemy* reads as an illustration of the perils of the twentieth century, made at a point — the inception of sound cinema — where the Great Depression called for a grand remaking as its only possible solution.

Under Paddy's guidance, Tom and Matt steal a massive amount of booze in a gasoline truck, linking prohibited alcohol and gasoline, illuminating the perspective of *The Public Enemy* with regard to the influence of the political to crime. Later, toasting their success, Tom is in his own world and well out of synch with Paddy's and Matt's cheer. Tom looks up at his friends, and viewers see the loner he will become, where his repressed and/or misplaced desire places him outside the social, like Walker in *Point Blank* or the Lieutenant in *Bad Lieutenant*.

Next occurs the most sexually confounding scene in *The Public Enemy* and one that was edited down for many of the movie's rereleases. Flush with money, Tom is being fitted for new clothes — gentlemen's clothes — by a crusty old Menswear Associate and his handsome, and very fey, Assistant. As Matt observes the scene unreactive, Tom gestures to his crotch and remarks to the Assistant, "Don't forget — plenty of room in there." Knowing Tom, viewers must wonder if it's a request meant to accommodate his gun, or his penis. It could also be posturing covering for impotency, something *Bonnie and Clyde* makes finally explicit in the gangster genre in 1967. Attentive to Tom's desires, the Menswear assistant responds, "Oh, no sir ... here's where you need the room," and more than flirtatiously squeezes Tom's arm. The Senior Menswear Associate keeps his

In a publicity shot dramatically different than the scene in the film, *The Public Enemy* (William A. Wellman, 1931), Matt Doyle (Edward Woods) looks on as the Menswear Associate Assistant (Douglas Gerrard) fits Tom Powers (James Cagney) for new clothes — gentlemen's clothes — while the Senior Menswear Associate worries at the exchange. (Jerry Ohlinger's Movie Material Store.)

eyes glued to his notepad, solemnly announcing the numbers he is recording, as the flirtation continues with the Menswear Assistant taking groping measurements of Tom, climaxing with his "inside leg." Neither Matt nor Tom seems to be made uncomfortable by the apparently homosexual assistant — they are not especially friendly to him, but in no way do they openly mock him. It is possible to read into the Menswear Assistant's homosexuality a class difference suggesting a conflation/confusion of "Queerness" and upper-class "dandyism" wherein Tom and Matt would not recognize a Queer man of a higher social station. However, this reading is unsupported because Tom has already alluded to his brother's "night school" activities, and because seconds later in this very scene, the Menswear Assistant follows Tom out of the store like a smitten puppy. Apparently the flirtation between the two has given way to a sexual date, and the scene fades as Tom tips his hat "good-bye" to presumably either the Senior Menswear Associate and/or Matt. The defiance of Cagney's hat tipping eerily recalls young Tom's "How do you want 'em this time? Up or down?" and viewers again see traces of the physical abuse (or probable incest) which the movie suggests contributed to Tom's homosexuality and/or criminality.

Perhaps Tom dares so public a display of homosexuality because his success as a gangster has allowed him to live large — remaining in his undereducated social station while adopting the airs of his "betters." After the incident with the two tailors, Tom pulls up to the "notorious" Washington Arms Hotel in his new Rolls Royce. He admonishes the valet, "Hey stup, that's got gears, it ain't no Ford"— his automobile unmistakably equaling status.

Matt and Tom enter the speakeasy at the Washington Arms Hotel and are warmly greeted by a black maître d'.

> MAÎTRE D': Ah, Mr. Powers, Mr. Doyle. Alone as usual —
> TOM: I am. Matt's all fixed up; he's got me with him.
> MAÎTRE D': The night's young. You'll wind up with something —
> MATT: Yeah, the morning paper.

The conversation seems to underline Tom's, and presumably Matt's, homosexuality. It also proposes the two as a couple, and what is shocking is not the idea of a homosexual relationship between Tom and Matt, but the incestuous relationship it presumes between them. The theme of incest as the product of distorted family is remade by Howard Hawks in the gangster spoof *Scarface* (1932) between Tony and his sister Francesca. Complicating the sexuality of *The Public Enemy*, later that night at the speakeasy, Tom and Matt meet two women, Mamie (Joan Blondell) and Kitty (Mae Clarke), toward whom they make heteronormative advances. Matt and Mamie hit the dance floor and immediately lose themselves to physical passion while Tom is left to flirt with Kitty, who is first revolted, but then titillated by what he whispers into her ear. This bisexuality of the characters takes us back to Shakespeare as the forerunner of Freud. Harold Bloom sets up the affinity toward Kleinian developmental theory, writing, "The human endowment, Shakespeare keeps intimating, is bisexual: after all, we have both mothers and fathers. Whether we 'forget' either the heterosexual or the homosexual component in our desire, or 'remember' both, is in the Sonnets and the plays not a question of choice, and only rarely a matter for anguish."[11] Bisexuality in the Shakespeare-Klein line is a natural state that is unlearned, or remade out of individuals under pressure from society or influence from family construction. As in Shakespeare, bisexuality does not seem to cause outward anguish to Tom and Matt, but rather allows them to further construct and repair their lack of parental love. In this way bisexuality presents itself as the most enlightened and truly knowing/healing of social postures.

The gangster film removes the barriers of social class as illustrated when Matt and Tom are introduced by Paddy to "Nails" Nathan (Leslie Fenton), a gang boss way out of their social league. Needing Matt and Tom's muscle, the quartet plan to reopen Leehman's Brewery and establish a territory wherein all must buy their hooch. Nails is suave and debonair, though clearly homicidal when provoked. Fenton is the opposite of Cagney, and his performance is equally indelible. Remarkably, there is no tension between Nails and Tom, illustrating how Tom's criminality is more or less a sequence of events that leads up to his being a "public enemy" rather than the rise to the top and hard fall chronicled by *Little Caesar* and *Scarface*. By this point in *The Public Enemy*, something of a freak, Tom has stepped outside class and continues in his trajectory of isolation caused by greed and desire.

Also something of a "freak," Tom's brother Mike returns from the war unwell and brooding. A family celebration dinner goes foul around the beer keg sitting on the dining room table. Tom, Matt and Ma enjoy a drink, while Mike contemptuously glares at the alcohol, understanding the beer keg to have literally brought criminality into "his" home. Mike is the straitlaced one during the Roaring Twenties, saturnine with post-traumatic stress incurred during the Great War. In Mike exists the response to Tom — that is, neo-conservatism, where archaic social order is upheld and the politics of self-denial privileges perspective, granting, at least in Mike's mind, a moral superiority not otherwise present. Perceived moral superiority allows boys and men to be trained as killers — soldiers — by governments and further indoctrinates society into the "necessity" of upholding the political, when oftentimes the political is the true usurper. This neo-conservatism escalates from on screen to off screen with the Hays Code created to stop frank films like *The Public Enemy* from being produced. It can be suspected that the social "danger" of *The Public Enemy* is not in its alleged glamorization of criminality but its attack on the systems of wealth that seeks to expose the political on screen, as well as in the home, here represented by the beer keg. Mike cracks up at the dinner table, refusing a drink and screaming, "You think I'd care if it were just beer in that keg? I know what's in it. I know what you've been doing all this time. How you get those clothes and those new cars. You've been telling Ma you've gone into politics. That you're on the city payroll. Pat Burke told me everything. You murderers! There's not only beer in that keg — there is beer and blood. Blood of men." Once again, the political rears its head, yet Mike cannot comprehend the political as being truly criminal and that makes him a sucker in Tom's — if not the viewer's — eyes. Mike hurls the beer keg across the dining room with rage. Tom remains cool, remarking, "You ain't changed one bit. Besides, your hands ain't so clean. You killed and *liked* it. You didn't get those metals by holding hands with those Germans." Mike exemplifies the problem of turning men into soldiers and killers — for once they return to the home front, it is not so easy to shed the regimented violence of army life. Rather, that violence enters the culture and seeks to reinforce its alleged normalcy. Tom again suggests his doubleness, with Mike acknowledging that they are both killers and that they both "like" it. Killing becomes another form of perverted intercourse. Tom's killing, however, is more financially rewarding, which to his (and the viewer's) logic makes it normalized, whereas Tom seems to insinuate that Mike's killing is an escape for personal frustrations that his brother has repressed. These threads converge in the *Forced Entry* movies (1973 and 1981) — with the protagonist liking his killing and being emotionally rewarded by his homicidal actions — while these two socially unacceptable films return American cinema full circle to the positioning of cinema as moral object lesson as touted by Warner Bros.' 1931 opening and end title cards, but unfashionable by the final quarter of the twentieth century.

The row at dinner leads to Matt and Tom moving from Ma's to the Washington Arms Hotel. Installed there with dames Mamie and Kitty, the duo continue to enforce for Paddy and Nails. Nails calls Tom from the stables and complains of receiving rubber checks. Tom and Matt are instructed to bring back "cash or his heart." Matt can be clearly heard foolin' around with Mamie next door while Tom is frustrated at his apparent lack of sexual chemistry with Kitty. Their relationship ends as Tom pushes a grapefruit half into Kitty's face. Tom's next girlfriend, Gwen Allen (Jean Harlow), seems to be right for Tom as she's more of an object than a person or a woman, and her femininity is as constructed as a drag queen's. Harlow herself features many "drag" elements, and she is remade in subsequent decades as Marilyn Monroe, Jayne Mansfield and — most post-modernly — as Divine. Matt and Mamie, who have the type of romantic bliss that Tom is apparently not capable of, wed. At a dinner after Mamie and Matt's wedding, Putty Nose is uncannily glimpsed at the very same club where they are celebrating, having finally resurfaced after running away years before. Both Matt and Tom are immediately focused on Putty Nose and revenge as their masculine needs derail the wedding festivities. Later that night — what is still Matt's wedding night — Putty Nose leaves his garage, and a black cat crosses his path just before Matt and Tom surprise him. Putty Nose acts as if he is glad to see Tom and Matt, but it soon becomes apparent that the boys' reunion with him is not nearly so sentimental an occasion. Tom and Matt pressure Putty Nose to let them into his place for a drink, and Putty Nose puts them off, saying he has a woman — a "Jane" — waiting for him upstairs. Tom will not relent:

> TOM: We've got a little business to settle, Jane or no Jane.
> PUTTY: You ain't sore, are you, Tom? I've always been your friend.
> TOM: Sure — you taught us how to cheat, steal and kill, and then you lammed out on us.
> MATT: Yeah, if it hadn't been for you, we might have been on the level.
> TOM: We might have been ding-dings on the streetcar.

Tom and Matt blame Putty for their criminality, and it must be again considered if "criminality" is code for homosexual orientation. If it is, it would certainly be within the findings of Klein, who writes, "One of the bases of psycho-analysis is Freud's discovery that we find in the adult all the stages of his early childish development. We find them in the unconscious which contains all repressed phantasies and tendencies. As we know, the mechanism of repression is mostly directed by the judging, criticizing faculties — the super-ego. It is evident that the deepest repressions are those which are directed against the most unsocial tendencies."[12] Much analysis has been given to Tom and Matt's probable "repressed phantasies and tendencies," and applying Klein to *The Public Enemy*, it can be seen that the "deepest repressions are those which are directed against the most unsocial tendencies," which suggests that criminality is again masking homo- or bisexuality. If Queerness is read as these "unsocial tendencies," it is a good thing — not an exclusion of the LGBT community — but rather an illustration of how Queerness, from Oscar Wilde's time onward, is one of the most formidable attacking forces against oppression. Fluidity of sexuality is akin to the dream state of cinema, where it is not a matter of what orientations are, but what impulses can be gratified, thus remaking sexuality as fetish.

Revenge, from *Hamlet* onward, is an unmaking, wherein assuming the role of vengeance overwhelms the act of play and thereby threatens to supersede the individual (never more explicitly than in Hofmannsthal's *Elektra* based on Sophocles). A majority of gangster films focus on revenge and provide examples of playing revenge, be it here with Putty Nose, Walker with Mal Resse, or the Lieutenant with the two Nun Ravishers. Moments from his execution, Putty Nose pleads for his life, invoking how he was Tom and Matt's "friend" in childhood. Uncharacteristically silent, neither Tom nor Matt responds as they are stunned at Putty Nose's wormy spectacle. Matt seems torn at what actions to take, but Tom fills Putty Nose with lead slugs, a moment of bravura filmmaking from William Wellman that Kubrick will later appropriate for the opening of his version of *Lolita* (1962).

The death of Putty Nose in no way appears to ease the aggressive anxiety of Tom or Matt — rather it fully cements their personalities, and it seems as if their anxiety now needs another object to graft itself onto. Tom visits his mother for the first time since being thrown out by his brother Mike on the occasion of the beer stein incident at dinner. Tom gives his mother money, which she eagerly accepts. No sooner than she does this, Mike enters and, calling Tom's gift "blood money," forcefully gives the money back to Tom. Tom challenges him, saying, "Hiding behind Ma's skirts like always." Mike replies, "Better than hiding behind a machine gun." This frankness stuns Tom, for again fraternal duality — and mutually shared secrets — force Tom to recognize that part of him which is "playing" a role with the phallic-substitute machine gun. Tom mutters to Mike, "Yeah, you're too smart," and Mike seeing an advantage grabs Tom's money and follows him to the door, taunting, "Don't forget your money." Seeking to once again hide in plain view, Tom declares, "Money don't mean nothing to me," but again brother Mike gains the upper hand with truth, remarking,

"No, I guess not, but with no heart, and no brains — you'll need it." Here the role of money is directly linked to Tom's pathology, as is the link between Tom's homosexual/criminal impulses and the way money allows him to remake himself into something socially acceptable.

Gilles Deleuze writes that "[Robert] Bresson shows that money, because it is of the order of time, makes impossible any reparation for evil done, any equivalence or just retribution, except of course, through grace. In short, *the cinema confronts its most internal presupposition, money, and the movement-image makes way for the time-image in one and the same operation.* What the film within the film expresses is this infernal circuit between the image and money, this inflation which time puts into the exchange, this 'overwhelming rise.' The film is movement, but the film within the film is money, is time."[13] Deleuze's denial of a Kleinian reparation with the uses of money is exactly the predicament that Tom finds himself in and one that the genre exacerbates, as with the absurdity of Walker's quest in *Point Blank*, or the difficulty that Michael Corleone has in maintaining legitimacy in *The Godfather Part III* (1990). "Grace," always achievable in Bresson, is a concept largely absent from American English–language cinema because the cinematic systems of dream and politics both cannot quantify the human as being capable of extra-human instincts, as it would defeat the imitation of life that is core to sound cinema's makeup. Therefore there is always the "internal presupposition," which Deleuze correctly cites as being "money," that remains. What the gangster film offers viewers is a fantasy of how wealth can be (re)made, but what the genre is less forthright about is how the individual can never reimagine him- or herself without money. In this way, the specific dreams created by gangster films are less important than the fact that capitalism is placed as part of its central and unremovable ideology. English-language sound cinema can therefore be understood as becoming the underlying tool of political propaganda. It can be witnessed — especially moving out of the 1930s — how capital embraces the spectacle of money and how that drive becomes the death drive for future gangsters, such as Walker or the Lieutenant.

The deepening relationship between Tom and Gwen is puzzling. She seems half a projected male fantasy — her aforementioned "drag queen"–like nature — coupled with a genuine feminine mother instinct that appears to be the true bond between her and Tom. Clearly, the relationship has not developed normally, and their dialogue presents a reoccurrence of the sexual problems that have plagued Tom before in his relationships with the opposite sex. Tom, reduced to the submissive feminine by Gwen, broaches the subject of marriage with her, perhaps trying to figure out the lack of sexual spark between them.

> TOM: I figured you were sort of different, too. That is, er, different than the kind of girl I was used to. I don't go in for these long-winded things, but with me it was always yes or no. And I could never figure you out.

GWEN: Now you can?

TOM: No, and I guess I ain't your kind. I think I'd better call it quits.

Tom's frustration leads him to his impulse of flight, which recalls the premature ejaculation of his gun at the primal scene in the fur factory. Even in this relationship talk, Tom says "I" not "we," and the viewer has yet another indicator of psychotic self-absorption and the possible fantasy fulfillment that Gwen offers because she is not the traditional female seeking a heterosexual partner, and the fact that she is not interested in money (visually coming from a place of affluence). Gwen nixes Tom's plan for a breakup, coddling him and ultimately pressing him to her (motherly, "good") breast.

> GWEN: Oh, don't be like that, Tommy. Of course, I "go for you" as you say. Maybe too much —
>
> TOM: You know, all my friends think that things are different between us than they are.
>
> GWEN: Yes?
>
> TOM: Mmm-hm. They figure they know me pretty well and, um, they don't think I'd go for a merry-go-round —
>
> GWEN: Do you think I'm giving you a merry-go-round?
>
> TOM: (*genuinely flustered*) Well — no.
>
> Gwen: Then do you want things to be different? To please your boyfriends?
>
> TOM: No. How long can a guy hold out? I'm gonna go screwy. (*He goes to leave.*)
>
> Gwen: Where are you going?
>
> Tom: I'm gonna blow —
>
> GWEN: You're a spoiled boy, Tommy. You want things and you're not content until you get them. Well, maybe I'm spoiled too — Maybe, I feel that way too. But you're not running away from me. Come here. (*She holds him to her breasts.*)

The conversation is intensely ambiguous as to what Tom and Gwen are concretely discussing, and since *The Public Enemy* is pre-code, it cannot be written off as coyness to avoid the censor. What does Gwen go for? Is it a casual relationship, or is it that Tom, in his sexual confusion, his lack of potency, and his inability to be part of the community completes Gwen's already dominant personality? Tom's emasculation before Gwen subdues her maleness gained from having used capital to transcend her social gender station, while also allowing her to play at heterosexuality, and so this exchange is consistent to Debord's observation that "the more powerful the class, the more it claims not to exist."[14] Tom's counter that "all my friends think that things are different between us than they are" hints at the (sexual) abnormality of their relationship, and the audience understands here that Tom is trying to remake himself as Matt who enjoys an active and sexual relationship with Mamie. Gwen asks Tom if he wants things different and relates this difference to Tom's "boyfriends," again pointing to their non-heteronormative relationship. Gwen does not try to compete with the men in Tom's life, for she is in a synonymous position. Is "being spoiled" a libertine pursuit of pleasure, or is it the recognition of what the secret of supposed aberrant sexuality infuses in its ashamed suffers? Tom's reply to Gwen of, "How long can a guy hold out?" expresses his frustration with being unable to reconcile these parts hidden away within himself.

The scene between Gwen and Tom is a turning point in the movie, one that is the start of Tom's final tragedy and death. Tom is a tragic hero who is undone not by a fatal character flaw, but by what of his character he has repressed. Later, repression (such as this) will be linked to Klein's examination of individuals unable to experience mourning. Tom must expel outward, to — as Klein theorizes — preserve the good within, and so *The Public Enemy* asks the viewer to consider this, as in the movie's final epigram, when judging Tom. Klein writes that "if we have become able, deep in our unconscious minds, to clear our feelings to some extent toward our parents of grievances, and have forgiven them for the frustrations we had to bear, then we can be at peace with ourselves and are able to love others in the true sense of the word."[15] From the conversation with Gwen, which crescendos to her calling him "my darling boy," it is clear that Tom is not in that place, and the trauma from his childhood continues to undermine his maturity. Tom's "frustration" continues to unthinkingly motivate him toward crime, as he is unable to love others, only to recognize their similarity, judge their acceptance, or rejection. In this way, Gwen becomes a surrogate for not only unachievable heterosexuality, but for brother Mike, which then allows Tom's homosexual impulses to be grafted back onto a woman — a move, which as mentioned before, is remade in *Scarface*, and which in *The Public Enemy* explains why Gwen is Tom's most compelling female partner. Klein observes

> The process by which we displace love from the first people we cherish to other people is extended from earliest childhood onward to things. In this way we develop interests and activities into which we put some of the love that originally belonged to people. In the baby's mind, one part of the body can stand for another part, and an object for parts of the body or for people. In this symbolical way, any round object may, in the child's unconscious mind, come to stand for his mother's breast. By a gradual process, anything that is felt to give out goodness and beauty, and that calls forth pleasures and satisfaction, in the physical or in the wider sense, can in the unconscious mind take the place of this ever-bountiful breast, and of the whole mother.[16]

Gwen is the whole mother in that she can gratify Tom while expressing the (hyper-)feminine repressed within him. Yet at the same time, the symbolic object has been removed from the human, and in Tom's case is an unreplaced part whose void is filled with anxiety. Klein commands our attention, illustrating that "at the bottom our strongest hatred, however, is directed against the hatred within ourselves. We so much dread the hatred in ourselves that we are driven to employ one of our strongest measures of defense by putting it on to other people — to project it. But we also displace love into the outer world; and we can do so genuinely only if we have established good relations with the friendly figures within our minds."[17] Sadly, for Tom, none of this has been accomplished, and like homosexuality stemming from Klein's view of the equality of mother and father, he cannot project it, only use it as the impulsive motivation for his self-absorption and what might be phrased as his mono-bisexuality. Klein refers to this phenomenon in one of her female patients — who might as well be Tom Powers — observing, "In her play at this period there appeared, in contrast to the attitude of the paranoiac child, the tendency to recognize reality only in so far as it related to the frustrations which she had undergone but had never got over."[18]

Nails Nathan is thrown from a horse and dies. Indelibly and defiantly after the funeral, Tom and Matt buy the horse that threw him and execute the beast in its stable stall. The fall from the horse is a grand literary tradition here remade into the realm of the gangster, and one that anticipates the famous horse's head in bed scene from *The Godfather*. Nails' demise sparks headlines, and the perceptive audience must wonder if gangsters make headlines, like the celebrities of the media era, or if Hollywood is here being lazy with its construction of narrative. The newspaper reporting does, however, equate the value of life and value of actions with their cost, as the headline screams, "GANGLAND BURIES ITS OWN — 'NAILS' NATHAN'S FUNERAL STOPS TRAFFIC; FLORAL PIECES AMOUNT TO $75,000. CROWDS LINE STREETS FOR BLOCKS TO WITNESS PASSING OF NOTED GANGSTER."

Tom and Matt's decent escalates. Paddy commands the duo into hiding after a mob war breaks out and his saloon is bombed. Paddy takes Tom and Matt's guns and cash money, hoping to keep his boys off the street and protected until he can gather more support for a counterattack. Once again money, which, as Deleuze writes, is always itself, and the gun — the penis surrogate — are summarized as Tom and Matt's agency into the world, just as Paddy has become "the good parent." Paddy's Girl (Mia Marvin) looks after the fugitives but takes advantage of Tom when he is drunk, forcing him to have sex with her. A shockingly unusual female-on-male rape in American cinema, this encounter is the last of the external impulses that drive Tom to his criminal doom. Tom pushes Paddy's Girl away several times, climaxing with his plea, "Get away from me. You're Paddy's Girl, "but the woman presses on and has her way. Again, Tom becomes the victim of sexual abuse, and like so many victims of sexual abuse, he does not recall the coitus the next morning. Paddy's Girl, on the other hand, is glowing, which is surprising, for as drunk as Tom was the night before, it seems unlikely that he would have made much of a lover. However, the possibility also arises that the sadism of the rape turned masochist Tom on in the same way that he erotized his parental beatings during boyhood. Tom's intoxication might have also allowed the forced sex to channel the subconscious into physical actions wherein gender is removed from the pleasure of the orifice. Paddy's Girl gingerly serves breakfast and asks of Tom, "You aren't sorry, are you?"

TOM: Sorry? Sorry for what?

PADDY'S GIRL: For last night —

TOM: (*suddenly angry*) Whaddya mean — for gettin' drunk?

PADDY'S GIRL: Aren't you the little play actor!

TOM: (*overcome with a look of shock and horror on his face*) Wait a minute. Do you mean? (*She puts her hand to his lips.*) Why you —(*He slaps her face, and she likes it.*)

Perhaps unable to have sex with a woman, or possessing the need to be drunk to do so, Tom storms out of the safe house with no money and no gun. The betrayal of Paddy's Girl has become a betrayal of Paddy himself and fully suggests the level of sexual surrogacy (what Paddy's Girl calls "play acting") that must have been in the exchange the night before. However, Tom has remade himself into a world where, without money and a gun, he stands very little chance at survival. Ever the loyal partner, Matt follows Tom outside the safe house, saying to the latter, "We're together, aren't we?" However, almost immediately after this expression of supreme loyalty, machine guns open fire on the duo. Tom escapes, but Matt dies. Revenge overwhelms and replaces the sexual urge, giving Tom a renewed, clear purpose. Greed pivots between capital and revenge. Tom goes to a gun store, where he acts the naïf long enough to throw the proprietor of the shop off guard and get a hold of a loaded gun, which he immediately uses to hold up the establishment.

Now totally isolated, only a pure instrument of vengeance, and without a thought of the beardage that is Gwen, Tom hunts and stalks his prey. It is not clear whom he specifically seeks, but it can be assumed that it is the mobsters who are responsible for Matt's demise. Rain envelops Tom, and — like the rain in *Psycho*— it becomes a cloak for the psychic interior. Tom arrives at what must be his antagonist's hideout and bursts in. The movie's frame is empty of actors as gun blasts explode from inside, dimmed by the sound of rain. Tom staggers out, wounded. He turns back and throws his guns at the headquarters of his enemies in a final act of defiance before collapsing a few blocks away, admitting, "I ain't so tough." Thus Tom falls into the gutter still the hurt little farting boy of *The Public Enemy*'s opening minutes.

That should be the end of the movie — a true clean ending — however, classic Hollywood often gave false happy (or, "socially tenable") ends, and so viewers are presented with the final sequence of *The Public Enemy* wherein Tom is patched up in the hospital (like George Minifer will be in the studio remade cut of *The Magnificent Ambersons*) long enough to apologize to his mother and brother/double Mike. However, any unity of forgiveness is soon forgotten as the ailing Tom is kidnapped and held for ransom by irked enemy gangsters. Paddy strikes a deal with the rival mob for Tom's safe return, but it is Tom's bound corpse that is dropped off at his mother's house to be received by Mike. More grotesquely than the beer on the table, Tom's body brings criminality into the home once more, again shattering the family with violence as the only modern language with any true meaning.

Point Blank (1967)

In the final minutes of *The Public Enemy*, Tom Powers transforms into a lone and hunted animal, snarling in the shadows, doused by heavy rain, which totally isolates him from the social. Metro-Goldwyn-Mayer's 1967 film of Donald E. Westlake's 1962 novel, *The Hunter*, retitled *Point Blank* for the screen and directed by John Boorman, remakes *The Public Enemy*, turning Tom into Walker (played by Lee Marvin), a doubled-crossed gangster "bent" on revenge and the recoupment of stolen money. More a (supernatural) force of nature than an individual, Walker is defined only by how he has been betrayed, and his purpose is only revenge, as everything else has been repressed. Walker does not play "Revenge" like Tamora in *Titus Andronicus*, or Matt and Tom in *The Public Enemy*, but becomes "Revenge" as in Greek and Roman drama, as Walker is literal, and there is nothing to him that is not always manifest. In the source novel, Westlake categorizes Walker (there named Parker) as this force unto himself: "He didn't know if he was going to make it, if he was going to hold up the syndicate and get away with it, and he didn't really care. He was doing it, and rolling along with the momentum, and that was all that mattered."[19] By the 1960s, American society had accepted gangsters, and the pull between the moral and the social was superseded by their mutations into the culture industry of the middle and late sound era. The irony of *Point Blank* is how normalized the gangsters are — they are businessmen and a corporation like any other. It is this portrayal which illustrates the extent of nonthinking that assumed the individual's (and viewer's) active self-consideration in mid–twentieth-century America.

Deleuze writes, "Money is the obverse of all the images that the cinema shows and sets in place, so that films about money are already, if implicitly, films within the film or about the film."[20] It is important to understand gangster movies as movies about movies and the cinema of the middle and late sound era as being about money — that is, as fantasy exploring the potential of capital. This fantasy, which overwhelms cinema as it moves toward the media era, is described by Debord as the relationship between money and the society of the spectacle:

> The spectacle is the flip side of money. It, too, is an abstract general equivalent of all commodities. But whereas money has dominated society as the representation of universal equivalence — the exchangeability of different goods whose use remain uncomparable — the spectacle is the modern complement of money: a

representation of the commodity world as a whole which serves as a general equivalent for what the entire society can be and can do. The spectacle is money one can *only look at*, because in it all use has already been exchanged for the totality of abstract representation. The spectacle is not just a servant of pseudo-use, it is already in itself a *pseudo-use* of life.[21]

Cinema can be understood as "spectacle," and the absence of representation is what evolves from *The Public Enemy* to *Point Blank*, where the characters are themselves absent of representation because of cinema-spectacle. Cinema begins in the silent era as a reaction to theater, but with the sound era it becomes reactionary and a display of money — capital that "one can only look at." *Point Blank* follows Walker's quest to regain ninety-three thousand dollars — his share of a heist, which was immediately stolen from him by his (even more) crooked partner Mal Reese (John Vernon). Modernly, *Point Blank* remakes itself before viewer's eyes by filtering the tropes of the gangster drama through memory and dream, decentralizing the concrete social realism of *The Public Enemy* and proposing how marketing replaces content in post–World War II America along Debordian lines.

The Player King in *Hamlet* orates that "purpose is but the slave to memory,"[22] and what informs Walker and the characters in *Point Blank* is an inescapable past, partly chosen, yet presented as decided by unknown forces. The characters in *Point Blank* are almost Shakespearean, but also something of a return of the caricatures of Christopher Marlowe who are unable to listen to themselves and therefore change within relation to themselves. The opening heist in *Point Blank* — Walker's primal scene — takes place on Alcatraz Island. The prison is closed but is ironically used as the location for covert "drops" by an all-powerful syndicate of organized crime. Alcatraz is an uncanny place, like the hotel in *Last Year at Marienbad* (1961), or the Overlook in *The Shining* (1980). Deleuze quotes Andre Labarthe, referring to *Marienbad* as "the last of the great neo-realist films."[23] Labarthe is incorrect to see *Marienbad* as the "last" of anything; however he is correct to identify Resnais' film as a cinematic watershed. The stylization of realism in *Point Blank* connects it directly to *Marienbad* and makes it a neo-realist movie because the psychological has been removed from the physical as a result of the shift of sound cinema from dream state to the tool of the political. Earle writes that "Alain Resnais' films also proceed to dissolve any assurance in a public reality by demonstrating the ambiguity of the meaning of the present through its dependence on the past, a past moreover which is itself ambiguous through its significance for the present. Memory here becomes the artist whose materials are always on the verge of losing any independent reality whatsoever,"[24] and Boorman adopts this method for his crime fiction adaptation. *Point Blank* has no reality other than memory, yet because of its lack of psychoanalytic introspection, the characters are unable to be remade and remain terminal cases, or in Walker's situation perhaps already prior.

At the opening of the first reel of *Point Blank*, nondiegetic psychedelic lights — the phenomenon of pure cinema — bathe Walker's face, and as the face comes into view, gunshots are heard as he is shot at "point-blank" range. Walker staggers into a cell, and his voiceover tells us his thought process in the present moment — that is, his fleeting thoughts after his betrayal and serious injury. "Cell. Prison cell. How did I get here?" He asks, "Did it happen?" and then mutters, "A dream, a dream." The memory state of *Point Blank* is thus established, and Boorman — with great assistance from skilled and creative editor Henry Berman — is able to weave the viewer in and out of Walker's fugue. The implication is that the audience is watching a dream — perhaps Walker's death dream — and the fantasies of revenge he will not live to fulfill. Significant in its irony, the spectacle has robbed cinema of dream, but the absurdity of the spectacle forces the adoption of dream as the prism to decipher spectacle's meaning. Like so many doubles, the false reality of dreams thus becomes "true" in a world where fantasy and perception obscure actual reality. Walker's flashback continues to a drunken reunion, where he meets up with Mal Reese. Reese is desperate and clamors after Walker, finally tackling him to the ground. Depending on whose subjective flashback is witnessed, the "friendship" between Walker and Reese changes, and the relationship seems less and less about fraternity and

In *Point Blank* (1967), Walker tells Reese, "We blew it," and it is that same line, and situation, that Peter Fonda and Dennis Hopper will remake two years later in *Easy Rider* (Dennis Hopper, 1969). (Courtesy the Chestnut Hill Film Group.)

more about opportunity. Despite Reese' claims to the contrary, Walker and he were never Matt and Tom. Rather, Walker has what Reese does not — he is a successful gangster with a long-term female companion, Lynn (Sharon Acker). Reese insists to Walker, "You're my friend," and explains that he will be killed if he cannot repay his mob debts. And so the duo partner, and the Alcatraz heist is set where the two "independent" gangsters will rob the mob. However, the heist does not go as promised because trigger-happy Reese executes the mob's bagmen, and Walker senses — but does not act on — the first hint of his undoing. Reese is delighted by the money, but Walker is clearly not. Reese's methods are sloppy and "unprofessional." Walker tells Reese, "We blew it," and it is that same line, and situation, that Dennis Hopper will remake two years later in *Easy Rider* (1969).

After rewitnessing Walker being shot point blank, the opening credits run and are a highly unusual mix of freeze-frames and tableaux, stressing *Point Blank* as a gangster remake of Herk Harvey's *Carnival of Souls* (1962) by way of Ambrose Bierce and Resnais. In *Carnival of Souls,* the protagonist pivots in a surreal undulation between life and death, and the action of the drama is the

In *Carnival of Souls* (Herk Harvey, 1962), the protagonist Mary Henry (Candace Hilligoss) pivots in a surreal undulation between life and death, and the action of the drama is the moment of one's life flashing before one's eyes just before extinction — certainly one way to read *Point Blank* (1967). (Photofest.)

moment of one's life flashing before one's eyes just before extinction — certainly one way to read *Point Blank*. The opening credits of *Point Blank* track Walker's dreamy, uncanny escape from "inescapable" Alcatraz, finally leading him into the deadly San Francisco Bay waters that surround the prison. The audience next sees Walker, repaired, on a boat taking a sightseeing tour of the old prison site. Walker here circles in on his own memory, until he is interrupted by a Mysterious Man (Keenan Wynn), named "Yost" in the credits, who asks, "How did you make it, Walker?" *Point Blank*'s questions are never resolved, but Walker's revenge is helped by the Mysterious Man who becomes a recreation of The Ghost of King Hamlet, thereby remaking Walker as a modern inverse of the Danish Prince who is now all action and no introspection. The Mysterious Man tells Walker, "I'm going to help you, and you're going to help me." What remains the same between *Hamlet* and *Point Blank* is the parental manifest destiny that threatens to assume identity. Walker's revenge quest — the reclaiming of his ninety-three thousand dollars stolen by Reese from the mob to pay the mob — becomes Walker's Kleinian "destructive interjections." Like both Tom Powers and Hamlet, there is seething hatred, or in Walker's case, the intense sensation of having been "wronged," that replaces the ability for any other type of relationship. *Point Blank* is important in the sound era's transformation into media for the many reasons already illustrated, in addition to being the beginning of the streamlining of archetypal narrative that leads to first-person shooter video games, where object (quest) becomes object (object) and social definition is unthinkingly given over to aid the objective.

Walker's vengeance is as spectral as his personage because he doesn't kill things intentionally so much as break them, like an angry child whose first language is violence. Walker lives in a society where the objects are of more value than people — people are replicable, remakable, whereas an object appreciates or depreciates, or just "is." Reese sets up Walker and then steals money from him in addition to also "stealing" Walker's girlfriend, Lynn. Walker does not express concern at Lynn's betrayal, as it is superseded by the loss of money, and the tangibility of money replaces the ephemera of emotion. In flashback, the audience sees Lynn and Walker "falling in love" in a boozy dockside idyll, which, apart from being emotionally vague, also seems subjective and untrustworthy — more of a constructed memory than an actuality. Because of the society in which he lives, Walker has, post-betrayal, placed all his feelings about Lynn onto object (money), which he then has "destructive interjections" with. Back in the "present," Walker tracks down where Lynn lives and bursts in shooting at her bed even before he registers that Reese is not in it.

Since Walker's shooting at Alcatraz, Lynn has become pill dependent, and like Walker — though in a different way — she lives in a vague twilight world. Lynn's drugs, ostensibly to correct a sleeping disorder, have made her waking and sleeping lives blur together into a dream state no more or less "real" than the confused late–1960s society around her. The intersection of business, crime and tranquilizers first appears most clearly in English-language cinema in the real estate office scenes of Hitchcock's *Psycho*, where Marion Crane's fellow administrative assistant, Caroline (Pat Hitchcock), is zonked and pushes tranquilizers on Marion as a cure-all for her ostensibly economic problems. *Psycho*, as much a crime film as a horror movie, prefigures the relationship to drugs in *Point Blank*, and in the gangster film from this point on. The most explicit example of drugs remaking society after *Easy Rider* is on display in Brian De Palma's 1983 remake of *Scarface*, where cocaine is practically a character.

In *Point Blank*, Lynn confesses to Walker, "You ought to kill me," and that she "just couldn't make it" with him; but that with Mal it was "kinda fun" and she "just drifted into it." Now an object herself, Lynn is unable to escape her role and live in a culture where what lies beneath is absent because it gives her no identity other than that of consumer. All Lynn can consume are pills to numb out conflict with nonthinking. Lynn continues voicing her tangled thoughts to Walker without prodding, not trying to change in relation to herself, but merely trying to understand herself in another example of *Point Blank*'s culturally telling short-circuiting of the Shakespearean tradition. "I loved you [Walker], then Mal happened," Lynn says. "You talked a lot about Mal Reese. He was very real to me — until I met him. The two of us. Then the three of us." Lynn's disconnect is an unreality, her letting go of the actual-psychological to seek meaning in object and function. Lynn kills herself with an overdose of sleeping pills rather than sort out her role in their tangled world. Reese and Walker are thereby proposed as doubles, and it is understood that what must have upset Walker first was that *he* did not do the betraying. However, as *Point Blank*'s ending proposes, wherein Walker "gives up the ghost," Walker is an "honest" criminal. Crime has been organized, and so the raw passion of Tom Powers and his ilk is removed in favor of conservation of what is established, which is the "mob" of capital. In a society where all business is criminal, gangsters are no longer acting out, but conforming — albeit in a technically illegal way. *Point Blank* suggests that it must have been a fantasy of Walker's to have Lynn kill herself, because it removes her from his vengeance and does so leaving his emotional repression fully and firmly buried.

The dominance of the material continues when Walker — still seeking Reese — tracks down Big John, a car dealer as smarmy as the one in *Psycho*. Big John (Michael Strong) ignores Walker at first, distracted by a busty blonde woman in the parking lot. Here, the film remakes Walker's distraction from Lynn by capital during the plotting of the heist, while she and Reese were becoming intimate and greed posed as sexual desire. Finally, Big John takes Walker for a test drive — as Walker buckles his seat belt, Big John tells him, "You really don't need that," underlining the capricious surface of 1960s America that removed gravity from decision. With Walker driving, the giant car tools down Californian streets with Big John as passenger. Like the stock footage in *The Public Enemy*, *Point Blank* has a tangible amount of mid–1960s location photography and a great visual tension between the movie's two opposing cities, San Francisco and Los Angeles. The former is the site of the primal emotional scene, and the latter is the "cultural" remaking. In a cunning display of the utility of capital, Big John points out the car audio system, asking, "Mind if I hear my commercial?" When the radio is turned on, he remarks, "Stereo — pretty good," performing the narcissistic, if not cannibalistic, act of listening to his own advertisement — his own myth. The advertising removes Big John from the present sale personally and again illustrates the simulation of reality, caused by capital, adopted as identity. Without asking questions, Walker begins to drive recklessly, taking out his frustrations on the car — speaking with violence — finally gaining the true attention of, and information needed from, Big John.

Remaking the detective movie's plot archetype, Walker follows his clues and goes to Lynn's sister Chris' nightclub ironically called the "Movie House." Here, like Deleuze linking money and film, or earlier when Walker and Yost saw each other through the texture of an actual window "screen" (racking focus) after Lynn's death, *Point Blank* presents itself as allegory of moviemaking — the obsessive, unexplained quest and insignificant struggle in front of controlling economic forces enormously larger and more powerful. The club is in the middle of a frenetic floor show, clearly inspired by Andy Warhol's *Exploding Plastic Inevitable* performances (1966–1967), where one must shout to be heard over the music — a sort of illustration of Friedrich Nietzsche's belief in power of music chronicled in *Ecce Homo* and revisited by David Lynch in the subtitled Roadhouse sequence of *Twin Peaks: Fire Walk with Me* (1992). At the "Movie House" of *Point Blank*, Chris (Angie Dickinson) wants revenge for her sister ruined by Reese, or needs to express the rage within her and so latches on to the idea of revenge. She tells Walker that Reese is holed up in the Huntley Arms Hotel and describes the place as "like Fort Knox." With this detail not found in the novel, *Point Blank* here remakes *Goldfinger* (1964) and, using that affinity, links the next set piece with the aforementioned James Bond adventure. Walker's plan becomes penetration into the Huntley, using Chris as live bait and sexual sacrifice to Reese. Chris asks Walker why she should help him, and he nonchalantly says, "It's up to you." Chris is the only character in *Point Blank* who seems to be able to respond to the world around her; however her susceptibility to Walker still presents her on the precipice — the same one the United States itself was on the edge of in 1967 — that is, of falling like Lynn into being a tool of the political, accepting false reality.

To cause a distraction for the police and Reese's bodyguards across from the Huntley hotel, Walker breaks into an apartment and finds two homosexual men whom he holds at gunpoint. The men are helpful, so much so that they

Chris (Angie Dickinson) and Walker (Lee Marvin) in the loveless revenge drama, *Point Blank* (John Boorman, 1967) that Andrew Saris once aptly dubbed "Last Year at Alcatraz." (Courtesy the Chestnut Hill Film Group.)

lend a hand with their own detainment, tying themselves together. It is not totally clear if the homosexuality is represented cruelly or if the film is suggesting gender-sexual construction within the genre. Like "abnormal" sexual desires that manifest in dreams, the scene with the gay male couple serves two purposes within *Point Blank*, providing wish fulfillment (Walker and Reese's "romance") as well as the expression of fear linking sadism and revenge. *The Public Enemy* equated criminality with homosexuality and can be read as a cry for the acceptance of the homosexual as a product of his or her environment. In *Point Blank*, the Queer men are one of only two functional couples portrayed — the other being the young lovers at the automat who offer an equally ironic commentary on Walker and Chris' "romance." Walker's obsession is first Reese, and then the money — the other men in the movie seem unconcerned with anything other than the homosocial pecking order of the mob's "boys club." In a time just at the birth of the national feminist movement, *Point Blank* represents men as separate and unequal to women, and the film is decidedly and definitely anti-heterosexual union and anti-marriage. Movies against marriage offer one of the most taboo fantasies — that of living outside the structure of normative social life — and with this *Point Blank* again remakes *The Public Enemy*'s social problems.

Following Walker's plan, Chris gains access to Reese, and as she offers herself to him sexually, he sends his bodyguards away. That Walker's cunning works so well makes it clear why it must have been so personally shocking for him to be double-crossed back at Alcatraz. Because of Chris' seduction of Reese, Walker has his opportunity and enters the penthouse pulling Mal off Chris mid-intercourse. Reese is terrified of Walker, and he names names: Fairfax, Brewster, and Carter, the three men running the organized crime syndicate — "the Multiplex Corporation" — whom Reese paid back his debt to with Walker's "stolen" money. Reading *Point Blank* as an allegory of Metro-Goldwyn-Mayer circa 1967 — which Deleuze's theories encourage — the business of the motion picture studio is dwarfing the product it is producing, thereby making the studio hierarchy ostensibly "the Multiplex Corporation." Furthermore, the phenomenon of multiplexes in the 1980s and 1990s forever changed the way movies were released and brought cinema closer to the world of cable TV and the Internet, and all the other remade tropes of the media era.

Trying to escape Walker, Reese falls to his death from the roof, and Walker leaves. Outside the Huntley, Chris waits for Walker like a streetwalker loitering for a trick. Her fucking Reese has absolved her in Walker's eyes — for his forcing someone to have sex with Reese is tantamount to remaking when Lynn had sex with Reese and Walker had so little control that he didn't even know. However, because Walker exists for vengeance alone, Chris cannot remake her sister for Walker, and any hope of emotional healing is absent and sterile as the chrome, mod world around them. Walker pays Chris outside the Huntley, saying, "This money belonged to your sister; you'd better take it." *Point Blank* thus comments on how tangible ownership is, as well as the mad, contemporary world where profit is the only principle and one that removes the individual from the process. Nowhere is this exchange more evident than in the lonely night scenes between Walker and Chris that follow their adventure at the Huntley.

Reese's information leads Walker to Carter (Lloyd Bochner). A payoff is arranged for Walker, but it is another double-cross, illustrating that business now has no ethics. Remaking his previous error, Walker double-crosses the double-crossers, and Carter is killed by his own sniper. Walker kills the sniper professionally and with detachment. Even the payoff "money" is blank and clean, underlining the obscenity of currency in the midst of bloodshed.

Carter leads Walker to Brewster, and Walker stakes out Brewster's house waiting for his return. Chris comes to Brewster's expecting a romantic evening with Walker but finds him in the middle of a grueling and obsessive deathwatch. She sees the emptiness of Walker's vengeance and tries to grab his attention by turning on a multitude of kitchen appliances. However, even the hum of the modern age cannot penetrate into Walker's empty, hypo-manic focus. They fight — Chris literally tries to beat her struggle into Walker — and here this fight remakes the roughhousing between Reese and Walker in the reunion flashbacks, but Walker cannot be penetrated with ideas and cannot serve any purposes other than his own after Lynn's betrayal. That night, Walker and Chris make love, and the sex is a blurring, with the various couples of the movie remaking their liaisons — Walker on top of Chris becomes Walker and Lynn, which becomes Lynn and Mal, which becomes Mal and Chris, before finally returning to Chris and Walker. What is left out here is the pairing of the men and women together, an incestuous act that would fully return the viewer to Tom-Matt/Tom-Mike dichotomies of *The Public Enemy*. All *Point Blank*'s love affairs are past, however, and the meaninglessness of the present is illustrated to further force the character back to memory. At this moment in *Point Blank*, the romantic tragedy overwhelms the allegory of capital-spectacle, and Walker's emotional anguish is finally presented as rooted in the fact that he was not only double crossed by his best friend but by his woman as well. Such betrayal delineates an end of true society — of true fraternity being possible — and so all that is left for Walker is the expression of his identity as Revenge.

Walker is able to take Brewster (Carroll O'Connor) hostage with ease, as Brewster is such a mod(ern) criminal that he possesses no muscle. Likewise, Brewster has no cash and can only offer Walker his credit cards. Finally, fearing for his life, he agrees to take Walker to Alcatraz, apparently the only place where the Multiplex Corporation has any cash dealings. Brewster agrees that when the helicopter drop comes, he will pay Walker the ninety-three thousand dollars he seeks. The finale of *Point Blank* becomes Walker's ultimate wish fulfillment as he is able to go back and remake the botched heist that began his odyssey at the start of the film. The proximity of closure is in the air for Walker, raising the stakes of this Alcatraz remaking. True to this, the old prison seems even more ghostly than *Marienbad* in the final sequences. This time, Brewster is shot, not by Walker but by another hidden sniper. As Walker disappears into the shadows, renouncing his claim to the money which is finally his, the Mysterious Man — reveled to be Fairfax — comes forward from the darkness. The partner of Brewster and Carter, Fairfax has used Walker to seize control of the syndicate and dispatch his competition. Here the Fairfax/Brewster-Cartier double cross remakes the Walker-Reese double cross. Either disgusted by the absurdity of it all, having fulfilled his quest, or having reached a catharsis in the remaking, Walker disappears. It does not matter if he was a ghost all the time, or a hired killer with a vivid imagination, as his story represents money as ultimately meaningless, as well as violence (and war) as being a totally symbolic but nevertheless universally understood language.

Bad Lieutenant (1992)

Deleuze quotes Sade, remarking, "I have infinitely less reason to fear my neighbor's passions than the law's injustice, for my neighbor's passions are contained by mine, whereas nothing stops or contains the injustices of the law."[25] Abel Ferrara's *Bad Lieutenant* released at the end of 1992 takes place in a mythical New York City Indian summer of the recent past — that is, the recent cinematic memory. It exists in the realm where "neighbors' passions" are expressed through the law's injustice. Not so much a morality play as a failed appeal to God, *Bad Lieutenant* follows a nameless Lieutenant (Harvey Keitel) in the sordid days just before his murder out front of Penn Station for unpaid gambling debts. In *The Ancient Tragical Motive as Reflected in the Modern*, Kierkegaard writes, "The wrath of the gods is terrible, but the pain is not so great as in modern tragedy where the hero bears the whole weight of his guilt, is himself transparent in his suffering of his guilt."[26] Indeed, it is hard to have anything more than empathy for the Lieutenant, for he is the victim of his own compulsions and not social influences — other than society's existence itself. The Lieutenant is a collection of base impulses interwoven with a Christian hangover and ravenous compulsive behaviors, suggesting a parallel to Kierkegaard — in that to live is to suffer. It is this selfsame transformative suffering that fosters the cultural archetype evolution of Tom Powers into Walker, and Walker into the Lieutenant.

Schoolly D's (aka Jesse Bonds Weaver) "Signifying Rapper" is *Bad Lieutenant*'s theme song, but the movie's opening credits are instead underscored with sports talk radio. The Mets are in an imagined series with the Dodgers, three games down, and face the seemingly impossible task of having to win four straight. Sporting games, with a very different psychoanalytic value than cinema, do provide the sense of daydreaming that movies can, as sporting events, offer emotional surrogacy and a very graspable substitute for confrontation. However, sports remove any trace of Shakespearean listening, returning to the bread and circus days of Ancient Rome. Best personified in the early media era with the 2006 movie *Zidane*, directed by Douglas Gordon and Philippe Parreno, movement can return cinema to a pure place akin to the silent era; however, movement without text/language has no actual psychoanalytic meaning other than suggestion, and therefore it presents its viewers with false possibilities indicative of current times. For the sports viewer, the team can win for you, even if you, yourself, cannot win. With the dawn of the media era, sports on television became an outlet for advertising and so perpetuated the remaking of the individual into a post-literate — but inclusive — state removed from self. Adding gambling to sports fuses the sports-media-advertising triumvirate to the change of catharsis of mid–twentieth-century cinema. Thus, the concept of "remaking the odds" is forever intertwined with the "American Dream"

Not so much a morality play as a failed appeal to God — the nameless Lieutenant (Harvey Keitel) at the scene of the Nun's and the church's violation in the sordid days just before his murder for unpaid gambling debts in *Bad Lieutenant* (Abel Ferrara, 1992). (Courtesy the Chestnut Hill Film Group.)

because of its unrealizability — and so patrons buy the concept, and catharsis retreats from the climax of the drama to the act of (ticket) purchase.

The Lieutenant lives in working-class Queens with his wife and their two sons along with various relations — presumably of the wife. As he drives them to school, the Lieutenant rages at his pubescent sons about their tardiness that morning. They stutter a defense about an aunt in the bathroom, which only serves to make their father more irate. Teaching masculinity to his offspring — undoubtedly colored with his fierce attitude — he asks his boys if they are "men or mice." Impulsively, moments later, as he is about to follow his brother out of the car, the remaining son hugs and kisses his father. Like the late twentieth-century viewer, the Lieutenant is so removed from his humanity that he is unsure of what to make of this display of affection. After the children have gone to school, his compulsions become action, and, snorting some cocaine, the Lieutenant goes to "work."

Bad Lieutenant begins with the baseball game, and then moves into the home. Tension and violence stem within both, and the next sequence of the movie adds to this the perversion that police officers are the greater criminals at large. It is as if the syndicate in *Point Blank* became so refined that its hoods were forced to take jobs with the police department — something on display late in the Anthony Burgess adaptations discussed in Chapter 5. Klein helps the viewer to understand that Tom Powers sought to express his repressed hatred and rage at his parents via his criminal activities, but in a world where everything is criminal due to the forces of big capital, the Lieutenant performs the inverse by becoming a cop and his vocation is therefore a further repression. Illustrating the perversion of the NYPD, the cops at the crime scene of a shootout, joined by the Lieutenant, talk sports in a huddle rather than the details of the investigation at hand. The Lieutenant takes bets from the cops to place with a bookie, and the audience is made aware of the extent of the Lieutenant's gambling problem as he hustles his fellow officers to try to catch up on his own losses. As he makes the phone call to place "their" bet, the Lieutenant watches a guy across the street break into the trunks of a line of parked cars. The audience doesn't know what the Lieutenant will do—bust him, take the stolen goods, or, as he chooses, ignore the crime. Later in *Bad Lieutenant*, thieves, followed by the Lieutenant, rob a corner store and are all witnessed by a young Asian girl who will not look away. She cannot ignore the injustice as she is yet not part of the system and—like the other children in the movie—on the verge of being corrupted by the adults who have already given themselves over to the combine of big capital. As on display in *The Naked City* (1948), to *Wise Guys* (1986) to *Goodfellas* (1990), et al, the greatness of the New York City crime movie is the inhumanity of the city itself. It is not one element that is the menace, but the very atmosphere that is corrosive. Fear does not totally rest on the traditional boogieman-sicko but something far worse—something inside everyone—that kills unconsciously a thousand times each day via self-perceived moral authority, a casual callousness to the environment, and an indifference to unequivocal social justice for all. If certain audiences are occasionally unresponsive to the value of *Bad Lieutenant*, it is probably because the film wants viewers to make choices in how to watch it, or the fact that the material may hit too close to home.

Bad Lieutenant is photographed (by Ken Kelsch) on location in the last moments of New York City before Times Square was sold to Disney and the boroughs re-gentrified in the 1990s. This change removed the character of the city, turning Manhattan into a white person's outdoor shopping mall, almost a police state, served by a colored underclass. Ironically, *Bad Lieutenant*'s "remake," *Bad Lieutenant: Port of Call—New Orleans* (2009), must remake post–Katrina New Orleans to achieve the effect Ferrara captures through authenticity of storytelling. When Zoe (*Bad Lieutenant* screenwriter Zoë Lund, aka Zoë Tamerlis) shows heroin to the Lieutenant, saying, "Fine, brown shit," the viewer wonders—because of Ferrara's commitment to perceived "naturalism"—if actor Keitel is doing real drugs. When he and Zoë smoke dope off some tinfoil, it must be considered if they are actually getting high, as well as exponentially increasing their chance of Alzheimer's from the warmed, heated silver menace. *Bad Lieutenant: Port of Call— New Orleans* is mostly interesting because it can be considered the second or third remake of *Bad Lieutenant* — if the censored "R-rated" cut of 1992's *Bad Lieutenant* issued on VHS home video is counted along with the new transfers of *Bad Lieutenant* currently circulated on DVD where "Signifying Rapper" is lamentably expurgated from the soundtrack because of copyright issues regarding the sound samples contained within.

In the unedited 1992 movie, "Forever My Darling" plays on the soundtrack as the audience sees the Lieutenant in a squalid room participating in a threesome complete with faux lesbian bondage. The women mime a show for the Lieutenant, yet — save for the nudity — it is removed from the sexual. The three hug, and the viewers sense that they are beyond sex — more than just post-coitus, the trio resembles the people in J.G. Ballard's *Crash* who have the need to feel *something* in the shadow of lurking oblivion and therefore must push beyond the usual. Wound fucking is just another form of mainlining. In the same way, and seeking to make Kleinian destructive interjections and express repressed hatred, a white Nun (Frankie Thorn) in her late twenties is raped by two unidentified men of color on the alter of a Catholic church, and the crime is intercut with images of Jesus Christ suffering on the cross. This rape is the central action of *Bad Lieutenant* as it is the one event that perhaps allows the Lieutenant to change in relation to himself. While the agony of crucifixion seems a very different experience than the horror of two-on-one, no-holes-barred rape, Ferrara illustrates in this sequence how religion — especially Christianity — provides the same type of fantastic, seemingly meaningful daydreaming that early twentieth-century filmmaking also offers via spectacle.

Unable to dream, only to "sleep it off," another next morning finds the Lieutenant passed out on the couch at his home in Queens. When the Lieutenant wakes, he does not tend to the child watching television by herself but switches the channel on her from cartoons to sports. The baby mimics the Lieutenant despite his lack of interaction with her, and viewers here sense the greater tragedy of *Bad Lieutenant* echoing back to *The Public Enemy*— that of the children sure to grow up dysfunctional as a result of largely absent and/or abusive parents. In addition to the plague of compulsive behavior, the Lieutenant is clearly at the mercy of his addiction to drugs. It can be interpreted that the Lieutenant is not himself because of this — that he is something other than himself, as all his decisions stem from a nonintellectual place altered by substances. The move to stimulants and narcotics offers another type of interjection, but ones that quickly devour themselves, as demonstrated by the long scenes of Zoe getting the Lieutenant high and speaking of vampires being "lucky" analyzed later in this chapter.

At another crime scene, the Lieutenant steals a large bag of coke, but he drops it and must let his subordinate log it as evidence. The other cops seem

outraged at the Nun's rape, as if the act crossed some sort of line that other violence against women (including their own) does not. The Lieutenant seems
aware, if unconcerned, with this hypocrisy and correctly calls the church "a
racket." However, the racket of the church offers the Lieutenant a chance at a
reward, one that is enough to pay off his bookie if he can restrain himself from
trying to make up his gaming losses with further gambling. The Lieutenant
goes to the hospital and spies on the raped Nun's examination. The Nun is eroticized, and with this animal impulse the Lieutenant is able to make a connection
to her. But the Lieutenant's connection to the Nun is not totally sexual as —
more stimulatingly — it ignites the plan of self-reparation wherein he will reclaim
his losses as victories and — more problematically — wealth. Sex is another compulsion of the Lieutenant, one removed from real pleasure or emotion, save for
the release of orgasm, which is not unlike the momentary rush of getting high.

The Lieutenant's self-hatred is expressed in his sexual acts and drug use.
On the prowl — "on duty" the viewer assumes — the Lieutenant pulls over two
young women in an old car with little cause. The girls are out for a night of
clubbing in a "borrowed" automobile. Immediately afraid of the police, they
admit their cannabis use earlier and beg the Lieutenant not to run them in
because of an (abusive) father who will "kill" them. The Lieutenant tells them,
"I'll do the right thing, if you do the right thing. I know what it's like to get
stoned a little." He compels the one young woman to show her panty-swathed
ass, and the other young woman to simulate the act of fellating a penis with
her open mouth. The Lieutenant here enters a nebulous area of sexual violence,
and the viewer must question what gratification other than the use (and abuse)
of his power the Lieutenant is receiving, as well as what differentiates the Lieutenant from the Nun Ravishers.

After the assault on the two girls in the borrowed car, the Lieutenant goes
to church — not to seek absolution or to search for clues, but because he has no
place to go, as his world and mounting debts and addictions are fast closing in
on him. He naps in the pew but finds no solace. The fabled Mets-Dodgers
series continues and, back in his car, the Lieutenant shoots his radio with his
gun, cursing player Darryl Strawberry's success against seemingly impossible
odds. Then he manically puts on his flashing lights and siren and drives forward
in an unthinking rage. The Lieutenant's reality is dawning on him and yet he
is unable to act out any more than he is already doing. This end-point frustration
harkens back to the American mythos of one's success being on one's own shoul-
ders, and so the Lieutenant — while unable to break his patterns — is still able
to hold himself responsible in failure. As in Kierkegaard, "the hero bears the
whole weight of his guilt, is himself transparent in his suffering of his guilt."
What is portrayed is a failure in the construction of society where positive introjections are no longer possible because they must refute all that is established
and thereby have no official voice or advocate.

The Lieutenant is drawn back to the church for a first communion, and this sequence is the start of the Lieutenant's attempt at "rebirth" — that is, his attempt to crawl out of the hole he has found himself in. Later, the Lieutenant eavesdrops on the raped Nun in confession to a priest, where she refuses to name her attackers — even though their identities are known to her. The Nun expresses her desire to see the transformation of "bitter semen, into fertile sperm" — to turn hatred into love. Here, Catholic transmogrification is the ultimate "remake" and shows the narrative archetype of remaking that thusly underscores Western civilization. However, the Nun's comment that her rapists "did not love me, but I ought to have loved them" also illustrates the "slave morality" of Christianity which is why *Bad Lieutenant*'s Christian "bent" is so illustrative of the reasons for the emergence of the media era in the late 1990s. As the Lieutenant sits drunk in a bar, "his" baseball team makes a comeback, and it is the same hope against hope that the Nun holds to, and which intriguingly presents the Lieutenant and the Nun as doubles.

Perhaps the Lieutenant is not looking for rebirth but death and is in that way a character like Herman Herman in *Despair* (1978), a movie — like *Bad Lieutenant*— also produced by Edward R. Pressman. The Lieutenant's Bookie tries to collect his money and, failing, screams at the Lieutenant that his debts "ain't no fucking joke no more." The Bookie warns the Lieutenant that his badge will not protect him. To this, the Lieutenant responds, "No one can kill me. I'm blessed. I'm a fucking Catholic." Here, the Lieutenant takes steps backward into personal darkness as the dementia of his (self) perception rises. It is not that the Lieutenant feels "blessed," but — like the baseball game about to be played — the Lieutenant has the potential for last-minute redemption, something always proselytized by the Catholic Church — or another sports game — surrogating what is absent in real life. Troublingly, all these factors wrongly suggest existence as a game.

The Lieutenant lies about being at the playoff game, when in reality he watched it on a TV in a bar. The false reality of television — of the encroaching media era — further isolates the Lieutenant in his compulsions. Like organized religion, television provides the simulation of reality as false as the one the Lieutenant tries to conceive around his increasingly sloppy police work and unhappy home life. The Lieutenant drunkenly says he knew Strawberry "struck out on purpose. And that he's saving it up, for the big one — tomorrow," and here, even the surrogacy of sports metaphors start to fail the Lieutenant in his downward spiral. The Lieutenant's Bookie recognizes this, telling him, "You're sick in the fucking head, you know that?" In late twentieth-century America, hard work will not fairly reward, and so viewers see the lure of gambling — of "getting rich quick." The Lieutenant defiantly tells another bookie, who will not take his over-the-phone bet, "It's my money," when it is clear to everyone — save for the Lieutenant — that it is not. Of course, all property can be viewed as theft, but in addition to that, what the Lieutenant experiences is what it is to lack money — that which he can quantify and define himself with. What has not been understood by the Lieutenant is the remaking of capital into credit, which also is not worth anything because of the lack of real resources behind it.

The Lieutenant's time becomes more and more fragmented, and the movie moves further into the Lieutenant's own reality, increasingly influenced by his anxiety concerning his gambling debts. The ritual of drug addiction mirrors the rituals of religion, and the scenes in Zoe's windowless apartment become the Lieutenant's Mass. In a scene seemingly ripped from the pages of a Donald Goines novel, Zoe shoots up the Lieutenant with heroin, cooing, "Oh, it's a beautiful vein." Again, *Bad Lieutenant* confronts the viewer with cinema's remaking as well as the ambiguity of whether what is being watched is truth or "playing." Along the Deleuzian line, films about money—like *Bad Lieutenant*—are films about filmmaking. The indications that these scenes are not "play" points to this film as being another unique landmark on media assuming cinema—that is, captured reality assuming created fictions. The Lieutenant cannot find words as Zoe compels him to shoot up. The Lieutenant's repressions have led him to seeking the purity of the primitive—much like Ferrara's cinema itself—and this is the expression of the hope for clarity in simplicity. Viewers see the inexpressibility of the Lieutenant's grief and guilt, and this inexpressibility of the modern is what draws 1990s culture into the post-literate era. Zoe tells the Lieutenant (and the viewer), "Vampires are lucky, they can feed on others. We've got to eat away at ourselves. We got to eat our legs, so we got the energy to walk, we gotta cum so we can go, we've got to suck ourselves off. We got to eat away at ourselves until there's nothing left but appetite. You give and give and give, crazy, why—?" Here Zoe expresses the hunger at the root of humanity, at the root of the search for the Kleinian breast and the mother—the need for devourment. Feeding leads to self-cannibalism, as in culture where the political has taken over as the only true tangibility, and which becomes the ever more redundant self as a result. "Cumming" leads to "going," and orgasm remains the primary form of individual expression because without orgasm there is only appetite left.

As the Lieutenant nods out from the smack, Zoe talks about how no one understands why Christ did it, and Ferrara treats the viewer to another montage of Christ's suffering, which seeks to connect the mythological agony of the Son of Man and the Lieutenant. Tom Powers ultimately sacrifices himself for the family that never loved him, whereas Walker becomes *only* an instrument of a higher power, and here, the Lieutenant seeks to be a man who can perform Christlike acts and thereby redeem himself with identity. That all of these Christ figures are morally dubious illustrates the incompatibility of the myth of religion with actual mankind, which nevertheless is presented by organized religion as the ideal model of human behavior.

Again back in his car, the Lieutenant canvasses the streets with the baseball game on the radio. Ever more desperate, the Lieutenant goes to see the Nun.

He pleads for her help with identifying the rapists. Unknown to her, his plan is to claim the reward money and use it for his debts and more gambling. As if she is one of his sons, the Lieutenant asks the Nun to "get with the program," barking, "Don't you want this crime avenged?" The Nun has no desire to play Revenge and announces her "ultimate revenge"—that she has forgiven her attackers. Hamlet is here confronted with Prospero of *The Tempest* and nonplussed by this, and unaccustomed to not having his way, the Lieutenant challenges the Nun, asking if she has the "right" to forgive her rapists. It is clear that what the Lieutenant actually seeks in this moment is his own forgiveness, that which neither he nor the Nun can offer himself.

Outside the church, an older black woman, with connections to a local pawnshop where a chalice stolen from the scene of the rape was hocked, tells the Lieutenant who the men who raped the Nun are and where they live. The Lieutenant travels into a rundown building, which is mostly used as a shooting gallery for addicts. There, the Lieutenant finds the two rapists who are watching the final game of the Mets versus Dodgers series. The only human identity of the rapists and the Lieutenant in this scene is from New York City itself, as the trio is only defined by the urbanity around them and the surrogacy of sporting franchises. Remaking Walker and the homosexual couple across from the Huntley Arms, the Lieutenant has the two rapists handcuff themselves. Sitting on the couch, the three share smoke from a crack pipe, watching as the Lieutenant's team loses and his enormous gambling debts again double. Knowing now that his death may perhaps be imminent, the Lieutenant takes an opportunity to gain the same power the Nun has gained with her acts of anti-vengeance and—ever the compulsive gambler—attempts a double-or-nothing "win," giving the rapists cash and putting them on a bus out of New York City, presumably to start over. Even if the Lieutenant cannot reach a state of grace himself, he can feed his compulsion's needs to the very end, as here he gambles not with currency but with actual lives, and his actions are about power, not intellect or emotion. The Lieutenant travels from the Port Authority Bus Terminal south to Penn Station and waits for his Bookie, who drives up to the Lieutenant's car and with a "Hey, cop" executes the Lieutenant with bullets fired at point-blank range and speeds away. Several yards away, the camera holds on the Lieutenant's car, and a crowd gathers around it to see the spectacle of the victim of a drive-by shooting. There is the sensation that the Lieutenant will have an undeserved hero's funeral, for to truly indict him would be to indict oneself, and for the movie to turn on its sympathetic audience members. *Bad Lieutenant* is a reminder of Kracauer's remarks about how revolutions may only be depicted as successful if they are in the past, for in Ferrara's cinema the recent past of *Bad Lieutenant* only serves to slyly suggest what layers of corruption have been added since the movie's creation. The viewer is also reminded how cinema as the dream state gave way to the cinema of politics, which robs everything of everyone for the sake of making them more violent, faster consumers.

CHAPTER 3

"In the grimace
of intense desire"[1]

Remaking Women with
Imitation of Life (1934 and 1959)

Susan Sontag writes that "the earliest *theory* of art, that of the Greek philosophers, proposed that art was mimesis, imitation of reality."[2] But more than an "imitation of reality," art, or what is understood in this study to be the popular culture of cinema, becomes its own reality. Parker Tyler remarks in *Magic and Myth of the Movies* (1947) that Hollywood produces "a magic of dream creation that far transcends its literal messages,"[3] and so cinema is understood as a double — the conscious and subconscious. Julius Caesar Scaliger writes in his *Poetics* that "imitation, however, is not the end of poetry, but is intermediate to the end. The end is the giving of instruction in pleasurable form, for poetry teaches, and does not simply amuse, as some used to think."[4] This removes the idea of an actual reality and so leaves cinema as being a learning play. Again the dichotomy between cinema as phantasy and cinema as propaganda is explored, and it illustrates what Scaliger understands as truth being an "agreement between that which is said about a thing and the thing itself"[5] *Imitation of Life* is instead about untruth because there is no reconciling "what is said" and "the thing," and this split is subsequently the same rupture that allows media to commandeer cinema in the late 1990s.

Fanny Hurst's 1933 novel, *Imitation of Life*, follows the life of Beatrice "Bea" Pullman, née Chipley, of Atlantic City as she is widowed early and forced to provide for an infant daughter and stroke-crippled father. By assuming her husband's boardwalk maple syrup supply business, and his name, "B. Pullman," Bea is able to build a comfort-food empire. She does this through much hard work, sacrifice and the help of an African American woman — Delilah — whom

Nicolas Rodriquez, Pedro Infante and Pita Montaner in a publicity still from the 1948 Spanish language adaptation of *Imitation of Life* made in Mexico entitled, *Angelitos Negros*, directed by Joselito Rodriguez. Director John Stahl's 1934 version of *Imitation of Life* features more overt "cooning" from Delilah, but the 1948 Spanish language adaptation and the 1959 portrayal directed by Douglas Sirk all contain elements of stereotypes based on ignorance. (Photofest.)

Bea first takes in as a nanny and cook. With a daughter herself, Delilah becomes something of Bea's double as well as Bea's most significant relationship after the death of her (unloved) husband. While her name changes in the three screen adaptations to date, Delilah herself is never remade and does not change in character or role. Director John Stahl's 1934 version of *Imitation of Life* features more overt "cooning" from Delilah, but this, the 1948 Spanish-language adaptation *Angelitos Negros* (directed by Joselito Rodríguez), and the 1959 portrayal directed by Douglas Sirk all contain elements of stereotypes based on ignorance. In contrast to Delilah in the two English-language editions, Bea is constantly remade, yet she always becomes so caught up in financial success that her emotional life suffers greatly and remains incomplete. By the novel's end, Bea is a very rich woman, but alone with the realization that she has never truly lived. This is different in the 1959 version where Bea triumphs, but Sirk's film nonetheless places its drama in ironic or satiric brackets that subvert the actuality of what is on surface display. This technique of contrasts — what is often called "Sirkian" — is brought to a totality of method by Rainer Werner Fassbinder, especially in *Despair* (1978), which is examined in Chapter 7.

Hurst's first-person novel charts how Bea must remake herself to survive in the man's world of the 1920s and 1930s. It furthermore displays how, when capitalism becomes tangible, it creates for Bea aspirations that compromise her humanity. While ultimately a prosperous woman of business, Bea never behaves cruelly; however, the desire for wealth and empire and expansion place Bea in her own "lost generation" where, because of her gender, she suffers and becomes a social-emotional outcast. As Bea's neighbor Mrs. Hanson admonishes soon after the death of Bea's husband, "In the nasty eyes of a lot of men a woman who is out to earn her own living a man's way is either a freak or don't mean any good."[6] Bea denies herself in order to succeed, ostensibly to support her burdens (family), but also because success is an identity for a girl forced to be a woman prematurely. Bea's equating of this mirrors the race toward modernity prevalent in so much of 1930s culture, and as examined with regard to *The Black Cat* or *The Public Enemy*.

Even before her remaking, Bea is described by Hurst at the novel's start as "over-anxious."[7] Bea's mother's premature demise is coupled with Bea's shock at the recent revelation of her own first menstruation and the "mystery" of human sexuality. Later in life, Bea recalls the home she grew up in, and how "you could scarcely lie abed in one room in the house on Arctic Avenue and not overhear a conversation going on in an adjoining."[8] It is the emotional withdrawal of her parents (one by death, the other by stroke) that instills Bea with a sense of her own unlovability and her "inadequacies."[9] That the Chipley house offers so little privacy also suggests it as the primal scene of Bea's repression, thereby suggesting her ignorance of her parent's coitus as being feigned. From sex to silence, here the metaphoric tensions of a house of incest, as examined by Klein, are remade as the business of (a) marriage and the same internal forces that shaped her parents' emotional distance at Bea's primal scene. Remaking Shakespeare again, Polonius' theory that "The origin and commencement of his grief / Sprung from neglected love"[10] can be traced through to Klein, writing that "it is evident that the deepest repressions are those which are directed against the most unsocial tendencies."[11] It is this "neglected love" that perverts Bea's idea of the social, starting with her parents and continuing into her business practices.

Bea is able to mourn her mother and come to terms with her death. This instills in Bea what Klein would call a "desire to restore" and sets Bea up for many early failures. Klein explains Bea's driving need for success, writing,

> Let us now consider what happens when the feelings of guilt and fear of the death of his mother (which is dreaded as a result of [the child's] unconscious wishes for her death) are dealt with adequately. These feelings have, I think, far-reaching

effects on the child's future mental well-being, his capacity for love and his social development. From them springs *the desire to restore*, which expresses itself in numerous phantasies of saving her and making all kinds of reparation. These tendencies to make reparation I have found ... to be the driving forces in all constructive activities and interest, and for social development.[12]

Bea wants to restore the home her mother tended, but in a society where the genders are not equal, Bea's social development, which takes her from the home, is what removes the emotional. In this way, Bea can better "be a man"—yet this act also results in an inferiority complex created by capital. Klein writes that this sensation is "more deeply rooted than is usually supposed and [is] always connected with unconscious feelings of guilt. The reason why some people have so strong a need for general praise and approval lies in their need for evidence that they are lovable, worthy of love. This feeling arises from the unconscious fear of being incapable of loving others sufficiently or truly, and particularly of not being able to master aggressive impulses toward others: they dread being a danger to the loved one."[13] Bea resents the burdens of her family but at the same time wants to provide for them, all the while overcome with a type of repressed self-loathing that results in self-denial and living an "imitation of life."

In *The Little Shopgirls Go to the Movies* (1927), Siegfried Kracauer writes, "Life is an invention of the haves, which the have-nots try to imitate to the best of their inability. Since it is in the interest of the propertied classes to maintain society as it is, they must prevent others from thinking about that society.... This leads to such tragedies, which really aren't tragedies. But for society's sake, it's imperative that they appear to be tragedies."[14] However, Bea Pullman's story *is* a tragedy because as an adult she subsists on fantasy alone, imitating the imitation of life, and does not consider the costs of her remaking herself for business and society. When Bea finally does—with regard to her doomed crush on her business assistant Flake—it is expressed in the novel in the language of capital, "It was as concrete as this: I've got to get over being penny wise."[15]

As a teenager at her mother's viewing, Bea is unable to fathom her parents engaging in intercourse and her conception. She wonders how two people "ever become sufficiently well acquainted with one another"[16] to have sexual relations. Her sexual awakening unreconciled, marriage becomes the first tool of survival for Bea as her widowed father arranges with the Chipley's long-term boarder, Mr. Pullman, to wed his daughter. Bea so understands marriage as business, perhaps the business of sex. Bea believes that "marriage established you. Gave you a sense of security and being cared for in a special private way that meant everything"[17] and comes to understand sex as being "wonderful, it was beautiful, it was being a goddess, to be able to bestow, even though within yourself no fires were lighted, only the willingness to endure."[18] Bea's ability to "endure"— to remove or ignore her desire—feeds her masochistic self-loathing and drives her to success, further displacing her from herself and her sexuality. Later, "jealousy of Delilah smote her, dying instantly, as it always did, of self-loathing,"[19] and Hurst alludes to the repression of a homosexual impulse — born like Tom Powers' out of a dysfunctional home — as existing in addition to Bea's desire to restore and connect. Klein writes, "Since the tendency to make reparation ultimately derives from the life instinct, it draws on libidinal phantasies and desires. This tendency enters into all sublimations, and remains from that stage onwards the great means by which depression is kept at bay and diminished."[20] Bea's drive is coupled with the rise of modernity in the 1930s and the drive to fascism that was its by-product. As Bea becomes more successful, her thought process becomes increasingly mechanized, and she sees her franchise of pancake restaurants as a type of invasion.[21] Ideas for success come to Bea "on the impulse of one of her flashes,"[22] and while she must deny her body and self to achieve, the spark of her genius — her unique "taste" — is rooted in her gender's singular menstrual cycle and its cramps.

In Hurst's novel, Bea has an active internal life, and it is these flights of fantasy that make her life bearable. Bea recalls reading David Hume, and that "the one passage, reminding her more and more of herself, had stuck. 'There, mind is a kind of theater, where several perceptions successively make their appearance, pass, repass, glide away and mingle in an infinite variety of postures and situations.'"[23] Bea's fantasy life, conjoined with how she must remake herself to achieve success, is only a temporary pleasure; however it is a real pleasure for her as it is filled with the real potential of hope. Toward the climax of the novel, Bea has "the strangest nostalgia for something she had never known,"[24] and here the truth of her fantasies is juxtaposed with the unreality of her actual business success. "Love and happiness ... made what had been going on through years of a petty and mundane routine seem imitation of life."[25] The problem at the end of the novel is that a heterosexual woman cannot be both liberated and successful in a capitalist economy/society.

Based in his unhappy experience with the culture industry, Bertolt Brecht writes in *The Three-Penny Trial: A Sociological Experiment* (1931) that cinema "exhausts itself in matters pertaining to taste and, in so doing, remains entirely beholden to preconceptions provided by class. It does not recognize taste as a commodity or the weapon of a particular class, but rather posits it as an absolute (something everyone can buy is attainable by everyone, even if in reality not everyone can buy it)."[26] Connecting to Brecht, Bea's escape from Atlantic City and rise in the business world is therefore motivated in class elevation, which is a further example of the power of the political that forces Bea to denude her gender for the capacity of reparations that capital promises a "buy in" to.

Hurst's *Imitation of Life* has, as of this writing, been twice adapted into English-language cinema by Universal Pictures — both films are "woman's pictures" or "women's weepies," a subgenre of melodrama geared especially for female viewers. Heide Schlupmann writing on *Melodrama and Social Drama in the Early German Cinema* (1990) remarks that "melodrama offered a genre which began to establish itself as one that lent the commonplace an 'eventful' character. Melodrama represented the social problems of women in a stylized manner which lent them a metaphysical dimension by focusing on the particular tragedy of a single and unique woman."[27] Kracauer's sense of tragedy from *The Little Shopgirls Go to the Movies* thus comes full circle, as what is relegated by class is made metaphysical when portrayed through cinema. From Schlupmann's study applied to *Imitation of Life,* viewers see the story as a parable or learning play and sense the greater implication of Bea Pullman's narrative as voicing (increasingly) common gender discrepancies. Schlupmann's thesis is that "melodrama had from the very beginning a disciplinary function."[28] Connecting this to the movies — which, unlike the novel — offer a happy resolution for Bea, Bea's "imitation of life" takes on a cautionary nature and returns it to Kracauer's first assumption where propertied classes must "maintain society as it is," preventing "others from thinking about that society."[29] If Bea ends *Imitation of Life* unhappy, as she does in the novel, then she is punished for the remaking of her gendered role; however, if she ends the work "happy," then the movies' changes to Hurst must be examined to see what facilitated this and how the encoded message, sent directly to female viewers, changes and is remade.

Imitation of Life (1934)

The first image of *Imitation of Life* 1934 is the crest of the newly invigorated MPPDA looming over a whirling charcoal background. Superimposed is the text, "This picture approved by the Production Code Administration of the Motion Picture Producers and Distributors of America. Certificate No. 412." After a moment, this multilayered image dissolves into a National Rifle Association (NRA) member seal bearing the legend, "We do our part." Created to curb prurience on screen in cinema, the MPPDA was one of the industry's first enforced censorships. Linked here to the militarization common to the 1930s — and distinctly American in its right to bear arms — the doubling of the MPPDA and NRA also offers early evidence of sound cinema answering not to a psychoanalytic dream state but to the political forces of capital. An argument can be proposed that the transformations that culminate around *Psycho* 1998 and sound cinema's end begin with the enforcement of the code mid–1934. The opening credits in *Imitation of Life* 1934 are presented by the "New Universal," and the newness here is the studio cleaning up its act, distancing itself from movies like *The Black Cat* released six months before, when the code was not so stringently enforced. The culmination of this social effect, and indeed what the enforcing of the code represents — apart from giving newly defeated alcohol prohibitionists a new cause to lick their wounds with — is what Philip Roth's

As Elmer Smith (Ned Sparks) looks on, Delilah Johnson (Louise Beavers) hesitates to legally accept her financial windfall from the pancake business for fear it will take her away from keeping house for Bea Pullman (Claudette Colbert) in *Imitation of Life* (John M. Stahl, 1934). (Jerry Ohlinger's Movie Material Store.)

narrator in *The Human Stain* calls "America's oldest communal passion, historically perhaps its most treacherous and subversive pleasure: the ecstasy of sanctimony."[30] Sanctimony being the fuel of the media era's digestion of culture into nonreconcilable, commercialized fragments.

The remaking of Universal, and films made after the mid–1934 value shift, sensorially reduce sound cinema to a more confined and limited place, where the still primitive nature of the sound medium is compounded by cagy presentation of the so-called "vulgar realities" of modern life. Made for visually less sophisticated viewers than the ones of the post-literate media era, crude techniques like primitive jump cuts are assumed invisible and result in what the twenty-first century clearly identifies as mismatched, noncontiguous action. The static necessities of early microphones and sync-sound recording add another level of disconnect. Yet while the visual lexicon of another time may seem off-putting — as no doubt much of the movies' handling of race is — what cannot be denied importance is how the problems of women have not radically changed in America since the 1930s. The shocking resonance of *Imitation of Life*'s remaking of female gender illustrates how few sincere advances there have been in granting women equal rights.

Taking its cue from the pages of the Hurst novel, *Imitation of Life* 1934 focuses on pathology rather than psychology, as Bea (Claudette Colbert) is presented as an implacable force or "Earth Spirit" (in the classic Wedekindian sense). In 1934, her suffering, unhappiness, and canny menstrual cramps are expurgated, so what motivates Bea is pure drive, perhaps a race for sainthood with Delilah, but even more clearly and concretely it is cinema remaking the individual out of the consumer. The Karen Blixen (Isak Dinesen) short story collection *Anecdotes of Destiny*—from which Orson Welles derived his 1969 film, *The Immortal Story*—could also serve as an apt subtitle for *Imitation of Life* 1934, as Delilah Johnson shows up at Bea's house by mistake and the majority of the plot turns on happenstance, again removed from the actions and/or desires of the protagonists. Delilah is an absurd character, and yet Bea is willing to trust her almost immediately. Bea's rise to the top is an "anecdote of destiny," her free-market acumen presented as a ping-ponging of relations and assemblages. The servants in *Imitation of Life*, *The Parent Trap*s and *The Immortal Story* perpetuate the concept of servant-friends. The purchase of someone's time for wages is presented as a totality — an all-or-nothing affair akin to buying a slave. In post–Civil War times, the message to be gleaned here — truly a warning of the removal of the individual and the needs of the flesh — is that all economics become prostitution and therefore slavery. After the scene of Bea hiring Delilah to keep house, Bea comes home from a hard day of work and Delilah rubs her feet, telling "Miss Bea" that she needs (sexual) "lovin'." In the novel, this conversation takes place toward the end of the narrative when Bea is just awakening to her libido's hungers, whereas with Colbert's portrayal — who is never nonsexual in *Imitation of Life* 1934 — the conversation is remade as an attempted seduction of Bea by Delilah. In the novel, however, Delilah is clearly trying to coach Bea toward a male lover:

> Miss Bea, whyfore doan' you go git yourself some one who will make your mawnin' and your evenin's de way God meant for dem to be. Filled wid de right kind of man-lovin' which is something you deserves and doan' know nothin' about. Even if you has to take a husband thrown in, Miss Bea, I's for man-lovin' to make a body forgit life ain't all beer and skittles. Some one for to make over you and for you to make over, even if you knows in your heart ain't no man livin' worth makin' over.... Lawd, honey, if I do say it as shouldn't, in mah day I shore could make over 'em. What you want ridin' around evenin's with ole "Lilah? Go cotch yourself a beau."[31]

It is interesting that in the novel Delilah understands sex as an individual's remaking, a mutual "makeover." Hurst here links herself to another 1930s author, Philip Barry, with the concept of the saving power of expressed sexuality, which can — as examined in Chapter 4 — augment, save, or even replace community dissipating rapidly in the face of technology and big capital.

In the 1934 film, Bea rebukes Delilah's advances by reminding her of her Oedipal bond with her daughter; "I've got Jessie — that's enough." Bea here is aligned with the "single" parents A.N. Lewis (*Peeping Tom*), Isabel Amberson (*The Magnificent Ambersons*), Rufus Collier (*One More Tomorrow*), Virginia Cartwright (*Strange Illusion*), Mrs. Bates (*Psycho*), Mitch and Margaret (*The Parent Trap* 1961), and Nick and Elizabeth (*The Parent Trap* 1998) as the cinema's psycho-Oedipal bond is again reaffirmed. Colbert's Bea admits that her first husband was her father's choice and that she was too young to know any better. This reinvents her as having "never been in love before." Coupled with the sexual agency of her not having to protect her hymen because of her consummated marriage to the conveniently deceased Mr. Pullman, "never being in love before" gives Bea a "virginity" of spirit appealing to the sanctimony of 1934 viewers.

Bea remakes Delilah (Louise Beavers) as "Aunt Delilah" — the "Aunt Jemima" of her day — and uses Delilah's image as the face of her company in *Imitation of Life* (John M. Stahl, 1934). Bea's servant is so "branded" — not literally with a hot iron as she might have been during the era of American slavery — but as a commodity nonetheless. This commodification becomes Delilah's inescapable and dehumized identity — from this point forward she can never not be "Aunt Delilah." (The Museum of Modern Art/Film Stills Archive.)

However, such sanctimony is very different from the actual gray moral attitude that brings people through a Great Depression and a Second World War. This hypocrisy attitudinal to the New Universal — and motion pictures blessed by the code — creates further distance between what is represented as reality on screen and off. When Bea is congratulated, "It's really good to see someone go ahead and make a success" — the picture is speaking to the 1930s' Depression recovery, offering an escapism where near-overnight success which remakes the individual is viewed as possible. The 1934 film is less than forthright about how much Bea may, or may not, "put out," as Bea's success in the first Universal movie version is the result of her being able to sweet-talk and charm a series of horny men circling her widowed femininity for trade.

Bea's first husband, Mr. B. Pullman, is killed in a train accident — "destiny" leaving her a maple syrup consignment as the result of the intervention of faulty technology. The "crash" remakes Bea and her infant daughter Jessie's life, and — as in the Hurst novel — it is the reason for Bea's entrance into the world of business and capital. In the 1934 movie, Bea does not pose as her dead husband "B. Pullman" to take over the syrup concern but is defiantly herself, and uses herself to establish a boardwalk eatery. Combining her maple syrup business with Delilah's out-of-this-world pancake mix recipe, Bea bottles lightning, and the industry of breakfast blooms for her, as it does for the United States in the twentieth century because modernity puts more people on the go and eating fast or outside the home. In Hurst's novel, Bea's success is caused by surrogate sons, one-night (emotional) stands — "doughboys, with body scars and deeper, more subtle scars deep down in the wells of their eyes, [who] had, during those strange days of the strange orgy of going off to war, literally rioted her B. Pullman [café] into prominence."[32]

In the 1934 motion picture, the "strange orgy of going off to war" is expurgated — being both too real and too painful, as well as too far removed from the Depression-era zeitgeist. Bea still remakes Delilah as "Aunt Delilah" — the Aunt Jemima of her day — and uses Delilah's image as the face of her company. Bea's servant is so "branded" — not literally with a hot iron as she might have been during the era of American slavery — but as a commodity nonetheless. At her shop, Bea meets Elmer Smith (Ned Sparks) by chance, and, taking pity on the wet, unemployed man who boasts of his abilities as a "pancake surrounder," offers him a free stack of wheat cakes. They make small talk, and Elmer tells Bea the story of Coca-Cola's success — "bottle it," here telling Bea to "box" her pancake flour, which is mixed according to Delilah's secret but, we are told, "simple" formula. The move toward prefabrication is another harbinger of the media era, one taken up again by Andy Warhol's pop art Brillo boxes of the 1960s. In the 1934 film, in keeping with the swank style of fascist art, an arresting montage of box production displays multiplicities of Delilah's iconography flying off the press. Again thinking ahead to Warhol, the connection of fascism and pop art is clear, and the flirtation with fascism played with in the United States in the 1930s now tangibly evokes sound cinema morphing into propaganda learned from the Third Reich.

As with the novel and the 1959 edition, *Imitation of Life* 1934 is a movie of dualities, remaking the era after the stock market "crash." Bea's daughter, Jesse, and Delilah's daughter, Peola, are twins — one white, the other passing for white. Bea is an absent mother in a way that Delilah never is. Bea cannot think outside herself and see the difference between her and Delilah and so remarks to her servant, "Oh, it's been nice for them to have each other all these years we've been so busy." Both almost wealthy from their pancake flour sales, Bea dreams of "college" for Jessie, whereas Delilah dreams of "no housework" for Peola. It is no wonder that Peola is ashamed of her mother, for in the Hurst novel and the 1934 movie Delilah is presented as a saintly but shuffling mammy, mentally simple or subhuman, undignified in her frequent invocations of "de Lawd." Yet Delilah has "brought up, not drug up," Peola, and clutches onto her with the same misplaced Oedipal love tendencies as Bea to Jessie, declaring, "I just can't be separated from my Peola." It is possible that it is her mother's obsessive needs and clinginess that repulses Peola as much as Delilah's dark skin color and lack of education. Few would claim that *Imitation of Life* 1934 has much profound to say about the matter of race in North America. Rather, the movie grafts what should be the issues at play with race into a Christian mythos. Therefore Peola's denying the parental identity of her mother when Delilah comes to bring her an umbrella at school become an anti-recognition scene — if not a burlesque — of Peter's denial of Christ. Bea is shocked at Peola, tensely asking, "How can you talk to your mother that way?" However, perhaps Bea completely understands why but, fearing such rebellion from Jessie, wishes to suppress such an outburst from Peola. Delilah, very distraught, looks in the camera — apparently breaking the fourth wall — remarking, as much to the viewer as Bea, "I don't rightly know where the blame lies." In this moment, the transference to the audience is profound because the movie addresses what it elsewhere avoids, and when it does finally confront the matter, it implicates everyone.

Elmer introduces Bea to Stephen "Steve" Archer, played by Warren William, who will remake Steve malevolently as "Brett Curtis" in *Strange Illusion* in twelve years' time. As Cecelia mistakes Rufus for an unconcerned party guest in *One More Tomorrow*, or how George does not consider that Lucy may be Eugene Morgan's daughter at the ball in *The Magnificent Ambersons* when he speaks derisively of him, Steve dances and flirts with Bea, telling her that his old friend Elmer has begged him for years to meet "the pancake queen." Bea leads Steve along, and they are kissing in each other's arms by the night's end. In the final reel of *Imitation of Life* 1934, Bea chooses not to sell her empire. Knowing her daughter Jesse to also be in love with Steve, Bea renounces him, breaking their engagement to spare her daughter's feelings. Bea promises Steve a reunion after Jessie's emotions have healed, but the separation seems as permanent as it is illogical. This is very different from the type of "tragedy" thrust upon Bea in the novel, wherein Bea's love object Flake is mutually in love with Jesse, and Bea has no choice but to surrender him to her daughter and continue her imitation of life crushed at the reality of the young couple being "so young ... so right."[33] In the 1934 movie it is Bea's choice to suffer and that thus aligns and guarantees Kracauer's "irrevocability of social structures" promoted by cinema. The final scene of *Imitation of Life* 1934 takes place after Delilah's funeral, and after Steve's departure. Bea is alone with her daughter, "in a garden." Jessie asks Bea about the afternoon she met Delilah, and Bea tells her daughter about her being in the bathtub, saying, "I want my quack-quack." This is a final remaking, as the audience was present for this primal scene at the movie's opening and heard that what Jessie really said was "wants my quack-quack." The importance of the change is that Bea's remake adds "I," suggesting infant Jessie as a separate unit from her mother, which she clearly was not. That Bea thought of her daughter as so removed, even in infancy, explains the trauma — oft described by Klein — no doubt inflicted upon Jessie by her mother. Given the context of *Imitation of Life* 1934, this final mother-daughter scene and the recollection it contains is a warning of the dangers of an ambitious woman willing to remake herself when capitalism becomes tangible.

Imitation of Life (1959)

An extravagant opening title sequence — as lush as the wrappings of Herman Herman's fine chocolates in *Despair*— features the crooning lyrics, "What is love without the pity?" Diamonds stack on top of themselves in a shining pile, implacable to both love and pity, and so glitter a reflection of the imitation of life. *Imitation of Life* 1934 is a movie about people and their pathology, whereas the 1959 remake directed by Douglas Sirk is a projected fantasy, rendering an intoxicated dream state in which Kleinian phantasies resonate. Fundamentally, *Imitation of Life* 1959 is a movie about architecture, not people, though the architecture supports the illustration of how fictional characters remake themselves. As a director, Sirk is incredibly invested in object, be it the suburban house as sanctuary; the naturalistic sound design with music; or the environmental nature of the filmmaking, rich with the textures of sandy beach, wet snow, or, as with the diamonds in the credit sequence, "falling rocks." Actors meanwhile refract archetypes, and here John Gavin remakes Rock Hudson in earlier Sirk pictures, while Susan Kohner as Sarah Jane, age eighteen (the 1959 remaking of Peola), simulates the heat issuing forth from Natalie Wood in *Rebel Without a Cause* (1955), which was already iconic by the release of *Imitation of Life* 1959. To further the case of this doubling of Kohner and Wood, Sara Jane's racist boyfriend Frankie is dressed like James Dean in the Nicholas

Ray–directed picture. *Imitation of Life* 1959 partially remakes itself as a youth movie, and there is no doubt that the film is a crushing illustration of what it must have meant to be a teenage girl in the 1950s. Sirk's films are "movie-movies" and therefore, like many of the other remakes in this volume, cinema about money, and money's influence and final co-option of drama.

As so much of the architecture is created/faked on a soundstage in *Imitation of Life* 1959, Sirk's objects are disproportionate to their actual utilitarian form in real life. That the sets and colors take on such extravagant personality serves to alienate the characters from their environment, while never being anything less than a totally unreliable simulation of life always disorienting the viewer. Judgment must be made about how to view *Imitation of Life* 1959, as it is not a film that suggests allegory but rather demands interpretation. It is this satirical dramaturgy of Sirk's that both Kubrick and Fassbinder adopt in their movies. *Imitation of Life* 1959 is a comedy in the classical Shakespearean sense, and in the sense that Mr. Clay creates his "comedy" in *The Immortal Story* with Virginie and Paul the sailor. Comedy, says Cicero, "is an imitation of life, a mirror of custom, an image of reality"[34] The matter of melodrama and its disciplinary functions again arises, this time transformed into something close to a perfect Brechtian learning play, as in Sirk the visual mise-en-scène of the movie tells a different story than the one the actors play. Diderot elaborates on Cicero in his *Encyclopedia* entry on comedy and in turn suggests a reading of the 1959 credit sequence:

> From this propensity to seize hold of the ridiculous, comedy derives its power and its resources. It would undoubtedly be more beneficial if we could transform this vicious self-satisfaction into a philosophical pity; but it has proved easier and more certain to make human malice serve to correct the other vices of mankind — much as the sharp edges of the diamond are used to polish the diamond itself.... This is the goal which comedy sets for itself, and the theater is for vice and the ridiculous what the court of justice and the scaffolds are for crime — the place where it is judged and the place where it is punished.[35]

What is so elegant about Sirk's directorial style is his warm embrace of the ridiculous that achieves the "philosophical pity" sought after by Diderot. Indeed it may be this element that makes Sirk so appealing to Queerly oriented artists of the next generations like Fassbinder, John Waters, Charles Ludlum and Todd Haynes. *Imitation of Life* 1959 itself does not correct, judge and punish — uniquely to the "woman's film," it records the events around when such an individual is corrected, judged and/or punished by (usually) her, but sometimes his, community. Again, as with the production design, Sirk's use of the Brechtian alienation effect manifests itself. As Jean Eustache remarks in his seminal work, *La Maman et la Putain* (1973), "The more you appear false ... the farther you go, the false is the beyond," and in this way Sirk can be linked to Lucio Fulci's extravagant remaking of his former master Edgar G. Ulmer as well as the subsequent generation of Queer directors mentioned above.

A depression picture, *Imitation of Life* 1934 illustrated how people remake themselves into greatness — in Colbert's case, through sex, gumption and, most of all, lying, followed by a near-religious devotion to her business. The transition doesn't make sense in the film, as a "star" has overwhelmed the logic of the narrative — for if Bea really looked and acted like Colbert, she would be a movie star, not a pancake queen. Yet *Imitation of Life* 1934 is a movie of pancakes, and therefore industry, and viewers today can see the iconography of female role models still prevalent in the early media era. *Imitation of Life* 1959 is cinema of the post–World War II "jet age" wherein the "greatest generation" has matured, and, as it has matured it has set up a cult of fame, which the culture industry — spearheaded by Hollywood features — perpetuates. *Imitation of Life* 1959 is the film about how to enter into the f/phantasy world presented — a movie about Hollywood, the industry as a dream state, and the frames with and around movies.

Until *Forced Entry* 1981, remakes afford social progress, and true to this, *Imitation of Life* 1959 is a more progressive movie about race than the one made in 1934. In the Hurst novel, Peola, passing for white on the West Coast, has herself sterilized and renounces her mother, never to be seen again. In the 1934 and 1959 film versions, Peola's character returns to make manic reparations at Delilah's funeral by throwing herself onto her mother's coffin. While Sirk ends an early scene of the 1959 version by portentously dollying in on a black doll, the issues of race in the United States are not given sophisticated agency elsewhere in the film. The argument could be made that what *Imitation of Life* 1959 addresses in terms of race is a more sincere allegory of homosexual desire in the United States, one that often metaphorically appears in Sirk's other Universal Pictures of this cycle and is personified in the Bea-Delilah relationship in 1959. Going back to Klein, homosexual desires must be seen as separate from sex acts, as homosexual desires are not about action but the reshuffling of an individual's emotional needs. While linked to the sexual, the action of sex only compounds desire — it does not create or remove it. A homosocial domestic arrangement leads Bea-Delilah to their homosexual impulses. Repression becomes the expression of the disparity of their ambition and natural states — versus the greater society around them with its increasing domination by the political forces of capital.

In *Imitation of Life* 1959, much of Hurst's plotting is jettisoned — Bea is rechristened Lora Meredith (Lana Turner), and Delilah, Annie Johnson (Juanita Moore). Rather than use her sexuality to open a pancake store as Colbert's Bea did, Lora Meredith — an actor before becoming a regional theater director's widow — lies to get an agent, who is immediately attracted to her comeliness. When he finds out her fibs, he is charmed at her guile and enticed; he remarks, "All actresses lie, but I believed you." The world of wealth and privilege and fame which *Imitation of Life* 1959 sets up as aspiration is thus again codified as unreal in its nature. Sirk's characters question their own reality but are also aware of their own unreality — a sophisticated conception of character advancing the Shakespearean model to another dimension, that of the virtual, a cornerstone of the media era. This Sirk-Fassbinder technique is adapted to fragment the nature of the movie itself in David Lynch's cinema after *Twin Peaks: Fire Walk with Me*. Unlike Lynch, Sirk movies never rupture within themselves because of the aforementioned split of actor and object directives and the total unity of masterfully photographed production design. Sirk uses the logic of paperback novels as Fassbinder does not, but Lynch does. For *Imitation of Life* 1959, this means that the movie — being a copy of a copy — doesn't have to make sense and that it may lose the novel's core elements as well as constantly remake itself, and its emotional state, chapter by chapter, reel by reel. The multiplicity of this cornucopia results in the viewer's identification with what is on screen, and this is also the true viewer catharsis experienced in a successful Sirk movie.

The diamonds of the opening credits of *Imitation of Life* 1959 give way to people on an Atlantic City beach in 1947. Bea's daughter Jessie is remade as Susie (played as a six-year-old by Terry Burnham and as a young adult by Sandra Dee). She has been lost by Lora in the furor of a hot day at the shore. Susie finds Peola's 1959 remake, Sarah Jane, age eight (played by Karin Dicker), and their affinity as doubles of each other is established from this point to the film's climax. At the end of the movie both daughters are left humiliated — for Susie it is that her mother's boyfriend Steve (John Gavin) does not return her romantic longings, and for Sara Jane it is her return from "passing" to throw herself on her mother's coffin, thus finally publicly acknowledging her heritage. Sara Jane's mother is Annie, the renamed 1959 remake of Delilah. But as with her counterpart in the Hurst novel and the 1934 movie, Annie confesses, "We just come from a place where my color deviled my baby," and the trajectory of her story remains her daughter's disavowal of her so that she may pass as white. This (melo)drama in 1959 is set against Lora's struggle as a single mother seeking to succeed as an actress. Like Colbert's Bea, Lora's widowhood remakes her virginity, while importantly retaining her sexual knowledge and power. In both English (but interestingly not in the Spanish) language movies of *Imitation of Life*, this state of hedging the sexual fence is presented as the one most advantageous to women, when in reality this bifurcation leads to sexual repression or the sexual expression of anxiety. Added to this power, Lora is remade as having the agency of being an actual actress, for, as a woman who never stops "playing," she thereby gains the tool of her success. Unlike the Bea Pullmans, Lora does not want to remake herself but does so as part of her occupation, which is a twenty-four-hour-a-day, seven-day-a-week role. For Sirk, Bea becomes Lora just as the character becomes object. The slightly exaggerated nature of Lana Turner's beauty contributes to the drag queen quality of her work along the lines of Jean Harlow's intervention in *The Public Enemy*. The audience is told

The family unit of *Imitation of Life* (Douglas Sirk, 1959): Sara Jane, age eight (Karin Dicker); Annie Johnson (Juanita Moore); Susie, age six (Terry Burnham); and the two irreal Loras — the one in the mirror and the one in the living room (both Lana Turner). (Jerry Ohlinger's Movie Material Store.)

that Lora's deceased (first) husband was a regional theater director, and this gives Lora both the knowledge of advanced creation as well as proposing her as the creation of the dead man. Lora's all-consuming role rivals the Oedipal tension carried over from Hurst and the 1934 film; however — expressing a real break from Hurst — Lora declares, "I never wanted anything but the stage and Susie," so remaking Colbert's Bea who simply states, "I've got Jessie — that's enough."

Like Colbert's Bea, Lora is a largely absent mother who leaves her child to the charge of Delilah/Annie. Not unaware, Lora remarks, "Maybe I should see things as they are. Not as I want them to be," but then — not able to listen to herself and change within herself — Lora blindly demands, "Susie's going to have everything I missed." Things, not personal interactions, are what are valued and desired by Lora. Starting here in the 1950s, the rule of the child — as examined in Chapter 6 and later in Chapter 7 — begins, and "entitlement" culturally becomes a richer gift to bestow than love. Like so many parents with a Kleinian need to restore within themselves, Lora remakes herself with her child; but as she remakes her child, she alters its development, and the child imitates impulses as opposed to responding to impulses naturally occurring, just as mid–century society shifts from being a representation of individuals as a unit to the dissolution of the individual by propaganda. The falseness of the world — and the need to become false oneself— is thereby confirmed for Susie at an early age. For megalomaniacal Lora, a mother's love is remade, Mama Rose Havoc–like, as a mother's ambition to style and/or wealth. The harm this creates for daughter Susie is that she is further made into an object, and that when she fails her mother's ambitions, it creates the need in Lora to further restore her own inner child, thereby contributing to her own self-obsession. Lora's manic reparations fail to make up for a lack of true, giving love, and what does succeed finally — and pointedly for Sirk, no doubt — is when Susie is denied. Susie's climatic "losing" of Steve ultimately results in a feeling of independence for the young woman. The growth that results from Steve's rejection is healthy, and in this case, a long-overdue severing of the mother-child infant bond, protracted because of wealth in *Imitation of Life* 1959. Up until now, Susie has been a possession of Lora's, with the mother continually remaking her daughter as an object like any other that gives her status. The movie offers no indication if Susie is prepared or can survive this break, yet the break and Annie's death at the end allow Lora to restore within herself favored parent status, while not changing in relation to herself and remaining her own favored love object.

In *Imitation of Life* 1959, the Great Depression is remade as the struggle for Lora to come (and make it) in New York City. The great 1950s tension in culture between the psychoanalytic and propaganda is reflected in the movie's twin obsessions of Broadway versus Madison Avenue — of the theater versus advertising. There, Lora meets her love interest who is remade in the 1959 motion picture as a photographer named Steve Archer. Prefiguring Mark Lewis by only one year's time, Steve's seduction lines to Lora include, "My camera could have a love affair with you." An object herself, Lora is captivated by the machinery of fame more than the hunk of man operating the technology. Yet when Steve gets a full-time job photographing for a beer company, Lora surprisingly asks him if it is really what "he wants." Up until this point she has given every indication of desiring steady income, but in this moment Lora reveals that what she has really sought all along is the uncertainty that continuously springs hope and fantasy within her and thereby restores what must be the deficit at the primal scene which roots her self-absorption. To Lora's question of wanting, Steve replies, "Well, it's not the Museum of Modern Art, but they pay you in the nicest-looking, green folding money. Which reminds me, this is the season for spending it. Let's go." Steve commands her, but Lora resists and rebukes him and Sirk links this moment to capitalism, revealing that it now has a season that assumes identity, use, and bond with Christianity.

After the breakup with Steve, Lora is cast in a small part in the play *Stopover* by playwright David Edwards (Dan O'Herlihy). Sirk here remakes himself, as his preferred original title for 1953's *All I Desire* was *Stopover* but was changed by the picture's producer. David remakes Steve, as he is a man who must by nature of his profession remake himself in relation to himself with each production. On the opening night of *Stopover* the audience demands that bit-player Lora bow with the play's leads. Soon love has blossomed between Lora and David — muse and poet. Acknowledging his unreal nature and the fleeting present, David tells her, "I'm in love with you, Lora. I must hasten to add that I always fall in love with my leading ladies." She is not taken aback by his admission of planned obsolescence but responds in a crescendo of expressed desire, which — like the remaking of catharsis from the climax of the drama to the purchase of the ticket as the sound era became the media era and cinema ended — so removes orgasm from the climax of sex and places it in Lora's performance/presentation/imitation of her love for David. She responds to him, "Maybe that's all it is, but I don't care. Because I'm loving you. Now. Tonight. Thank you." Together Lora and David will play the part of writer/director and actor who are lovers, and the potential of this "playing" informs and ignites the sexual tension of this scene rather than sexual desire. The removal of sexual desire from love in *Imitation of Life* 1959 presents the audience with examples of how modernity removes the actual from the individual as well as linking love to being about confirming self as opposed to giving to the other. This great imitation of life allows Lora to disapprove of Steve's "commercial job" while spending the next ten years — 1948–1958 — doing one after another of David Edwards' breezy Broadway comedies. The delightfully spoofy titles fly by in a montage — *Summer's Madness, Sweet Surrender, Happiness, Always Laughter, Born to Laugh* — and when the narrative returns to Lora, she is being dragged out for a night on the town on the arm of David who is wooing investors for their next show. Annie remarks, "Doesn't he ever stop?" and Lora expounds on the iconography of the "self-destructive director" — which no doubt feeds the popularity of Sirk's movies among film directors like Fassbinder — responding, "He can't Annie. If he did, he'd be sure to find out how sad he really is. And I know that feeling." Lora has grown tired of the part she is playing and wants to remake herself for new times. She breaks up with David to do a play called — ironically — *No Greater Glory*, wherein the "colored angle's positively controversial." *Imitation of Life* 1959 again reveals itself as a movie-movie by imitating itself just as the place of race in the film is again revealed as a surrogate for other concerns — here, as something that gives importance, rather than being something that actually *is* important. The 1959 *Imitation of Life* is controversial, not because of its depiction of race (other than the real but surface concerns of the potentially hurtful representation of stereotypes within), but in its commentary on wealth and the nearly complete absence of realistic femininity represented. That *Imi-*

tation of Life 1959 is a "woman's picture" and features so many female cast members is thus especially perverse and again anticipates Fassbinder and projects such as *The Bitter Tears of Petra von Kant* (1972). Lora's frustrations at David's Broadway comedies must have been close to what Sirk himself felt at the end of his Universal Pictures run in which he had predominantly directed a sequence of very interchangeable women's weepies.

Sirk's frustrations are expressed with caustic wit, which makes *Imitation of Life* 1959 nimble and delicious viewing today. Susie asks, "Was Jesus white or black?" and Sarah Jane replies, "He was like me ... white." Both the notion of passing—and the even more extreme concept of coloring Christianity black—must have been deeply unsettling concepts to the movie's original audience as the ambiguities of interpretation in *Imitation of Life* 1959 become apparent. However, *Imitation of Life* 1959 retains the Christian allegory of the 1934 movie that is only somewhat present in Hurst's original source novel. Annie postulates between fool and saint; and while the Delilahs were certainly more of the former, Annie is remade as a lesbian seeking full domestic partnership— her masochistic need to serve rooted in a Kleinian need to restore. In the case of the 1959 movie, this may be the self-acceptance that her daughter clearly lacks. Slavery is remade with Annie's willful submission to Lora, and as a result she is not "branded" as she was twenty-five years prior. The only way Annie can express her homosexual impulse is in her submission to Lora—that which must replace the sex acts which are not allowed in the home—making Annie the Countess Geschwitz to Lora's Lulu "Earth Spirit." In *Imitation of Life* 1934, cunning White Americans take advantage of African Americans who are fools— here African Americans need White Americans' oppression for identity, and it is the oppression which is imitated culturally from the movie (produced—it should never be forgotten—by White Americans). Annie's morality is best expressed in her remarking that there's "no sin in looking prosperous," which serves to seduce Lora as much as David's promise of the Broadway high life. Yet Annie is denying herself sexually just as her daughter is denying herself racially. She tells Sarah Jane, "It's a sin to be ashamed of what you are. And it's even worse to pretend, to lie." Yet all the women lie—play—living their imitations of the role that they believe, and are societally told, will grant them fulfillment.

Sarah Jane's inability to accept being black is never explained other than the heredity-infused notion that the same issue of looking-white-while-being-black "deviled" her father who is never represented. As Sarah Jane insists to Susie, "I'm white too—and if I have to be colored, then I want to die!" *Imitation of Life* 1959 thereby suggests Sarah Jane as a "bad seed" in the way many villains are presented classically—such as Aaron the Moor or Othello in Shakespeare— who are largely defined and motivated by their skin's darkness. While Sarah Jane makes every effort to establish her dominance over Susie by demanding a good-night kiss from Lora as if she is her daughter too, the equality at stake is familiar — not racial — and Sarah Jane remains *Imitation of Life* 1959's villain. There is a punitive nature to *Imitation of Life* 1959 that cannot be denied, especially at the funeral finale where Sarah Jane publically punishes herself for passing. Before she dies, Annie remarks that "an empty purse can make a good girl bad," and what is proposed by Sirk in this reactionary domestic drama are the economic factors of why — very logically — Sarah Jane does not want to be identified as "colored" in 1950s America. But in rejecting Annie, Sarah Jane is also rejecting Annie's wealth. The 1959 movie suggests that capital is a force as great as race and one that cannot be overcome. This is underlined with Sarah Jane's declaration to Susie, "Your mother doesn't own me." Fighting the race–capital dichotomy, Sirk transforms Sarah Jane's villainy to anti-hero status, making her a force like Milton's Satan who is willing to defy convention, presenting herself — like the society around her — as what seems and appears to be. By making Sarah Jane a burlesque dancer in *Imitation of Life* 1959, she is allowed to express sexual agency and so is afforded a personal honesty none of the other characters have. It is in these matters that Sirk's subversive satire is most apparent. However, the satire is dulled by the fact that the only overt sexuality in the 1959 movie is Sarah Jane's exoticized otherness — an example of stereotyping of the "loose" sexuality of black women so as to make it both desirable and reprehensible while paramountly serving the purpose of "purifying" white women.

Annie's lavish funeral illustrates how capitalism eats the dead as it has created an industry of death. From income to inheritance tax, living is continually remade to cost something in the twentieth century. Prior to her demise, Annie remarks, "Our wedding day and the day we die — the great events of Life." It is telling that it is social events, not individual triumphs, which are privileged. On her deathbed, Annie asks "Miss Lora" to look after Sarah Jane, just as Eugene looks after George (as he feels Isabel would have wanted him to) at *The Magnificent Ambersons*' end. By admitting "murder" — throwing herself on her mother's coffin and acknowledging her lineage and blackness — Sara Jane is absolved of her mother's death by the public branding of an allegedly more tolerant society. However, Sirk tempers this with what is an unresolved ending; after all, Sarah Jane did achieve her fantasy — she wanted her mother dead and got her wish.

CHAPTER 4

The Bequests of Shadows

Remaking the Father in The Magnificent Ambersons *(1942),* One More Tomorrow *(filmed 1942; released 1946) and* Strange Illusion *(1945)*

With its flood of new émigrés remaking their lives in Hollywood and with the Second World War itself, the 1940s represent the height of Germany's influence on the culture of the United States of America in the twentieth century. The German dramatic touch, perfected by Brecht, lingers through the 1950s in the movies of Douglas Sirk and is compellingly reimagined, post–Fassbinder, by Paul Verhoeven's Hollywood masterworks, *Basic Instinct* (1992) and *Showgirls* (1995), but remains most perceptible on screen in 1940s American *film noir*.

Noir lies in the shadow of the great father of sound cinema, *Citizen Kane* (1941), which casts long shadows that fade shortly after the appearance of cinema's great prodigal son, cameraman-murderer Mark Lewis in *Peeping Tom*. *Noir* was a term coined by the French, and the classic, first period of the genre is often bracketed between *Blind Alley* (1939) or *Stranger on the Third Floor* (1940) and *Touch of Evil* (1958) or *Point Blank* (1967). Itself, the *noir* genre remakes the English-language "gray" gangster films of the 1930s — like *The Public Enemy* — elaborating on the gangster genre's allegory of capital by reframing the psychological focus to encompass a reality that is consuming its participants, as well as highlighting its psychoanalytic anxieties based in sex and family. *Noir's* icons, patterns of light, and deliciously imitable tropes now endlessly repeat themselves across culture, turning something that was modern, novel and poetic into stereotypes as potentially tiresome as they are endlessly remade. Therefore, post–*Blow-Up* (1966), *neo-noir* is a necrophilic act, often unbalanced with its enjoyment of cheap irony, obvious twists, and hyper-male posturing. What escapes most practitioners of *neo-noir* (that is, self-conscious, post-1967 *noir*) is that classical *noir* is unable to be reimagined because its graphic and/or archetypal patterns are behaviors locked in a specific past (i.e., the 1940s). The horror flick or the movie musical may be endlessly remade because its stereotypes are not grounded in a historical era, but Hollywood *noir* exists largely because of the Second World War. True to this, *noir* remains the most primal wave to come out of Hollywood since the heyday of the Universal horror cycle. This "twilight terror" of the 1940s would inform the generation to come, who would shake off Germanic shadow play only when color photography became the default, and hallucination a more appropriate state of expression than nightmare. This is specifically illustrated when *noir* gives way to *cinéma vérité* after Zapruder's document of the assassination of President John F. Kennedy renders all other types of cinema unreal matters of mere aesthetics.

In its pure, original duality — conscious but not self-conscious, alert but dreaming meta-reality — *noir* represents some of the finest craftsmanship and unity of production ever to come out of the Hollywood system and its Poverty Row imitators. The genre eagerly explored the link between dream poetry and philosophical psychology on the nation's cinema screens. *Noir*'s commercial popularity, namely that it was therapy for the (second) world war at the end of the Great Depression, allowed a visual, culturally repeated Oedipus/Hamlet myth catharsis to be popularly expressed and, at the same time, affirm dreams of commerce and technology to the motion-picture-going audience. Not only was *noir* all the rage in its day, but the fad allowed movies to continue the evolution begun by the German film industry's unparalleled silent pictures. Namely, Hollywood cinema, led by Karl Freund's great pupil Gregg Toland, developed, for the better part of a decade, in an overtly Expressionist manner. It was one that expressed then current anxieties and insecurities while elevating them to myth, namely that of a fused double, Oedipus-Hamlet.

Noir films are coded. That dark universe — actual and illusionary — offers nothing but free choice while at the same time presenting individuals as the hapless pawns of uncontrollable fate and/or desire. These behavioral codes, largely expressions of Oedipal-Hamletian desires, are social gestures. Characters say one thing to mean another, and the audience understands that the closest truth lies in the difference, denial or ignorance. The *film noirs* which are remakes, or more interestingly that remake the contexts of preexisting drama, are especially rich examples of 1939–1967's national obsessions. A closer look reveals how the anxieties and dreams of that postwar era illustrate the cycle of the twentieth century well on its way to the point where modernity becomes something that is imitated rather than experienced in any pure way.

Noir's classical apex in the 1940s fused the two great achievements of the Western literary canon — the *Oedipus* of Sophocles and the *Hamlet* of

Shakespeare — into the handbook for psychological character and situation writing. Both the sources, and their loose cinematic *noir* remakes, feature characters larger than the dramas they contain. Both plays are about fathers and sons — or, in a neo–Kleinian view where gender is removed in favor of "individuals" — parents and children.

Freud says, "According to my already extensive experience, parents play a leading part in the infantile psychology of all persons who subsequently become psychoneurotics. Falling in love with one parent and hating the other forms part of the permanent stock of the psychic impulses which arise in early childhood, and are of such importance as the material of the subsequent neurosis."[1] What Klein adds to Freud is the suggestion that psychic impulses remain in the psychic reality, thereby creating a split, where waking consciousness is guided by one set of impressions and the subconscious by others. Hamlet and his father, King Hamlet, may be doubles, but the son is an intellectual whereas the father was a warrior — the son feels compelled to avenge his father's death but subconsciously wants none of the bloody business as it is contrary to his nature. Hamlet is mocked by his other double, Fortinbras, who is so exactly his father. This point is explicit in Shakespeare's text, as Fortinbras' father is also named Fortinbras, and father and son are positioned to reflect the two Hamlets.

Heiner Müller sees Hamlet as "the intellectual in conflict with history, ... the man between the ages ... a self-critique of the intellectual.... It is the description of a petrified hope, an effort to articulate a despair so it can be left behind."[2] Clearly the Oedipus-Hamlet myth is cathartic: removing the royal trapping, the setups of familiar relations are so basic as to appear in most families. But the *noir* films of the 1940s also suggest that the Oedipus-Hamlet myths are relevant because they speak to the individual's neurotic concerns — specific to him or herself— rather than the actuality of familial relations.

This unreliability of attraction is accounted for by Sontag who writes that "love is an emotion felt by the solitary ego and mistakenly projected outward, the impregnability of the beloved's ego exercises a hypnotic attraction for the romantic imagination."[3] It not only defines the sensation of love, especially "being in love," but bears a relation to the viewer and cinema, as in both scenarios what is absent is most important, and *how* that surrogacy is reached is the primary goal. These elements become the foundation of the "underground" films of Andy Warhol in the 1960s.

In *noir*, this pattern begins with parents and infants. Sontag is compounded by Deleuze, who explores the misprision within individuals in the discussion of a masochist. The term "masochist"— which Deleuze correctly divorces from sadist — is specific and can be read as a synonym for the individual, for as in any consensual S&M scenario, it is the submissive "slave," not the dominant "master," who sets the limits of how far "play" will go, just as it is the individual who is ultimately responsible for his or her actions or inactions. Deleuze writes,

The love triangle: Son George Amberson Minafer (Tim Holt) looks on as his mother Isabel (Dolores Costello) reunites with former suitor, Eugene Morgan (Joseph Cotten) in *The Magnificent Ambersons* (Orson Welles, 1942). (Courtesy the Chestnut Hill Film Group.)

"There is no doubt that the masochist lives in the very depths of guilt; but far from feeling that he has sinned against the father, it is the father's likeness in him that he experiences as a sin which must be atoned for."[4] It is a type of self-hatred brought about by a disconnection with the physical world — a desire for self-annihilation fueled by cinema and its doubles.

Klein has more hope than Deleuze, perhaps because her patient "Peter," whom she writes about in *The Psychoanalytic Play Technique*, has "understood that his own aggressive feelings towards his father contributed to his fear of him, and also that he had projected his own impulses on to his father."[5] It is unfortunately not a breakthrough that the heroes of *The Magnificent Ambersons*, *One More Tomorrow* and *Strange Illusion* experience, for George Minafer, Tom Collier and Paul Cartwright are more indicative of the modern age than Klein's Peter, who was almost four years old when their sessions began in 1924. Klein's Peter is closer to Mark in *Peeping Tom*, born into the modern age, for like Mark, that generation grew up with twenty years of the sound era already having remade itself multiple times on screen and thus having already permanently mutated culture.

If the child being father to the man is the inverse of Oedipal–Hamlet anxieties, the other appeal of the myths are the story's problematization of marriage as an institution that inherently views people — largely women — as property. At the core of society, it is this union that commodifies the body, making it so vulnerable to technology in the twentieth century.

The axes of these concerns remake themselves most strikingly in the 1940s in *The Magnificent Ambersons*, directed by Orson Welles at RKO and released in 1942; *One More Tomorrow*, directed by Peter Godfrey, filmed in 1942 but released in 1946 by Warner Bros.; and *Strange Illusion*, directed by Edgar G. Ulmer, which emerged from Producer's Releasing Corporation (PRC) in 1945. All three are infused with wartime's *noir* archetypes and feature a marriage reflective of Gertrude's in *Hamlet* and parent-child dynamics rooted in *Oedipus*. Collectively the three movies illustrate the growing ailment of the nuclear family and a psyche whose dreams are uneasy and shaped by cinema — all setting the cinematic stage for children's dominance of the nuclear family from *Psycho* and *The Parent Trap* onward.

The Magnificent Ambersons (1942)

The story of *The Magnificent Ambersons* is built upon the neurosis of a son, George (Tim Holt), overcompensating for his father, Wilbur Minafer (Don Dillaway). First, the son is responding to his father's apparent lack of affection — perhaps even lack of love — for his wife and George's mother, Isabel (Dolores Costello). Second, Isabel is significantly more emotionally invested in her son George than in any other of her relationships, including Wilbur. Third, George must avenge his father by being intolerant of his mother's suitor, Eugene Morgan (Joseph Cotten), after Wilbur dies relatively prematurely.

Incest lurks in the corridors of the Amberson mansion as if it were Elsinore. George and Isabel resemble Hamlet and Gertrude, as Isabel and Eugene remake Gertrude and Claudius. Hamlet is unsure of when his mother and his uncle's affair (or "incest" as it is called it in the play) began — before or after the murder of his father by Claudius. However, in *Hamlet*, Gertrude, a type of Clytemnestra, is besmirchible, whereas in *Ambersons*, Isabel is not, for in the movie's post–Freudian conception, George has created and projected due to Wilbur's emotional reserve what Hamlet has experienced via his actual (i.e., witnessed) haunting by the Ghost of his dead father, King Hamlet. Because of that lack of specter, George has no choice but to focus anxieties inward to his family.

While published by novelist Booth Tarkington in 1918, *The Magnificent Ambersons* is primarily set before cinema had become popular. Elsinore had visiting players to psychoanalyze the court, but the Ambersons' mansion is devoid of any representational drama — tempestuously, every emotion is voiced, or not. The last ball, while filled with society, is more an illustration of how wealth isolates than a masque or Holy Communion. RKO's *The Magnificent Ambersons* is the second screen version of the Tarkington novel, the first being David Smith's silent *Pampered Youth* released in 1924. *Pampered Youth* is a very commercial "Hollywood" movie, wherein characters are renamed, and nearly all of the Oedipal anxiety of Tarkington is removed. Eugene's drunkenness that spurns Isabel in their youth, Sam, the African American butler, the last ball at the Amberson mansion, the ride where horse competes with automobile, Major Amberson's tangled estate, and George being hit by a car remain in the 1924 movie — yet events are reconstructed so as to eradicate any moral ambiguity. Therefore, in *Pampered Youth*, Wilbur dies before Eugene returns, there is no Aunt Fanny, and Isabel lives. At the climax of the film, after the rupture of the

Pampered Youth (David Smith, 1925). George Amberson Minafer (Cullen Landis) and his mother Isabel (Alice Calhoun) in the first screen version of Booth Tarkington's Pulitzer Prize winning novel, *The Magnificent Ambersons* (1918). (Courtesy Andrew's Video Vault at the Rotunda.)

Isabel-George-Eugene triangle, there is a fire where eavesdropping servants let pots on the stove catch fire, Eugene must rescue Isabel, and the onus of the characters' actions are thereby returned to the individual rather than societal. After her rescue, Isabel comforts her son in the hospital finale with Eugene and Lucy, and George begs forgiveness of Eugene, enlightened by his rival's selfless saving of his mother from the flames. The difference in the Smith movie, from Tarkington and Welles, is drastic and illustrative of how caustic and subversive *The Magnificent Ambersons* is in its original conception.

In the 1940s, new American theater was Tennessee Williams and *A Streetcar Named Desire*— Orson Welles was old news (along with the 1930s, the Depression, and the WPA) and viewed as something of a classicist. While still Hollywood's wunderkind (albeit with an irked William Randolph Hearst) at the start of production on *The Magnificent Ambersons* in the fall of 1941, the negative reception to the first versions of the finished film would begin Welles' cinematic exile from A-budget Hollywood productions. *Ambersons'* subsequent recutting

Aunt Fanny Minafer (Agnes Moorehead) looks down the staircase of the great Amberson mansion at George Amberson Minafer (Tim Holt) in *The Magnificent Ambersons* (Orson Welles, 1942). (Courtesy the Chestnut Hill Film Group.)

by the studio is legendary, but what is often not examined is how this studio remaking creates the film as the ultimate post-modern object. *Ambersons'* recut construction makes it visibly unfinished, a collision of several visions with moments that transcend the whole after the fashion in which corrupted Shakespeare texts like *Macbeth* are truly never less than the sum of their parts. Less sturdy triumphs of imagination, say, *The Second Maiden's Tragedy* or *Journey into Fear*, fare less well with extraterritorial editing. With *Ambersons*, the viewer must put it together and assemble each piece, rationalizing and considering a jigsaw puzzle with many baroque parts, centered around anxieties most Americans would rather avoid confronting. It is a situation somewhat analogous to the United States' national position just prior to the country's involvement in the Second World War, where uninvolvement was — like Hamlet's inaction in Acts 1 through 4 — becoming less and less of an option.

Rhythmically ignorant studio segues aid the meta-textuality of the *Ambersons* movie. For instance, the opening prologue, when the narrator's tone abruptly changes from an elegiac lamentation, "Too slow for us nowadays, because the faster we're carried the less time we have to spare," to tell us, "Darning the earlier years of this period," collides with Welles' experimental jump cuts (for instance in Eugene's shoe montage) which create cinematic tension by taking highly modern techniques and applying them to a text rooted in a much earlier era.

The doubling of technique by the studio's cut, while not in sync with directorial intention, allows for a dialogue with the medium in a way that Welles' original conception would probably have not. The weird ellipses created by the studio, which trimmed the movie by over forty minutes and inserted new material shaped by a myriad of hands, make *Ambersons* a more subversive work. Contrary to the studio's purpose, the connections and remaking the viewer has to engage in to stitch *Ambersons* all together highlights the very "somber" features RKO sought to play down.

Ambersons is a hotbed of taboo American subject in addition to incest. It is unrelentingly critical of capital, and its portrayal of the tragedy of poverty is unflinching. Because capitalism's ethics will not conform to the actual, it results in a society that must remake and so devour itself because — if inward hegemony cannot be achieved — outward homogeny is possible and may be surrogate for the internal.

Ambersons remakes its love attachments in a manner that shows the influence of Arthur Schnitzler's round dance of love and venereal disease, *Reigen*. First, there is the Isabel-Eugene-Wilbur-Fanny quad, Fanny Minafer (Agnes Moorehead) being Wilbur's sister, who is as histrionic as her brother is contained. Second, there is the Isabel-Eugene-George-Lucy quad, Lucy (Anne Baxter) being Eugene's daughter by an unknown, deceased woman. With the giddy glee of a merry-go-round operator, Welles spins these lovers about in a whirligig, remaking the Isabel-Eugene-Wilbur-Fanny quad on the Amberson staircase after the last great party with Isabel-George-Wilbur-Fanny, or suggesting the Isabel-Eugene-Fanny-Wilbur quad at the car factory with Isabel-Eugene-George-Lucy.

At the car factory, Lucy asks George, "Did you ever see something so lovely —" "As what?" George asks. "As your mother," Lucy replies, adding, "she's a darling. And Papa looks like he's going to *explode* or utter *loud* sounds." From this point on in *Ambersons*, George and Lucy's courtship is almost an act of spite toward parents Isabel and Eugene. It is understandable in the Welles conception of *Ambersons* why Lucy increasingly keeps her distance from George. But something about love cannot be rationalized — perhaps because the mentioned affection is a dream state, a poetic untruth. This is highlighted by the studio-mandated scenes in *Ambersons* wherein Lucy is waiting to fall into George's arms — ones which firmly link "love" to cinema's daydreams.

George's immediate reaction to Eugene upon meeting him at the ball after the pleasantries are exchanged is one of near pathological dislike. Examining the root of this hatred, it is apparent that it is not incestuous feeling toward the mother by George that causes this. Rather George's pathological hatred of Eugene is the result of Eugene being a self-made man, which George is clearly not. Tarkington and Welles tell the audience that the name Amberson has meant something since 1873, and the audience is equally aware that the surname Morgan never meant anything before Eugene linked it with the technology of the automobile at the dawn of the twentieth century. George is a Minafer (like his father) and must constantly remake himself as an Amberson in order to assume and confirm an identity defined by privilege — by Otherness. This urge for acceptance by capital connects with George's death urge and drives him to a point near extinction, at which the movie ends, its resolution far from totally clear.

When George finds out about Isabel and Eugene's broken engagement in their youth, he becomes nearly apoplectic with rage: "She was in love with him before — before my father died?" he screams, harping on the same tidbit well after the news should have sunk in. It is an obsessiveness that is only rivaled by the other Minafer who wishes to be an Amberson, Fanny. In truth, Fanny would rather be a Morgan; however her chance at that marriage grows more and more remote with each passing day, and Fanny's tragedy is that she becomes obsessed with remaking herself as an Amberson — something that she never truly wanted. It is her surrogacy of wealth for love. Fanny's unrequited love for Eugene motivates her so completely at times that it is hard to discern if she is manipulating events for her gratification or Eugene's, or if her desire is so devoiced from her actual self that she favors what she *thinks* are Eugene's needs over her own. To confound all this, the hospital ending added by RKO holds the absurd potential that Eugene will now fall in love with Fanny and she will become a surrogate for Isabel as both lover and mother. With all the different directions her character is scripted in, not enough credit can be given to Agnes Moorehead for the consistency, nuance and power of her performance, second only to her work as Charles' mother in *Citizen Kane*.

Eugene's approval of the kiss between George and Lucy on the afternoon of the sleigh ride redoubles his romance of years past with Isabel. Eugene is nothing but gracious toward George, a further sign of the psychological nature of George's hatred. In *Ambersons*, George turns Eugene away from the house twice, first after the dinner eruption, and second when Isabel is on her deathbed. George remakes Sam the Butler (J. Louis Johnson), and both — oddly — are the servants of Isabel's will. Like the masochist, it is Isabel who is ultimately in charge of her play scenes, and it is her choice to abdicate to her son's pathological jealousy. Isabel cannot give George her love for Eugene, and George is unable to accept this, just as Isabel is unable to accept having to deny George. Isabel's positional paralysis as depicted by Costello is indicative of Jocasta's fated role in the Oedipus tragedy. Within the structure of *noir*, it is a manifestation of the patriarchy's consumption of female agency.

The "turning away" is a theatrical gesture that Welles often repeated in his cinema — in *Citizen Kane*, Susan Alexander (Dorothy Comingore) turns away the investigating reporter Jerry Thompson (William Alland) the first time; in the pin-screen prologue to *The Trial* (1962), the story is introduced in terms of a turning away; and in *The Immortal Story* (1968), Virginie and Paul the sailor turn away from Mr. Clay, obeying yet defying him and his son/servant/double Elishama. Welles knows that something must always be denied, often for the good of a movie, but he himself is usually unable to be his own father and accept this disavowal and so leaves it to others by default. Reflective of the American National Character's desire for movement without meaning, it was in the case of *Ambersons* that Welles' flight to South America during post-production to make *It's All True* left confronting the *Ambersons* movie's actual and very real structural problems to the studio. Culminating in *The Immortal Story*, Welles' cinema is his child who seeks to represent what the father cannot conceive by the wishes of the very same father.

In the snow sequence at the end of *Ambersons'* first half, the horse-driven sleigh is juxtaposed with an early automobile. The car peters out but can be revived and kept going, whereas the sleigh crashes and the horses run off. The persistence of the automobile in *Ambersons* is essential. It is the collision of the technology of World War I — the era when the source novel was first published — and of World War II — the era when the Welles remake was produced. In *Ambersons'* story, the automobile is the physical manifestation of national and proto-environmental anxieties about the twentieth century's perpetual remaking by technology (i.e., the gasoline engine) — which leads to the remaking by capital (bigger streets) — as this excerpt from the dining room scene midway through the movie reveals:

UNCLE JACK: Gene, what's this I hear about someone else opening up a horse-less carriage shop, somewhere out in the suburbs.

MAJOR AMBERSON: Ah, I suppose they'll drive you out of business, or else the two of you'll get together and drive all the rest of us off of the streets.

EUGENE: Well, we'll even things up by making the streets bigger. Automobiles will carry our streets clear out to the county line.

UNCLE JACK: Well, I hope you're wrong, because if people go to moving that far, real estate values here in the old residence part of town will be stretched pretty thin.

MAJOR AMBERSON: So your devilish machines are going to ruin all your old friends, eh Gene? Do you really think they're going to change the face of the land?

EUGENE: They're already doing it, Major, and it can't be stopped. Automobiles are —

GEORGE: Automobiles are a useless nuisance.

MAJOR AMBERSON: What did you say, George?

GEORGE: I said automobiles are a useless nuisance. They'll never amount to anything but a nuisance, and they had no business to be invented.

UNCLE JACK: Of course you forget Mr. Morgan makes them — also did his share in inventing them. If you weren't so thoughtless, he might think you rather offensive.

GEORGE: (sarcastically) I don't think I could survive that.

EUGENE: I'm not sure George is wrong about automobiles. With all their speed forward, they may be a step backward in civilization. It may be that they won't add to the beauty of the world or the life of men's souls — I'm not sure. But automobiles have come, and almost all outward things are going to be different because of what they bring. They're going to alter war, and they're going to alter peace. And I think men's minds are going to be changed in subtle ways because of automobiles. And it may be that George is right. It may be that in ten or twenty years from now, if we can see the inward change in men by that time, I shouldn't be able to defend the gasoline engine but would have to agree with George that automobiles had no business to be invented.

At the end of *Ambersons*, there is yet another prefiguring of the musings of *Crash* when George is hit by a car and both of his legs are broken. The effect is manifold: it is the physical comeuppance his detesters have longed for, it (at least temporarily) absolves him of having to work for a living, and it is his rebirth, in that total fracture can now (possibly) allow real healing. This coupled with his parents' death — every child's secret fantasy contributing to anxiety — gives George something of a clean slate, as well as maybe an insurance settlement to return him to the fashion that he was born accustomed to. At the end of the RKO movie, viewers are unsure, however, if George is sorry for who he is, or if he is just sorry that he has missed out on Eugene's money via Isabel and Lucy. It is a "happy" — yet "down" — ending, for after all the characters have been through, and no matter how they have remade themselves, they are basically the same. The phoniness of the studio-imposed happy ending where Lucy hears of George's accident and says, "I'm going to him. You coming, Papa?" is a great example of *noir* saying one thing and meaning another, thus forcing the audience to look at the meta-film between, here in *Ambersons* exacerbated by the studio remaking.

One More Tomorrow (1942/6)

Battling the Universal globe for icon of the zeitgeist, the Warner Bros. shield looms with Max Steiner's thundering music behind it as *One More Tomorrow*—to date the second of four screen adaptations of Philip Barry's 1931 play, *The Animal Kingdom*—begins. Shot in 1942 but shelved because it was a commercial release ill suited for wartime, Warner's delay made *One More Tomorrow* even more of a period piece when it was finally released in 1946. The action starts with the intertitle, "Somewhere in Connecticut 1939," and *One More Tomorrow* can be understood as Warner's Nazi allegory — so precise in its depiction of national anxiety that it had to be suppressed for four years until the Second World War ended.

If it had been released in 1942, *One More Tomorrow*'s story would have started in the recent past, and the action would have advanced close to what was then "the present day." The movie's actual release in 1946 gave *One More Tomorrow* that much more historical perspective, as the outcome — that the Second World War would end — was already known, as it was not in 1942. From the perspective of that year, *One More Tomorrow* would have been an emotionally uncertain experience featuring the type of sourness that would heighten anxiety rather than relieve it. *One More Tomorrow* is a dark, mean, and hard-boiled picture, soaked in liquor and linking drink to dream, perhaps replacing dreaming with drunkenness, but all the while harkening dreaming as analogous to the cinema, which intoxicates as Hofmannsthal wrote in 1921.

Barry is the great American playwright of the first half of the twentieth century — more so than even Eugene O'Neill, who usually claims that mantle in the history books. Barry's work, idealist and fantastic, is filled with a uniquely American optimism. His theater texts exist out of time as a Shakespeare play does. Even though Barry's events may be grounded in a specific epoch (usually the 1930s, that is, between the First and Second World Wars), the heightened emotions of Barry's work are of a universal and mythic relation. Barry's plays float between myth and religiosity, but usually the cinema versions remake God out of their conception of his texts. Tom Collier, the hero of *The Animal Kingdom* and *One More Tomorrow*, is the Hamlet of the twentieth century. Like the Prince of Denmark, Tom is the opposite of his father but is also compelled to remake him in his action(s). For Hamlet, he must avenge his father's murder, and for Tom, he must come of age and marry. The Second World War transforms *The Animal Kingdom* so that *One More Tomorrow* removes Barry's idealism and reduces the story to focus on two wars — World War II and Tom's war with his father. While retaining a fair degree of philosophical similarity, Warner Bros. remakes Barry's idealism as propaganda — *One More Tomorrow* has a political agenda, whereas *The Animal Kingdom* does not. Barry's play — an object lesson about integrity — focuses on the difference between "selling out" and "cashing in." *One More Tomorrow* is the American movie of World War II, insomuch as Barry's romantic comedy of manners has been transformed into a Hollywood-Jewish-Brechtian learning play with roots in Barry's comedy. As with *The Magnificent Ambersons*, *One More Tomorrow*'s redoubling of repressed trauma was enough to sink the movie internally at the studio prior to release. In accordance with this, *One More Tomorrow* can be understood as Warner's *Ambersons*, and Philip Barry their Booth Tarkington. A witty gesture of this affinity is noted in *One More Tomorrow* in naming the heroine's camera assistant "Orson."

It is some thirty-nine minutes into *One More Tomorrow* before any dialogue from Barry's original play is heard. *One More Tomorrow* is a radical remake of its source — far more so than the 1931, 1957 and 2009 movie versions of *The Animal Kingdom*. Yet many elements of the story remain consistent in all three versions. Tom Collier is a wealthy man in his early thirties who does not get along with his father Rufus. He lives in a ramshackle old house out in the country with his butler, ex-prize fighter Regan, and an assorted, ever-changing entourage. Whereas father Rufus is conservative, the son, Tom, is extravagant. Lacking a mother, Tom is compelled to remake his father by being his opposite. Freud addresses this pathology in his paper *On Oedipus and Hamlet*, as referenced at the start of this chapter.

Because of the doubling, Tom has never outgrown his father as the healthy adult male must. For reasons that are fully unclear in all versions — but are perhaps Tom subconsciously obeying his father's will — Tom forsakes his long-term bohemian/counterculture girlfriend, Daisy, for a pretty poor girl with social ambitions named Cecelia Henry. In *One More Tomorrow*, Daisy is renamed Chris, and her twice-fold rejection of Tom — despite the fact that they act like soul mates — points to the same authorial intention as in *The Animal Kingdom*, namely that it is Cecilia, not Tom or Daisy, who is the story's central character.

Barry was no stranger to the application of psychology to theater. His use of it as a learning device and as social therapy is most successful in his play of the 1920s, *In a Garden*. Originally titled *A Man of Taste*, this three-act drama concerns playwright Adrian Terry literally (and unwisely) restaging in his Sutton Place living room a romantic moment between his current wife, Lissa, and her long-lost, recently reemerged one-time suitor, Norrie Bliss, to test the outcome of this remaking. For Adrian, his dabbling in psychology teaches him and the audience several bitter but potent lessons. The caustic nature of the ideas at work might explain why, from this point on, Barry toned down such insightful and challenging play technique, leaving the full exfoliation of marriage and money to the next generation of American playwrights, led best by Edward

Albee. Barry's work, as with the novel *War in Heaven* and its theatrical double, *Here Come the Clowns* (1938), is blisteringly personal. His psychological representation of theater and audience is split between more experimental work with short, less-commercial runs, and popular comedies that have earned a place in the world stage repertoire. Barry's greatest plays, *In a Garden, Holiday* (1928) and *The Animal Kingdom* reflect the psyche of the nation and challenge conformity, but do so so very lightly that an audience member (or heavy-handed director) could remake this sharp edge right out of the text, repressing the uneasiness back into the subconscious that Barry clearly culls his ideas out of.

The credits of *One More Tomorrow* give way to the outside of a 1939 house party, "somewhere in Connecticut." The radio brings the audience up to date while completing the Wagnerian transformation scene backward in time: "Twenty-one years after the war to end all wars, Europe once more stands on the brink of the holocaust. Tonight the conviction that war is inevitable has settled over all Europe." Aforementioned Daisy Sage is remade as Christine "Chris" Sage (Ann Sheridan), and her émigré violinist best friend, Franc Schmidt, is reimagined as Frankie Connors (Jane Wyman). In the case of Chris, her remaking is an improvement of *The Animal Kingdom*'s Daisy insomuch as Daisy/Chris is now an independent woman aware of her artistic voice. In the play, Tom is necessary for Daisy's identity as an artist. Here, Chris is a more fully developed individual, and her artwork is not rejected like Daisy's for being unready to show, but because it is ahead of its time and too political. This revision of the play is echoed in the fate of *One More Tomorrow*, which, while set in the recent past, was too ahead of its time (socially) and too political to be viewed as a commercially viable release by Warner Bros. in 1942. In *One More Tomorrow*, the occasion of Tom's surprise birthday party is Chris and Tom's first meeting — one where she has been sent to snap a photograph for the newspaper of the surprised playboy. As Chris remarks to Frankie of the potential meet cute "Murder in Poland, and a playboy's party in Connecticut."

Tom sneaks into the party via an unexpected entrance, but with his help, Chris winds up (re)staging her assigned "candid" photo for the newspaper, as another unpleasant truth is exorcised in *One More Tomorrow*— that of the unreliability of the photographic medium (i.e., technology) itself. *The Magnificent Ambersons* studio cutting made *Ambersons* a movie about cinema; *One More Tomorrow* making Daisy/Chris a photographer allows *One More Tomorrow* to become a movie about movies, or as the implications of Daisy's picture assignment represent, a movie about media. Twentieth-century war focuses cinema's connection with propaganda, and what is called media is a result of violence's direction of cinema and the evolution to the media era and the overtaking of the dream state it implements. As for the candid photograph, Chris directs Tom — so as to have the viewer think her Leni Riefenstahl — as she commands him, "Look astonished." For Barry, art is about remembrance and captured

Chris Sage (Ann Sheridan) and Frankie Connors (Jane Wyman) snap a staged picture on the occasion of Tom Collier's (Dennis Morgan) surprise birthday party in *One More Tomorrow* (Peter Godfrey, 1942/6). As Chris remarks to Frankie of the potential meet cute: "murder in Poland, and a playboy's party in Connecticut." (The Museum of Modern Art/Film Stills Archive.)

sentiment, whereas *One More Tomorrow* is about sentiment created for the advancement of social goals as illustrated in and by cinema.

While not socially devious like Cecelia, Chris' photographic skills, like Daisy's artwork before her, gives her an extra-body agency of spirit. Like *Crash*, and unlike *The Animal Kingdom*, Tom and Chris' affair in *One More Tomorrow* starts in the midst of trauma. Having fulfilled her assignment and taken the photograph of Tom, Chris starts to leave the party. Tom stops her, remarking, "You know you're leaving too soon. Things really begin to happen around here about midnight — you'll have a lot to shoot then. Wine stains on the carpet. Cigarette burns on the furniture. And somebody's sure to push somebody else into the pool!" Chris is unimpressed, as "by twelve o'clock Hitler might invade Poland. Then we'll have much more interesting pictures of death and destruction." Like *Crash*'s Helen Remington in her initial hospital encounter with Ballard, Chris needs a more radical form of stimulation — the stimulation of transformation that the sound era's cinema taught the body to crave as a (by-)product of war.

Tom follows Chris out of the party, and their love affair begins. After much passion, Chris breaks it off with Tom and then later returns to him to remake their relationship. It is Warner's remaking of the airport scene in *Casablanca* (1942). The screenplay to that movie, and the additional dialogue for *One More Tomorrow*, are both by the same team, Julius J. and Philip G. Epstein. Both Tom and mutual friend Jim Fisk (Reginald Gardiner) come to meet Chris airplane upon her return. Warner's redaction of the play has, until this point, suppressed Barry's bisexual undertones, but after the airport scene the pieces of Barry's story cannot be assembled any other way than to convey his message of polyamory being the social evolution that could augment, save, or even replace community dissipating rapidly in the face of technology and big capital. Having both Jim and Tom in attendance to greet Chris' airplane also signifies wartime's social neutrality, which — like *The Public Enemy*'s Great Depression — reaches not only across the gender line, but through various sexual orientations, allowing open homosexuality (and the "outness" of Jim), which in "normal" situations, post–1934 and pre–1970, would have to have been better cloaked for social, and therefore cinematic, acceptance.

One of the first things Tom's wife Cecelia actively connives to do once the ring is on her finger is to remove Tom's manservant and, implied sometimes sex partner, Regan from their connubial household. The scene where Tom and Regan say good-bye remains virtually and comparatively unaltered textually in all four screen versions of the play. If the erotics are removed from Regan's departure, the emotional impact is the equivalent of the scene in *Ambersons* where Uncle Jack (Ray Collins) says good-bye to George at the train depot. In *One More Tomorrow*, Tom and Regan's good-bye — which, to the happiness of both men isn't forever — is reset in a train station, again strengthening the Wellesian affinity.

Unlike Tom and Regan's relationship in *One More Tomorrow*, the male/female relationships are importantly altered from Barry's source play. When in *The Animal Kingdom* Daisy finds out that Tom has recently married Cecelia, she is heartbroken and implores him, "Does she love you?" to which Tom assuredly replies, "Yes," whereas in *One More Tomorrow*, Tom can only offer a weak "I think so." Making this change, *One More Tomorrow* points out the meaninglessness of everything in the compromised state of war. *One More Tomorrow* goes on to praise dissident propaganda as when Jim explains his left-wing literary magazine to Tom: "The Bantam is nothing more than a good American liberal magazine.... No one will advertise and very few people read [it]. ... It tells the absolute truth, but it tells it on cheap paper. It's controlled by no interest and is indebted to no one but the printer." For Tom, his feeling on becoming the magazine's underwriter are summed up with, "All I know about the Bantam is my father doesn't like it. That's good enough for me."

Tom's father, Rufus (Thurston Hall), and his peers are cheating the government — it is the type of scheme Kane would have exposed in early days of

The Inquirer. Tom is furious: "Cheating the government isn't a matter to be taken lightly. Who do these men think they are? Is a profit more important than a life? What makes them think they're beyond punishment? There's no separate Constitution for them and one for the rest of the people. They'll face the music all right and I'll be happy to beat the drums." No doubt the thought of war profiteering, on top of a depressed view of the institute of marriage, became another reason that *One More Tomorrow* was shelved.

On the night of the invasion of Poland by Germany, Tom's thirty-second birthday party remakes "the last of the great, long-remembered dances that 'everybody talked about'" in *The Magnificent Ambersons.* Tom changes in relation to himself after this night, and it turns out to be the finale of his ne'er-do-well youth. As he puts it, hours later, "if the world's going to war, the least I can do is go to work."

In *One More Tomorrow,* Cecelia Henry (Alexis Smith) arrives at Tom's fete on the arm of Owen Arthur (John Loder). Remade like something out of Laclos, the pair is scheming from the start. In Barry's play, Tom drives Cecelia toward monstrousness, where here for Warner Bros., she is already a monster. Owen, while ostensibly infatuated with Cecelia — or "C" as she is called by her intimates — nonetheless immediately tells her, "Tom's great at picking up people, in case you're interested." Informing her that Tom has "a life of leisure while it lasts," the romantic act is remade, as it is with so many American marriages, to feed financial desire and eliminate the physical-emotional. In the following exchange — not based at all in the Barry source text — Cecelia reveals her remade twentieth-century nature. As played by Smith, she is *noir*'s — already by 1942 — archetypical femme fatale reimagined as a capitalist gorgon.

OWEN: Tom and the old man don't see eye to eye about most things.
CECELIA: Not even money?
OWEN: The subject fascinates you.
CECELIA: Completely, I'm perfectly willing to admit it.
OWEN: Consistency thy name is C.
CECELIA: If I were mad about first editions, or collecting souvenir spoons, you'd see nothing wrong with it. I happen to like money. I like the power it brings. I like walking into the best restaurants and how every woman envies you. I'm sorry, Owen. I lived on a shoestring ever since I was born. And I hate shoe-strings.
OWEN: And where exactly do I fit in?
CECELIA: Owen, I'm fond of you. I think I've proven that, but, as far as the future goes — well, I don't know how to say it ...
OWEN: "Washed up" covers it nicely.
CECELIA: Stop being bitter and get me a drink.

In *One More Tomorrow,* Tom hates strings as much as Cecelia, and all strings are depicted so as to be clearly recognizable as capital's net. Cecelia's unhappiness of self— in all versions of the Barry play, she is filled with apparent self-loathing — is the result of the fantasy of wealth that cinema represents as the ultimate objective and that which has become her goal. Cecelia is a modern woman, raised in the sound era, who is trapped by its advancing demands. Marriage, the end of the individual and the beginning of the conscious double, is linked to fortune, an inheritance both Cecelia and Owen covet:

OWEN: Tom will come into a fortune one of these days and won't know how to use it. That's where I come in.

CECELIA: No, darling, that's where I come in.

OWEN: I don't suppose it would do any good to remind you that marriage has to do with other things besides spending money?

CECELIA: Really? Do tell.

OWEN: Well, making a home, having children —

CECELIA: For other people, perhaps.

OWEN: You are the most selfish woman I ever met.

CECELIA: Thanks for the compliment. (*She kisses him.*)

Perhaps overtly influenced by Ayn Rand, Cecelia is oddly nonetheless a feminist asserting her identity. Unfortunately, any resulting independence is reassumed by capital, making her the villainous central character of *One More Tomorrow*— a link between *The Public Enemy* and *A Clockwork Orange*. The Latin root of "monster" is "warning" (*monstrum* being derived from *monere*, which — incidentally — is the same root as "money"), and Cecelia is an amoral example of wartime and modernity's effect on personality as examined in the preceding three chapters. Cecelia has taken valuable Sadean absolutism and moral relativism and replaced the noble object of Sade's philosophy with currency, rendering the Marquis' philosophy truly obscene, as it is removed from the body and the mind is remade into lucre, which has no potential of imagination in and of itself.

Once married to Tom, Cecelia tries to pull Tom's "strings" by befriending his father, Rufus, and does so somewhat sincerely in all movie versions of the play, as Cecelia really does "like" money. Cecelia rationalizes the code of money by remaking it as love between father and son, hoping that Tom will be kind to his father, and thus encouraging Rufus' financial-emotional reciprocation. "All his life he's tried to do things for you —" Cecelia explains, and Tom snaps back before she finishes her sentence, "In order to own me."

Cecelia and Rufus meet in *One More Tomorrow* in a scene that echoes George meeting Lucy at the ball in *The Magnificent Ambersons*. There, George criticizes Eugene rather severely and is then embarrassed to find out that the woman with whom he is speaking is none other than Eugene's daughter Lucy. Cecelia meets Rufus at the party, speaks dismissively of Tom's zoo to him, and then finds out that Rufus is Tom's father — but unlike George, she has made a good impression, as Rufus tells her, "I'm not his friend; I'm his father."

Later, after the marriage, Rufus confides in Cecelia, "If there is hope for
Tom, you're it. I leave everything in your hands." Cecelia rises to the occasion,
but also protects her interests, adding, "Including the check?" Rufus laughs
heartily and remarks, "You and I should have been in business together, Cecelia,"
and she confirms the nature of marriage as depicted in *One More Tomorrow*,
answering him, "Well, we are in a way, aren't we?"

In *One More Tomorrow*, pregnancy and motherhood are a constant issue
with Cecelia from the early exchange with Owen quoted earlier onward. Money
renders marriage sterile, remaking birthing as accruing. The specter of Cecelia's
material pregnancy hangs over *One More Tomorrow* before she and Tom meet,
whereas it is not addressed between Tom and Cecelia until the final scene, in
Barry's source play. In *The Animal Kingdom*, Cecelia fakes headaches to get out
of things she does not want to do or talk about. Tom reads these attacks as
illness until the climax when he becomes aware of the totality of Cecelia's performance. In *One More Tomorrow*, Cecelia's spells are a shorthand to Tom that
she may be with child, and therefore that she must be indulged, and Tom's reading
of Cecelia's "headaches" is consistent with the social coding of 1940s films. This
coding has the power to remake metaphor and meaning as one, and *One More
Tomorrow* examines this phenomenon along with father-son relations.

Wars are fought ostensibly for the next generation. The cinema of the
1940s — especially from Warner Bros. — is filled with teaching dramas that
explain the fighting and (current) rules of international engagement between
fascism and democracy, man and machine, and on the homefront between individual and double, love and capital. War further removes the individual from
happy dreams, and the surrogacy that makes up the difference results in dreams
becoming the parental wish for the next generation.

Strange Illusion (1945)

Strange Illusion is the second film of director Edgar G. Ulmer to be closely
examined in this reading of English-language cinema. Not only is it a hugely
engaging motion picture but — as will become apparent — it is a bridge of sorts
between *The Black Cat* and *Peeping Tom*, between the generations, between
fathers Werdegast and A.N. Lewis and that next generation of sons represented
by Paul Cartwright and Mark Lewis.

"Dr." Ulmer is specially attuned to psychology, and his movies must be
thought of as belonging to the genre of "psychodrama," rather than to whatever
genre might first suggest itself (i.e., a western, a horror movie, a musical, etc.).
Coupled with Ulmer's often impoverished means of production, which mirac-
ulously serve to inform his ingenuity of theatricalism, this allows a certain
crude, but unmistakable, reality to enter his otherwise totally fabricated
Gesamtkunstwerks. Already it has been illustrated how Ulmer's psychodramas

are one step closer toward a truer representation of the nation's subconscious than most movies because of their inherent dream/discontinuous realities. The anthropological value of these unvarnished elements in Ulmer is of the highest interest because it is so authentic to the actual of the day the negative was exposed, making Ulmer the proto–Zapruder.

The opening credits to *Strange Illusion* appear over intersecting and twisting art deco staircases and columns, Oz- or Escher-like in their architecture. They twist and crash into one another and are representative of both Castle Elsinore and the inside of the human mind. Paul Cartwright (James Lydon) is a young Hamlet-Oedipus. The action of the movie starts in the middle of a dream, where Paul's voiceover remakes the scene, fostering psychoanalytic transference with the audience. "I am Paul Cartwright. My father was Judge Albert Cartwright, once the lieutenant governor of the state. He was killed two years ago in a mysterious accident. We were not only father and son, but friends. The shock of his violent death still haunts my mind. My nights are troubled by strange dreams."

Strange Illusion is an exceptional movie as Paul's dreams open and close the film and anticipate — rather than follow — events. Paul's precognition is representative of the sound era's precognizant cinema, offering both dreams and explanations that do not coalesce. The next great cinematic remake of Paul's situation, born of Hamlet-Oedipus, occurs in *The Shining* where the young son Danny is precognizant and Elsinore has been redecorated as the Overlook Hotel.

The portrait of dead Judge Cartwright looms over *Strange Illusion*, remaking *Laura* (1944) and prefiguring her remake as Laura Palmer of *Twin Peaks* (1990–1992). Hamlet is not surprised by his father's death in the play, but rather at the revelation of his mother's affair with his Uncle Claudius. Paul's letters from his dead father, which the Judge had the precognition to write before his death and which are mailed regularly, are greeted with a nonchalance the same as the Prince's. The Judge's letter echoes Hamlet's letter to Claudius in Act 4, because it is the father speaking through the son, the son assumed to be the father's surrogate:

> *High and mighty, you shall know I am set naked on your kingdom, Tomorrow shall I beg leave to see your kingly eyes, when I shall, first asking your pardon, thereunto recount the occasion of my sudden and more strange return.*[6]

The opposite of George Minafer, Paul Cartwright is compelled to remake his father by the letters, but unlike Hamlet, Paul has an affinity for the task at hand, and in this regard *Strange Illusion* remakes Paul as closer to the doubled Fortinbras than the Danish Prince. As with Hamlet's letter to Claudius, Paul is also remade as his father by the need for justice. Justice appears to be just until the final dream in *Strange Illusion* where the truth is shockingly associated as a mere element superseded by psychic reality. It is here at the Brechtian "happy end" of the movie that the proceedings enter into the perspective of Paul's delusion. Paul's reverie is a type of spiritual reward, like saints' experience — a rapture allowed by Paul because of the fulfillment of his obsessive-sacred quest. Like Walker in *Point Blank*, Paul has no reality outside of his paternal purpose. The dream that starts the film is not from Paul's perspective but a dream of the audience's, projected by Ulmer so as to attempt psychoanalytic transference and stimulate self-analysis. The dream ending of the movie is different; it is a projection from Paul of his psychic reality that then bizarrely awakens the viewer out of the world of *Strange Illusion*.

Like Hamlet, Paul is a student, and his investigations become obsessions because of his total certainty of understanding truth. But Paul's philosophy is also born of paranoia — however philosophical — rooted in one of Paul's father's last statements about the probability of there being a "lot of undetected crime." That paranoia is juxtaposed in *Strange Illusion* with the notion that family life is what removes privacy and that paranoia is built out of a desire for the child to remove sexuality and his/her body from the parent — less it be reswallowed into (Oedipal-Hamletian) incest.

Klein accounts for paranoia in an analysis of people who fail to experience mourning. "Feeling incapable of saving and securely reinstating their loved objects inside themselves, they must turn away from them more than hitherto and therefore deny their love for them. This may mean that their emotions in general become more inhibited; in other cases it is mainly feelings of love which become stifled and hatred is increased. At the same time, the ego uses various ways of dealing with paranoid fears (which will be stronger the more hatred is reinforced). For instance, the internal 'bad' objects are manically subjugated, immobilized and at the same time denied, as well as strongly projected into the external world."[7]

Klein's diagnosis does not apply to Paul but does fit his and his father's "evil twin" Claude Barrington, whose sociopathic impulses lead him to multiple murder. Like the murderous father Leland Palmer of *Twin Peaks*, Barrington is done in because he is an expressive — not obsessive — murderer. Barrington's lack of continuity-in-poise containing his drive and desire for young girls is his social undoing. In his *Strange Illusion* role, Warren William remakes himself as a villain after a career as a 1930s leading man, and Ulmer remakes the poetic murderer Bluebeard with the more Mabuseian Claude Barrington.

Replacing the evidence provided by *The Murder of Gonzago* in *Hamlet* are Paul's collected fingerprints. The movie's play-within-a-play is the content that unfolds between Paul's two different types of dreams which bookend *Strange Illusion*. Hamlet chooses to return from England in Act 5 and defy augury. True to the structure of *Hamlet*, Paul meditates over his father's case file on Barrington, as Ulmer's camera pans the room passing a globe, signifying that *Strange Illusion*'s Hamlet, Paul, has returned from his England and will now, enthused, end his Claudius' reign. It is after this point in the myth that Hamlet and Gertrude as well as Paul and Virginia, the son and mother of *Strange Illusion*, have their "closet scene" confrontation.

Paul's mother is closer to Gertrude than Jocasta because it is her "incest" that triggers Paul's precognition. Virginia Cartwright (Sally Eilers), nicknamed "Princess," is about to enter into a marriage not unlike the disastrous ones in *The Magnificent Ambersons, One More Tomorrow* or *Despair*. Her suitor is Brett Curtis (Warren William), who later is revealed to be Claude Barrington — the late Judge's nemesis. Before he is unmasked by Paul, Brett humiliates Virginia at a dinner party, mocking her faulty, "delightful arithmetic," and here *Strange Illusion* remakes when Eugene calls Isabel a "divinely ridiculous woman" in *The Magnificent Ambersons*.

Two characters who might be seen as Rosencrantz and Guildenstern or a two-faced version of Tiresias the Seer are *Strange Illusion*'s good doctor, Vincent (Regis Toomey), and his reflection, the wicked Professor Muhlbach (Charles Arnt). While initially appearing as opposites, they are both cut from the same ideological cloth. Dr. Vincent is all too ready and willing to offer Paul the council that, "to healthy minded people, a dream is just a dream" and that the Judge's uncanny letters are a "curious coincidence." The impression Toomey may project at first is an avuncular devil's advocate, but when the performance is examined multiple times, it becomes clear that Dr. Vincent does not have Paul's interests at heart because the "good" doctor recognizes Paul as too different from the society around him. This position of Hamlet being a man of the Renaissance in the world of the Middle Ages has been mentioned earlier in connection with Heiner Müller and Harold Bloom and certainly applies to forward-thinking Paul. Dr. Vincent further reveals his true nature when Paul is worried about Brett Curtis' origins, and he suggests they go to the local bank — the institute of deception through numerical accuracy. As Dr. Vincent testifies — incriminating himself—"a banker doesn't usually take people at face value."

A remake of the nefarious criminal doctor Caligari, Professor Muhlbach is sage enough to know Paul is a danger that may become an obstacle. Muhlbach speaks of "fools and children" and their super-intellectual abilities of (subconscious) connection. His binoculars are like Klingsor's magical implements and necromantic appliances — the whole impression of a Nazi wizard is completed by Muhlbach's nurse, who when busted at the end, defends herself with, "I know nothing, I'm just an employee," spoken as if she were a death camp guard.

Lydia is the Ophelia of *Strange Illusion*, and she feels that Paul is avoiding her as his pursuit of Claude Barrington and his distrust of Brett Curtis escalate. Paul pledges to Lydia that he is not-breaking-up-with-her, but that he must follow his hunch and protect the family as his father preordained. Lydia's dislike of Brett allows her to rationalize Paul's rejection — something that may well

In Paul's (James Lydon) climactic dream jouissance, Lydia (Mary McLeod) holds him in her arms and they so remake the Judge and Princess and the son is finally the father to the man in *Strange Illusion* (Edgar G. Ulmer, 1945). (Photofest.)

have saved her predecessor Ophelia from suicide. As Paul puts Lydia "on ice," her parting sentiment to Paul underlines *Strange Illusion* as being a movie about the greater power of dreams than reality when she coos, "Don't forget."

In Paul's end climactic dream jouissance, Dr. Vincent is joined with Virginia as Paul and Lydia remake the Judge and Princess — the son is finally the father to the man. Müller's quotation of Marx's *Critique of Hegel's Philosophy of Law* ends his *Hamletmachine*. The dictum of "the main point is to overthrow all existing conditions"[8] reverberates throughout Ulmer's cinema, which remakes through cinematic dreams the anxieties that are always a father's legacy and shape the next generation.

CHAPTER 5

"It's all very realistic!"

Remaking Image with
Vinyl *(1965) and*
A Clockwork Orange *(1971)*

In *On the Relation of Analytical Psychology to Poetry*, Carl Jung writes, "The work presents us with a finished picture, and this picture is amenable to analysis only to the extent that we can recognize it as a symbol. But if we are unable to discover any symbolic value in it, we have merely established that, so far as we are concerned, it means no more than what it says, or to put it another way, that it *is* no more than what it *seems* to be."[1] Most feature narratives produced during the sound era of English-language cinema are semiotic — often nothing but symbolic value — however there are the rare exceptions where the work just "is" and is impregnable to criticism because of total alignment of content and form. The films of directors Andy Warhol and Stanley Kubrick often fall into this rarefied category. To question the value of *Haircut* (1963) or *Barry Lyndon* (1975) is absurd because of their totality.

Despite many surface differences — Warhol was Queer, Catholic and performative; Kubrick was Jewish, relativist and obsessive — they hold many affinities. New York shaped their identities, and both mastered their craft being commercial artists in the 1950s — Warhol drawing ads, and Kubrick shooting pictures for magazines. When they started to make films, they did so independently, and their immediate brilliance was a fusion of the tools of documentary cinema with an emulation of the Hollywood studio model. Most paramount, Warhol and Kubrick are first and foremost both satirists. Opposites in technical productions — Warhol's movies are "sloppy" in a way Kubrick's are "studied" — both men evolved a highly idiosyncratic, visually pleasing, cinematographical lighting scheme. Of mid–twentieth-century filmmakers, Warhol is Dionysus, and Kubrick, Apollo.

Andy Warhol directing *Vinyl* (1965). (Courtesy Billy Name.)

Both Warhol and Kubrick filmed versions of Anthony Burgess' 1962 novel, *A Clockwork Orange*. Kubrick took sole credit for the 1971 screenplay, and Warhol worked from (and against) a scenario by Ronald Tavel. There is no record of Kubrick ever commenting on Warhol, but it seems likely that the master self-taught cineaste would have seen the Prince of Pop Art's work. The

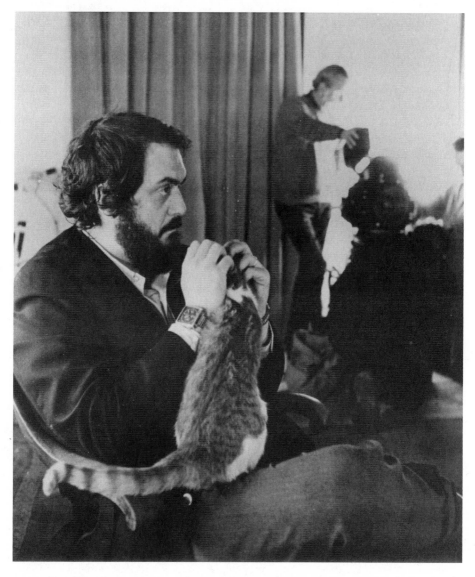

Stanley Kubrick directing *A Clockwork Orange* (1971). (Jerry Ohlinger's Movie Material Store.)

history of Kubrick remaking Warhol begins with the *Eric Says All (The Trip)* reel from *The Chelsea Girls* (1966) informing *Jupiter and Beyond the Infinite* in *2001: A Space Odyssey* and concludes with *Blue Movie* (1969) underwriting the bedroom scenes from *Eyes Wide Shut* (1999). The Warhol edition of *A Clockwork Orange*, renamed *Vinyl*, was first screened in 1965, and the Kubrick remake, reverting to the title of the source novel, was released in 1971. In *The Visible Human* (1924), Béla Balázs writes, "Film is a young, as yet unhackneyed art and works with new, primeval forms of humanity. For that reason, a correct understanding of it requires precisely that one be able to adapt oneself to the totally primitive and naïve. You will continue to laugh and to cry and will not have to decry it as a 'weakness.'"[2] Connecting with Balázs, both Burgess adaptations are primitive — Warhol's through its 16 mm technique and Kubrick's in its sadistic relish. Watching either movie, something is removed, or at the least reshuffled, in the viewer. The movies' transference with the viewer docks with such ferocity as to be the epitome of the cinema of vulnerability.

   Vinyl and *A Clockwork Orange* tell the viewer that if they watch what cinema is, it is as Arnheim remarks: "The truth is that man really likes evil and is born stupid; anyone who wishes to improve the world has to effect his purpose in spite not only of external opposition but especially of himself."[3] A most unique talent shared by Warhol and Kubrick — and perhaps somewhat explained in the twenty-first century as a matter of the postwar American era — is their ability to present ugliness in a way that their craft makes their films' object art impervious as tinfoil or monolith. Adorno mistakenly says, "It seems illusory to claim that through the renunciation of all meaning, especially the cinematically inherent renunciation of psychology, meaning will emerge from the reproduced material itself."[4] *Vinyl* and *A Clockwork Orange*, while "against interpretation," are nothing if not manifest meaning. Such is the nature of satire that it projects a grotesquerie of now.

   While "pornography" in the Deleuzian sense, that its erotic language can "be reduced to the elementary functions of ordering and describing,"[5] *Vinyl* and *A Clockwork Orange* are worthy of Deleuze's genre of "pornology," where those elementary functions cannot be reduced. Warhol and Kubrick's satire exists — no more or less — but the philosophies played with, within — as one is never presented as dominant — are endless enigmas harkening back to man's Arnheimian "evil" and "stupid" birth. In *Vinyl* and *A Clockwork Orange*, the filmmakers share the goals of pornological literature as presented by Deleuze: "Pornological literature is aimed above all at confronting language with its own limits, with what is in a sense a 'nonlanguage' (violence that does not speak, eroticism that remains unspoken). However this task can only be accomplished by an internal splitting of language: the imperative and descriptive function must transcend itself toward a higher function, the personal element turning by reflection upon itself into the impersonal."[6] Therefore the cultural value in pornography is affirmed in that it allows not only a Shakespearean remaking in relation to one's self, but also removes the individual while representing the individual, thus leaving a pure text ripe for interpretation.

Vinyl (1965)

Again aligning their duality, both *Vinyl* and *A Clockwork Orange*'s first frame of picture is a close-up of the protagonist's face. For Warhol his name is Victor, and for Kubrick, it is Alex, as in the source Burgess book. In *Vinyl*, Victor (Gerard Malanga) dips out of the frame of his close-up, lifting weights. Warhol's camera does not move to accommodate the individual. The frame is empty for several seconds, and as Victor returns, the shot pulls back to reveal the studio. Kubrick has the same sense of stillness as Warhol, and like a precognizant dream, it is as if one of Kubrick's photographs from *Look* could have been Warhol's silk-screen source photo — the same photograph which might have hypothetically illustrated a story on a magazine page with an ad for shoes drawn by Warhol.

Warhol's cinema is very close to journalism, not that cinema and journalism are very different. Cinema is quickly made, of the moment, firsthand history. Warhol's images look like newsprint lit with tabloid flash. Kubrick's reliance on artificial, but perfectly motivated source lighting gives his works an inherent, eccentric uncanniness that relates them to Ulmer's cinema. Warhol's cinema also functions as painting, the life-size-ness of the 16 mm framing contributing to his reputation as the twentieth century's greatest portraitist. Likewise with a Kubrick film there are often tableaux or close-ups worthy of being hung in an art gallery, for instance the opening of *A Clockwork Orange* in the Korova Milk Bar, or Billy Boy's close-up as he chews gum before he pops open his switchblade in the derelict casino.

Warhol and Kubrick's cinema thrives on repetition. For Warhol, it is the endless remaking of the Superstars and of identity being only a/his performance. For Kubrick his scripting (what can be understood as his performance) depends on repeats, of the hypnotic doubling back of narrative structure, which are where the juxtapositions of the script's ideas truly lay — a sort of epic theater born of Wedekind and Brecht. Warhol repeats music — "Nowhere to Run" plays through twice in *Vinyl*'s first reel — and Kubrick often picks a piece of preexisting music to use as a theme in a movie. In *A Clockwork Orange*, it is most famously "Singing in the Rain," which the audience hears three times — once when (masked) Alex sings it while raping the writer Mr. Alexander's Wife, second when Alex sings it to himself in the tub thus betraying his identity to Mr. Alexander, and finally as the credits pop on and off the screen at the movie's end.

Vinyl, like *A Clockwork Orange*, has a party-in-hell-like atmosphere indicative of the century and millennium's end. In *Vinyl*, the figures in Warhol's background torturing each other with molten candle wax are akin to Kubrick's witnesses loitering in the Korova Milk Bar. Kubrick's observing doctors, also in the background, are the closest Kubrick gets to screen surrogates of himself. He includes them, and doing so breaks the fourth wall as any true satirist since Christian Dietrich Grabbe does, and represent himself, like a Warhol, as a sadist behind the camera. Ergo, the whole of *Vinyl* is equivalent to the moment in *A Clockwork Orange* where Alex has to watch movies with eyes clamped wide open. Andy Warhol and his Superstars are forced to perform for identity, and the often inaudible audio allows no discernment of what to listen to, rendering the individual meaningless and revealed as a psychological primate. Misprision is key to Warhol's work, as it is not in Kubrick's — the former uses it to create and chart psychological space whereas the latter's movies are inherently ambiguous texts where misreading is impossible because everything is within a system of relative morality.

The highlight of *Vinyl* is the end of the first reel. Actors forget their lines, Edie Sedgwick walks off, and the viewer is trapped — like Alex undergoing the Ludovico technique — as the film cannot end until it all runs through the camera's gate. For Warhol, real time is reel time — the perfect alignment of cinema and theater and the ethical recursion of Mark Lewis of putting on the red light to murder Vivian in *Peeping Tom*. Inherently cinematic, *Vinyl*'s empty frame waits for potential action, and conversely *Vinyl* is inherently theatrical — the space itself is the subject. The antithesis of a Wagnerian transformation scene, Warhol takes Balázs' theory of the better egalitarianism of person and object in movies one step further, and his cinema here — most importantly — becomes about what is not represented. This is Warhol's monumental achievement within the feature film medium.

Warhol and Kubrick's movies are movies about the medium and unquestionably self-conscious works. Kubrick's are impeccably shot with every moment overripe with bravura. Warhol remakes the process from within, again commenting and discovering cinema evolving into media — where the very technical apparatus becomes the technique and this is the fission that propels drama. Warhol's whiteouts (or camera flares) and strobe cuts are cinematic punctuation-affirmations like Kubrick's use of dense grain in his later color motion picture events. Warhol's cue cards (whether used by the actors or not) are Brechtian effects, mirrored by Kubrick's frequent use of intertitles.

The highlight of *Vinyl* is the end of the first reel. Actors forget their lines, Edie Sedgwick walks off, and the viewer is trapped — like Alex undergoing the Ludovico technique — as the film cannot end until it all runs through the camera's gate. For Warhol, real time is reel time — the perfect alignment of cinema and theater and the ethical recursion of Mark Lewis of putting on the red light to murder Vivian in *Peeping Tom*. Inherently cinematic, *Vinyl*'s empty frame waits for potential action, and conversely *Vinyl* is inherently theatrical — the space itself is the subject. The antithesis of a Wagnerian transformation scene, Warhol takes Balázs' theory of the better egalitarianism of person and object in movies one step further, and his cinema here — most importantly — becomes about what is not represented. This is Warhol's monumental achievement within the feature film medium.

Vinyl's second reel is a more casual affair and the action remakes itself, and as it does so, it deteriorates like American culture between *Peeping Tom* and *The Matrix* (1999). In the second reel, *Vinyl* spins out into an intoxicated dance party as the movie becomes its own after party — another element adding to the totalities of Warhol's *Gesamtkunstwerk*. As in *A Clockwork Orange*, cinema, in *Vinyl* called "flickers," is therapy. Kubrick and Warhol have taken this metaphor to its extreme, bypassing psychoanalytic transference to represent total impulse, present and/or otherwise.

A Clockwork Orange (1971)

By nature of its advanced cinematic techniques, *A Clockwork Orange*, as directed by Stanley Kubrick, clarifies Warhol, as Warhol's ambiguity only lies in the murkiness of the shots, whereas for Kubrick ambiguity is suggested by juxtaposition between shots. Both Warhol and Kubrick's Burgess adaptations are rooted in the genre of the juvenile delinquent picture, albeit ones elevated to the garish level of tabloid-horror-show. Kubrick remakes his own images several times in *A Clockwork Orange*, as when the soundtrack to *2001: A Space Odyssey* appears in the record store, or when Alex is shown a droog rape reel as part of the Ludovico technique, and at the climax where Alex surveys his own press coverage in the newspaper. Of the Ludovico technique's big-screen imitation of his rape of the writer's wife, Alex's initial impression is that of fulfillment through cinema: "The first film was a very good, professional piece of sinny, like it was done in Hollywood. It's funny how the colors of the real world only seem really real when you viddy them on the screen." *A Clockwork Orange* has the thrill of a carnival, which in the middle of the second millennium AD, was occasion for masques and revels often tantamount to rape. As Alex (Malcolm McDowell) tells the viewer, no doubt speaking for both Warhol and Kubrick, "Viddy well little brother, viddy well."

Cinema in *A Clockwork Orange* is therapy and subversion, again harkening back to Arnheim's truth of the soul. But in the approach of the satirist, like Kubrick, there is the element of humor as being therapy because by creating an exaggeration of the viewer's anxieties, it seems less complex and therefore a more apparently manageable reality to the viewer. *A Clockwork Orange* has the tone of an especially edgy edition of *Mad* magazine, with outrageous James Cagney–sized performances all around, and the scenes playing as a succession of perverse and (a)moralistic blackout sketches, as if directed and starring Charles Chaplin at his most acrid.

Kubrick's cunning use of Warholian absence-as-presence is illustrated in this loaded but seemingly benign exchange, which affirms that Alex's vision — his clamped-open eyes — are the viewers, should they be unable to look away. It is a credit to the intellectual gentleness of Kubrick that he gives viewers that choice.

ALEX: What exactly is the treatment here going to be then?
DR. BRANOM: Oh, it's quite simple, really. We're just going to show you some films.
ALEX: You mean like going to the pictures?
DR. BRANOM: Something like that.

Dr. Branom's (Madge Ryan) and Dr. Brodsky's (Carl Duering) simplicity of explanation is that of cinema's allure. Pictures are dangerous because they deeply affect and have shaped anyone born in the last hundred years, yet at the same time pictures appear benign — a flat surface with clear borders. In truth, the escalating phenomenon of cinema is like Benjamin citing Duhamel, who says, "I can no longer think what I want to think. My thoughts have been replaced by moving images."[7]

Warhol's background torturers in *Vinyl*, almost stagehands, parallel Kubrick's observing doctors, who, like Warhol's observers, are directorial surrogates. In both movies, community rules politics and therefore the cinema. If Kubrick comes closest to stating a theme, it is not in any of the Prison Chaplain's speeches, so marvelously orated by actor Godfrey Quigley, but when Dr. Brodsky remarks to his colleagues in the back of the auditorium where Alex is forced to consume cinema that "it is during this period we have found that the subject will make his most rewarding associations between his catastrophic experience-environment and the violence he sees." As for Alex, he cannot escape Kubrick and pleads, "Leave me glazzies! Leave me glazzies!"

The background artists in the Korova Milk Bar are stoned zombies like the people in *Point Blank*, Sarah Palmer in *Twin Peaks*, or Alex's Mum who takes her "sleepers" nightly. In both movies, self-anesthetic against the world is the necessary tonic for the modern age. Korova milk will "sharpen you up and make you ready for a bit of the old ultra-violence" — it promises the impetus of heroically rebelling like Satan against a broken system while actually desensitizing the individual to environment's estrangement.

Corroborating this effect, Alex's rape victim, the writer's wife (Adrienne Corri), is referred to by her husband Mr. Alexander (Patrick Magee) as "a victim of the modern age," not Alex's victim as viewers concretely see her to be. The doubling of Alex as Mr. Alexander is unmistakable, and a reading of Burgess' twenty-first chapter of *A Clockwork Orange*, deleted from the American edition of the book until 1986 and not represented in the Kubrick screenplay, may be that Alex becomes Mr. Alexander after the end of the novel. It is an alignment also suggested in the Kubrick and Warhol film adaptations. For Kubrick, Alex and Mr. Alexander are similar in that they espouse the same sense of anarchistic freedom, repulsed by the world but from different perspectives — the id and the superego. As Mr. Alexander prepares to use Alex for his own political goals, he delivers this very cogent statement, but in an insane fashion over the phone: "The people — the common people must know, must see. There are great traditions of liberty to be defended. The tradition of liberty is all. The common people will let it go. They will settle for a quieter life. That is why they must be lead, sir, driven, pushed."

Alex is a cheerful pawn in a world that may soon need all its "prison space for political offenders." Like the boy heroes of those 1940s *noirs* examined in Chapter 4 — George, Tom Collier and Paul — Alex was born sullied by what the drunk Tramp (Paul Farrell) in *A Clockwork Orange* calls the "filthy songs of his father." Both Alex and the Tramp know that with "men spinning around the moon ... there is no attention paid to earthly law and order." Here, Kubrick presents a society disconnected from itself, a hyper-realized version of the world of Ballard's *Crash*. In 1996, what was outrageous in 1971 is still as potent, but the idea of subversion being a blasphemy is totally removed. Ironically from the Second World War on, it is a clearly Godless time, but one wherein organized religion — that great false god — is emphatically embraced. While commenting on the modes of cinema's disintegration, *A Clockwork Orange* undoubtedly contributes to it that which it consumes as the price of spectatorship — and that which is part of the film's great power.

Alex's stylized look of the future — the now iconic bowler hat, the trousers and white shirt with suspenders, the eyelash, and the guyliner — is half James Cagney in *The Public Enemy* and half Warhol Silver Factory proto-punk. Tom Powers' "affectionate punches" — first demonstrated by Cagney onto the viewer in the opening credits in *The Public Enemy* — are remade by McDowell's Alex drinking to the viewer in the first shot of Kubrick's film.

Like those two aesthetics, Kubrick has reduced everything in the world of *A Clockwork Orange* to its most basic element. If his preceding movie, *2001: A Space Odyssey*, is genuinely abstract, its successor is nothing if not literal. *2001: A Space Odyssey* can only be interpreted; *A Clockwork Orange* can only be experienced. The inverse is often thought to be true, but this is more or less to the credit of the MGM and Warner Bros. marketing departments — and Kubrick himself — rebranding Kubrick's studio-independent, iconoclast movies.

Kubrick reverts to the ur–Wagner, Beethoven, for Alex's musical tastes. The movie remakes itself and was blighted by real-life copycat crimes after the UK release, just as Alex copies his attack on "Home" in his attack on Woodmere Health Farm. Kubrick's endless delight in recursionary humor is evident in this copycat crime of Alex's being perpetrated on the Cat Lady. When she calls the police, who will arrest Alex thanks to Dim's treachery, she notes that Alex, when he knocked at her front door asking for help, sounded like something "quoted in the papers" with regard to the earlier crime. It is Alex's act of remaking which is the tipoff and his undoing, like the real individual trying to reenact the first, greatest high or first orgasm.

While not interpretive, Kubrick's movies are dreamy; perhaps they are even one step beyond dreams, becoming actual spiritual impressions. Kubrick acknowledges Warhol's contribution to the cinema — that which is outside the frame is most important — when he has the nude girl (Shirley Jaffe) run to safety from Billy Boy (Richard Connaught) and his gang into the wings of the theater on the stage of the derelict casino. Looking outside the frame, Kubrick here asks the cinema, "What is outside?" which can be answered in a very Warholian position of ambivalence. Kubrick presents Alex's most schizoid moment when Lardface forces Alex to lick his boot for the VIP audience, and Alex's voiceover describes utter confusion: "The horrible killing sickness has whooshed up, and turned the like joy of battle into a feeling I was going to snuff it." Both joy and death, but joy and death removed from orgasm — still totally essential, they are nonetheless relegated to the primal state of unknowing sensation. Remakes redouble trauma but are only truly terrifying when each experience is virgin. It is that illusion of revirginity that media offers and which is explored in *A Clockwork Orange*.

Revirginity flourishes in *A Clockwork Orange* as each scene resets in a way so as to highlight the serial and/or cartoon-strip nature of Kubrick's satire — never more apparent than when the Nurse and Doctor's coitus is interrupted by Alex regaining consciousness in the hospital after his suicide attempt. Alex's press coverage remakes Alex, even replacing the surname he gives in the prison, "de Large," as "Burgess." The Minister (Anthony Sharp) and Alex remake the scene between Mr. Deltoid (Aubrey Morris) and Alex in his parents' bedroom, but the homosexual sadistic subtext is replaced between the Minister and Alex with a true "understanding between two friends" so as to underline Kubrick's satiric jibes. Here, Alex looks like Tom Powers in the hospital at the end of *The Public Enemy*, and the viewer can understand that Alex's criminal instincts are also rooted in the same Kleinian primal scenes as Tom's.

With his parents' rejection, and the possible lack of parental availability in the first place, Alex questions what home is. In *A Clockwork Orange*, what is literally labeled "Home" is the sphere in which Alex may rape but also where he himself suffers the "tortures of the damned." Alex's bedroom in Municipal Flat Block 18-A Liner North prefigures Ferris Bueller's bedroom treasure horde, wherein the teenager is revealed as possessing everything he (or she) could desire as a moral right and confirmation of identity. It is the onscreen representation of the birth of the perceived value of "cool," and of the subsequent decades driven by child-directed consumerism. It is also this very expression of youth that makes Alex's crimes so appealing to real-life remaking. Who does not want to be Alex in theory? He is the rare teenage who can support himself, and, like Ferris, he is more successful than his parents. But Alex's (and Ferris') success is to the detriment of society, as it is the success of the media era, where culture rewards the ideology of "more, more, more" rather than of measured fulfillment. Alex's orgy with the two young girls he picks up at the mall is theoretical — as Alex's real pleasure is masturbatory; sex with himself the only form of lovemaking he knows. To know a truthful masturbatory fantasy is to truly know a person, as sexuality is rooted in phantasy and is a conscious dream as ripe for interpretation as is the cinema. It is truly as Alex says: "As I sloushed I knew such lovely pictures."

Like Duhamel, Alex can only think in moving images, and Kubrick — who may be like Duhamel himself too — shows viewers what Alex masturbates to. The only other scene that compares to this for Alex is the movie's climax when the photographers rush into the hospital room and his celebrity (for the moment) is confirmed as Alex daydreams of erotically frolicking with a woman while upper-class spectators applaud. This moment is precognitive of media and its interpretations as it claims the individual as special for conforming, both in its actions (being photographed) and within the person (Alex's new/old leaf). Here, Alex's mind state, his "cure" (being reborn like the star child in *2001: A Space Odyssey*), is one of sensation over fact. All Kubrick movies end at this precipice of modernity. To the director it appears all the same — be it the future of total annihilation, or of a new world order — as in either case the destruction is the same.

CHAPTER 6

Self-Deliverance

Children Unmaking the Family in Psycho (1960 and 1998) and The Parent Trap (1961 and 1998)

The myth of Oedipus haunts parents, as the most upsetting underlying trauma to those who have children is the fate of their offspring and its reflection on them. This leads to two primary cinematic archetypes — the parent who fails to mourn, as Klein explores in "Mourning and Its Relation to Manic-Depressive States" (1940), and the ones who engage in manic reparations as Klein starts to examine in "Love, Guilt and Reparation" (1957). Most often the films of the sound era tend to represent the parent who fails to mourn as the father — for instance the bad Lieutenant, Rufus in *One More Tomorrow*, or Dad in *A Clockwork Orange* — and, unrelatedly but concurrently, also represent the parent who indulges in manic reparations as either the father or mother — usually the mother, as with Isabel Amberson or B. Pullman/Delilah.

The cultural haunting of Oedipus in post–World War II America leads to widespread manic reparations on behalf of the parents to overcompensate for what can be considered their "original sin" — that which is culturally inherited, illustrated and predetermined by consumer society. As Klein observes, "This connection may also throw some light on the obsessional element which so often enters into the tendency for reparation. For it is not only an object about whom guilt is experienced but also parts of the self which the subject is driven to repair or restore."[1] Parents try to live through their children in a type of schizoid narcissism, which in turn allows them to refocus the good and bad within themselves.

Having reached a state of modernity where production — and crime, (and television shows) was syndicated, and knowledge of self-destruction a neurosis

136

of daily life, post–World War II American culture remade itself with each decade successive to the 1960s, through appropriation and nostalgia, with the end result of recreating the nuclear family unit. This refocused emphasis first from the extended family, to the "modern" concept of the nuclear family, and finally to a hyper-capitalized version of the nuclear family, where progeny-not-parents direct the family unit.

After the Second World War, cultural anxieties born out of the nuclear family dominate American culture, and the myth of Oedipus — of the separated family — is remade in sound cinema, removing divine providence and placing the onus not on Jocasta and Laius but their progeny. A world of children in bumper cars already, there are no minors or parents in *Crash*; however other movies from the 1990s featuring children and teenagers — for example *Home Alone* (1990), *Kids* (1995) and *Disturbing Behavior* (1998) — represent national upbringing as being in turmoil. What's more, 1990s-period youth movies like *Dogfight* (1991), *The Ice Storm* (1997), and *Whatever* (1998) — wherein the 1990s actually remake preceding decades — present tumultuous youth as a fact and perhaps a natural element of the world. *Psycho* and *The Parent Trap* bridge *Peeping Tom* and *Crash*, as *Strange Illusion* bridges *The Black Cat* and *Peeping Tom*. Themselves, both *Psycho* and *The Parent Trap* are key case studies of the remaking of family by cinema's myths.

The first movie of *Psycho* was directed by Alfred Hitchcock and released during the summer of 1960. *The Parent Trap*, first written and directed for the screen by David Swift, followed the release of *Psycho* less than a year later during the summer of 1961. These movies' remakes, both released in 1998, follow a similar but inverted trajectory — *The Parent Trap*, directed by Nancy Meyers, opened during the summer, and *Psycho*, directed by Gus Van Sant, closed the year in December. As noted in the introduction, *Psycho* 1998 is a landmark of the end of the sound era of cinema.

In *The Human Stain*, Philip Roth's narrator remembers 1998 as "a summer of exquisite warmth and sunshine, in baseball a summer of mythical battle between a home-run god who was white and a home-run god who was brown, and in America the summer of an enormous piety binge, a purity binge, when terrorism — which had replaced communism as the prevailing threat to the country's security — was succeeded by cocksucking, and a virile, youthful middle-aged president and a brash, smitten twenty-one-year-old employee carrying on in the Oval Office like two teenage kids in a parking lot revived America's oldest communal passion, historically perhaps its most treacherous and subversive pleasure: the ecstasy of sanctimony."[2] Matters of sanctimony aside, Clinton is a defanged Kennedy, and semen — the wet spectacle of the body itself— is removed from the personal by media and technology. In the 1960s, American spectacle was politicized violence. In the 1970s, that energy found its expression in new horror classics like *Last House on the Left* (1972), *The Crazies* (1973) and

Halloween (1978). However, by the 1980s, violence was dangerously and irresponsibly subverted into works like *Beverly Hills Cop* (1984), *Blue Velvet* (1986) and *The Stepfather* (1987). The alignment of *Psycho* and *The Parent Trap* and their remakes is essential for understanding how, from each decade after the 1960s, the United States remade the 1960s. Each time a previous decade is remade it is significantly declawed with the abstraction and commodification of the decade before. *Raider of the Lost Ark* (1981) was novel, *Indiana Jones and the Kingdom of the Crystal Skull* (2008) is not. Indicative of this cultural abstraction and commodification, nostalgia booms as an industry, and individuals come to expect certain gestures which are needed to reinforce their largely illusory status. Debord writes that "in societies dominated by modern conditions of production, life is presented as an immense accumulation of *spectacles*. Everything that was directly lived has receded into a representation."[3] *Psycho* and *The Parent Trap* represent, as Gene Youngblood essays in *Expanded Cinema* (1970), how, "by perpetuating a destructive habit of unthinking response to formulas, by forcing us to rely ever more frequently on memory, the commercial entertainer encourages an unthinking response to daily life, inhibiting self-awareness."[4] In the 1998 editions of both *Psycho* and *The Parent Trap* audiences meet characters less self-aware than in their 1960s counterparts.

Psycho and *The Parent Trap* are dually family comedies and horror films. As comedies, they toy with viewer's emotions with regard to their ignorance. As horror films, they exploit the perversion of children's domination of family structure, which became epidemic in the second half of the twentieth century. These anxieties harken back to Klein writing in *Early Stages of the Oedipus Conflict* that "the early feeling of *not knowing* has manifold connections. It unites with the feeling of being incapable, impotent, which soon results from the Oedipus situation. The child also feels this frustration the more acutely because he *knows nothing* definite about sexual processes. In both sexes the castration complex is accentuated by this feeling of ignorance."[5] Children need a certain type of symbolic castration complex — that is, they must be under the stewardship of an adult, under an ultimate authority. But in the late twentieth century this element of discipline is confused with punishment and therefore eschewed by parents, as parents — adolescent themselves because of an ever more stifling cultural landscape in America post–World War II — increasingly desire to be "liked" by their kids and perceived as "cool," etc, while children's levels of self-entitlement and self-actualization through consumerism results in these trends which are so popular *because* they tap into Klein's connections regarding the "early feeling of *not knowing*." To buy, or to buy for one's child to relieve the presupposed castration complex, manic reparations are indulged. The children of *Psycho* and *The Parent Trap* — Norman Bates, Sharon McKendrick/Susan Evers (as *The Parent Trap* twins are named in 1961) and Hallie Parker/Annie James (as the twins are named in 1998) — are largely sexually ignorant. As Klein writes in "Inhibitions and Difficulties at Puberty" (1922), "missed opportunities for enlightening children at an early age may never present themselves again; but if openings can be made, many difficulties can be alleviated or even removed."[6] Ignorance here at least partially motivates moral transgressions, like Norman's murder of Marion and the others, and the twins' deception and manipulation of the adults who should be responsible for them. The other side of this motivation is the stronger impression that the children's transgressions are represented in the movies as the result of parents who should have alleviated their children's symbolic castration further, perhaps "better"—for Norman, his mother should have realized that a "son is a poor substitute for a lover," and for the twins, they should have never been split up and kept in ignorance of each other's existence.

The line between comedy and horror is thin. Søren Kierkegaard neatly surmises, "The comical is present in every stage of life (only that the relative positions are different), for wherever there is life, there is contradiction, and wherever there is contradiction, the comical is present. The tragic and the comic are the same, insofar as both are based on contradiction; but *the tragic is the suffering contradiction, the comical, the painless contradiction.*"[7] Cinema is usually painless, and so it desensitized viewers to the truly tragic. In *Psycho*, audience members react to Marion being slashed but not necessarily the situation that forced her to steal money from her boss. In *The Parent Trap*, the secret of the other sister is absolved in the twins' remaking of the family's primal scene— that is the romance of the parents. The duality of joy and sorrow, exhalation and death, is not new (and better charted by Georges Bataille), but what *Psycho* and *The Parent Trap* show as cinematic learning plays is how the pursuit of this jouissance is something the individual strives for at an increasing earlier age. It is the illustration of the acceleration of cultural cycles by media and the resulting family unit breakdown.

Before the end of the sound era and the events of September 11, 2001, definitively sent the nation and its culture off in a new, previously unexplored direction, the 1990s remade the 1960s, and doing so illustrated how the balance of power both culturally and familiarly had shifted from the adult to the reign of the minor.

Psycho (1960)

Hitchcock's *Psycho* remakes the influence and mastery of Universal horror pictures for the second half of the twentieth century. The first Universal horror cycle charted the First and Second World Wars' contribution to the cinematographic medium, whereas the second wave—that of the influence of *Psycho*— envisioned technology's attack on the body, not as it was dispersed in a series of monster rallies, or *noir* descendants, but across the genre in remaking and by imitation of Hitchcock's film. In *Peeping Tom*, the camera adds a surrogacy;

in *Psycho* the camera causes the need for surrogacy, as it is that which castrates the viewer, denying the forbidden truth or reality — that is, excrement, (genital) penetration and snuff. *Peeping Tom* is about the reaction shot, whereas *Psycho* is about penetration. When coupled to machine and flesh, *Psycho*'s gruesome spectacles of murder-as-acts belie a culture-wide displacement of self. This is illustrated by what Deleuze cites in *Cinema 1: The Movement-Image* (1983) as Rohmer and Chabrol's thesis of Hitchcock's schema: "The criminal has always done his crime *for* another, the true criminal has done his crime for the innocent man who, whether we like it or not, is innocent no longer."[8] Apart from the astute Hitchcock ramifications, it is also Deleuze noting how movies instruct viewers culturally how to displace character. It is behavior often disadvantageous to the individual but desirable for those institutions that prey upon individuals like the forces of capital and media.

Psycho 1960 opens with a frenzy of gray, split lines of credits dancing to spunky, yet tense music care of Bernard Herrmann. The composer of *The Magnificent Ambersons* among many others, Herrmann's contributions to the success of the films he wrote music for cannot be over-valued, as feeling is evoked and elicited by the soundtrack, and the most totally successful movies surrogate what is absent from the pictures with sound. It is important to note how this allows a "lowbrow" genre like horror to visually take on a Warhol (and Bressonian) exploration of absence from the frame. In the media era, montage for the first time since the silent era takes precedence over sound, and in doing so remakes image as having to be actual. Ever influential, Warhol and Bresson are remade and expressed conceptually in early twenty-first-century phenomena like YouTube — which fuses Warhol's underground do-it-your-self technique and Bresson's use of "models" or nonactors and essentialization of tape recorder and camera. While as radically experimental a stylist as Warhol or Bresson, Hitchcock is easy to imitate but very difficult to actually authenticate and thusly has never visually entered English-language cinema culture deeper than multiple, some admittedly impressive, set-piece pastiches of what Deleuze terms his "weaving." Deleuze separates Hitchcock's images and his content, and this separation holds true for Van Sant, who remakes *Psycho*. "The essential point, in any event, is that action, and also perception and affection, are framed in a fabric of relations. It is this chain of relations which constitutes the mental image, in opposition to the thread of actions, perceptions and affections."[9] Hitchcock's (and Van Sant's) contribution to the cinema is the power of "chains of relations," which supersede the images, becoming images a la Duhamel's complaint to Benjamin.

Deleuze illustrates Hitchcock's influence via his theatrical concepts of story, which further point out the relative unimportance of Hitchcock's images in relation to the greater importance of weaving viewer and character relations. "What matters is not who did the action — what Hitchcock calls with contempt the *whodunit*— but neither is it the action itself: it is the set of relations in which the action and the one who did it are caught. This is the source of the very special sense of the frame. The sketches for framing, the strict delimitation of the frame, the apparent elimination of the out-of-frame, are explained by Hitchcock's constant reference, not to painting or the theater, but to tapestry-making, that is, to weaving."[10]

On the other hand, unlike Hitchcock, Herrmann is a truly influential figure like Warhol and Bresson, as Herrmann is very easy to imitate with some success. This is the result of Herrmann's purity of style, scoring being rooted closer to orchestration than composition, and because Herrmann, while immensely gifted, lay as much in Wagner's footprint as that other almost great composer, Richard Strauss. However, it cannot be denied that much English-language cinema music stems from Herrmann's work, whereas Strauss' contribution to twentieth-century opera is important but limited and easily superseded by Weill, Berg and Stockhausen.

From the music and opening credits, *Psycho* could be *North by Northwest*'s black-and-white twin. Saul Bass' skyscrapers and urban playtime have been assumed by symbolic gray — not white, it should be noted — lines representing both the skyscraper and the ledger. That it is the Jet Age, wherein global war has better informed culture and everything is a pulsing combine of assemblages, is the immediate evocation of both Hitchcock works. *North by Northwest* really is that film, whereas *Psycho* is not, but both represent, in different ways, the point of classical twentieth-century modernity — also on display in 1960's other big (but not quite as droll) summer comedy hit, *The Apartment*— about to be ruptured by the events of November 22, 1963. English-language cinema is led close to the totally pornographic by *Psycho* and *The Apartment*, however, it is the reality of *The Zapruder Film* that sets the new benchmark for spectacle and for technology interfacing with the flesh.

Like the leaves of grass on the grassy knoll, *Psycho*'s credits dissolve into a pan of Phoenix, Arizona. The rhythm of the gaze is so familiar, the viewer can almost hear the voice of the portly English director directly asking, "Who are all these dots below?" Seeking prurience on the viewer's behalf, the camera sneaks into a cheap hotel room. The cuts in Hitchcock's kino movements suggest stolen glances — a looking away, or a chance to look — as the camera moves closer and deeper into the rented bedroom space. In 1998, Van Sant's fluid CGI has none of the texture, or hesitation, in the peeping that the audience engages in with Hitchcock's 1960 movie. Hitchcock, like Ulmer in *Strange Illusion*, offers the audience a psychoanalytic dream transference with his mise-en-scéne in the opening scene. Marion (Janet Leigh) is either the woman viewers could be, or the woman viewers would like to instinctually be with. The slight discrepancy of matching shots in Hitchcock — while not as distractingly marvelous as the studio/location work of *Vertigo*— makes all of *Psycho* an uncanny, dreamy experience. Much of the 1960 movie's effects — apart from Herrmann's afore-mentioned contribution — is courtesy cinematographer John Russell. His black-and-white images remake newsreel yet also possess an artificial quality of gloss that denotes construction and fantasy.

With the first scene in the hotel room, Hitchcock ironically suggests that there is no great difference between stealing lunch hours and stealing money. Marion Crane's guilt is the same in either case, as no matter what, she persecutes herself for it as much as the coitus she evidently just enjoyed. As she says to her lover, Sam Loomis, "You make respectable sound disrespectful." The worse transgression than sex here might be taking off from her work routine, as Marion consciously recognizes that it is her numbing repetition of days that expedite her participation in culture, which results in "respectable" identity. At Marion's office, her fellow administrative assistant, Caroline (Pat Hitchcock), is zonked and pushes tranquilizers on her as a cure-all. As mentioned in Chapter 2, this prefigures the relationship to drugs in *Point Blank* and in the gangster film from that point on. *Psycho* is as much a crime movie as *The Public Enemy* or *Bad Lieutenant*, *Strange Illusion* or *A Clockwork Orange*. In all, crime is socially moti-vated from within the family unit, or from the outside the social structures they create and endorse. In the twentieth century, the pharmaceutical industry are like their nineteenth-century counterparts who sold their workers chocolate and sugar directly outside the factory, thus immediately taking back some of their workers' earnings, reducing the mode of production to slavery.

Marion's work is the only thing she can feel good about, as her life is so different from what she expected. Debord speaks for her when he writes, "The fetishism of the commodity — the domination of society by 'intangible as well as tangible things' — attains its ultimate fulfillment in the spectacle, where the real world is replaced by a selection of images which are projected above it, yet which at the same time succeed in making themselves regarded as the epitome of reality."[11] Caught up in late 1950s American culture, Marion is getting old; currently unmarried, she desires sex yet fears being promiscuous — things con-tradictory and unreconcilable. As a result, she is desperate for a happy end. "Respectable" is good capitalism where shared debt will underwrite the bond of marriage. Marion is a masochist in that her desperation is unleashed on her-self. She tells Sam, "I'll lick the stamps," with regard to his ex-wife's alimony payments and is willing to assume crime — as Deleuze explores via Hitchcock's schema with Chabrol and Rohmer's guidance. Sam himself is trying to get out of the system and — like a Philip Barry hero — understands that the rejection of the *fetishism of the commodity* erupts out of sexual pleasure. Regarding their possible marriage, Sam pleads with Marion, "If I can see you and touch you as simply as this, I won't mind" — what amounts to one-room poverty, as that is space enough for a love nest but not capital's cinematic illusions, appearances and "stuff."

Sam seeks the simplicity and purity of the real, not reel, and Hitchcock's cruel joke, best remade since in *Café Flesh* (1982), is that the viewers in the theater are denied the real, for cinemagoing is by nature irreal, an individual's filling an absence with illusion. Hitchcock understands this frustration cinema offers, and it is why the sexual sadism in his work is so resonant. Hitchcock's toying of erotic fascination and inaccessibility are the two tenets of prostitution, which is the business model for cinema. On screen, crime, these acts of commerce, are inherently alluring as they suggest and connote illicit behavior.

Hitchcock's English socialism runs amok at Universal and results in *Psycho* being marketed as "the picture you must see from beginning to end," so viewers understand that economics drive the plot of *Psycho* 1960 and that the spectacle of wet death is an illustration of capital's effect, shaped by its morality. At the conclusion of the motion picture, Norman Bates is almost absolved by *Psycho*'s screenplay when the Psychiatrist says that his were "crimes of passion, not profit." True to this hypothesis, the villain of *Psycho*, the manifestation of "Mrs. Bates," decries "cheap erotic minds," belittling the very eros that might truly liberate Norman. Free love is so powerful that it must always be devalued by capital.

Many of Marion's maladies are the result of the way women are treated poorly by men in the world of *Psycho*. In this regard, *Psycho* 1960 is one of the first movies to remake the myths of the 1950s, even taking one of its boy ingénues, Anthony Perkins, and presenting him as pervert Norman Bates. It is the type of negative depiction of the decade that starts from within in the Universal movies of Douglas Sirk and continues in the twenty-first century with TV shows like *Mad Men*. For instance, Marion has to endure that her male boss George Lowery's (Vaughn Taylor) office is air-conditioned, whereas the secretary pool is not. Marion is solicited by Lowery's associate Tom Cassidy (Frank Albertson), who believes in "buying off unhappiness" but only sees her worth as a commodity of amusement value. The morning after the theft, the Car Dealer is contemptuous to Marion, and this further results in Marion convicting herself, as when she imagines Lowery finding out about the theft on the soundtrack. Marion is so "psycho" as to actually hear voices, including Cassidy's speaking of the money and threatening, "If any of it's missing, I'll replace it with her fine soft flesh." Because Marion is always operating under the supposition of her guilt, her actions are guilty. By the time she is falling asleep at the wheel while driving to Sam in the rain on Friday night, she is at the breaking point psychologically — her theft a (final) cry for help.

Though blinded by the rain and oncoming traffic, no one ever seems to be driving in front of Marion, suggesting not only, as she herself says, that, "I knew I must have gotten off the main road," but illustrating the total isolation of self that pushes her to break. From this point on Hitchcock's *Psycho* can be understood as Marion's masochistic dream that she has while she is asleep by the roadside, or that she experiences, a la Paul Cartwright or maybe Walker, at the moment of her death, having fallen asleep at the wheel while driving. The interpretation depends on how the fadeout at the end of the night-drive sequence — mid-drive, mid–falling-asleep — is read. In her break — death or slumber — Marion's psychic reality jumps from being voices in her head to a fantasy of annihilation and then absolution by a murder more socially unacceptable than she feels herself to be.

What is apparent is that if Marion is not alive, then the remainder of *Psycho* is her nightmare of female castration where her penetration, first by her boyfriend (actual, emotional and physical), and second by Mother/Norman (metaphoric, represented by "mother's picture on the wall" and in the shower with the knife), renders her unfit or ineligible for marriage, while tauntingly, her younger sister Lila usurps her, achieving these social goals. Marion sees Norman in herself — she is the worst fugitive ever, and he too nearly gives himself away at every chance. For Marion, the car swap achieves nothing but the further loss of money, and when the Highway Patrolman (Mort Mills) suggests the motel to her, it is as if she is doomed to that brothel as he confirms her as the girl who will never marry and never get the house. Like the knife or camera, the house is another phallic substitute, but Marion Crane feels herself unfit to possess it because of her relationship with guilt, apparently fostered with her (dead) mother. Both Marion and Norman are trapped by dead mothers. Marion's mother is represented by a picture on the wall that Sam wants to turn over when they make love. Norman has dug up his mother's body, preserved it, and has it in his/her house.

The irrefutable evidence is that Marion is a "fast girl" — Friday afternoon during their almost-spat, Marion toys with the idea of leaving Sam if he does not make an honest woman out of her, and by Saturday night she is already out on an intimate dinner date with Norman Bates. From the minute he invites her with, "You're not really going to go out and drive up to the diner, are you? ... Well then, would you do me a favor and have dinner with me?" it is apparent that Norman is the only man Marion has met so far that she is able to dominate. As she can sexually entice anyone she wants, Norman is something of a pity/ mercy fuck for Marion. In a world of dominant men, Marion's subconscious dream has created an individual to whom she clearly has the upper hand. Marion dreams Norman because he is, within *Psycho*'s universe, the only figure imaginable more uptight than she — after all, Marion can say "bathroom," whereas Norman cannot, and Marion gets to fuck, whereas in Robert Bloch's source novel, as well as suggested by Hitchcock's movie, Norman is impotent.

In a relationship echoed in the dream reading of *Psycho*, Norman is Marion's psychological whipping boy, as Marion's conception of Norman's relationship with his mother (when and if she was alive) is only a slight grotesque of her own maternal relation. Klein underlines Marion's projection and representation in *Notes on Some Schizoid Mechanisms*. "Another typical feature of schizoid object relations is their narcissistic nature which derives from the infantile introjective and projective processes.... When the ego ideal is projected into another person, this person becomes predominantly loved and admired because he contains the good parts of the self. Similarly, the relation to another person on the basis of projecting bad parts of the self into him is of a narcissistic nature, because in this case as well the object strongly represents one part of the self."[12] Marion, the masochist-narcissist, sees Sam as the good ideal and creates Norman to project all the bad parts of herself onto.

When she is murdered by Norman, Marion removes herself from her own dream because of her anxiety at nonconformity. Seeking the stolen money, the private investigator Abogast (Martin Balsam) is searching for Marion. Tellingly, the montage of hotel and motel keepers he speaks to are all female, denoting the oddness of Norman's situation and how in *Psycho* mothers are iluminated like a "No Vacancy" sign. If Marion had been awake or alive and had gone to a real hotel or motel — one not of her imagination — Hitchcock reminds viewers that there would have been a female innkeeper. This is complemented in how Norman cannot let his mother die, because he'd have no oppressor, and in how Marion cannot absolve herself because of preexisting material guilt. Obviously perfect for each other in terms of romantic comedy, Hitchcock eschews a Marion-Norman love match, and makes Marion's murder one of many, as at the end of *Psycho* viewers are led to believe that there are at least two other missing girls at the bottom of the swamp who met their deaths at the hands of Norman Bates.

As early as in her afternoon tryst in the hotel room with Sam, Marion is aware of a manifesting psychological illness within her mind — as perhaps something overcoming herself. With her erratic action — that is, the theft — the voices in her mind increase to a nearly schizophrenic level. Perhaps she, not Norman, is the titular character, or more possibly, they are the same character with the same mother, split like the twins in *The Parent Trap* or brother and sister Michael Meyers and Laurie Strode in some of the *Halloween* sequels, and the remakes and their sequels. The fear of madness in Marion is symbolized by how Norman can't say "bathroom," yet calls foul when Marion utters the euphemism "someplace" (i.e., "put her someplace") for an institution for his problematic mother. Marion's fear of her anxieties getting the best of her — which would ostensibly make her Norman — or of having to suppress anxieties like Caroline in the office with the use of drugs, informs her nightmare with its suicidal, self-annihilative bent, as anything is better than that terrible "someplace."

Already noted, the influence of *Psycho* was a pebble thrown into the horror genre's melting pot — one that rippled outward in influence, finally ending what could be looked upon as the classical era of so-called slasher films with the release of *Scream* (1996) and *The Blair Witch Project* (1999). Those movies again chart cinema's remaking as media: in the first one, the characters act like they are in a horror movie — they have become Marion and Norman — or in the latter, the viewer's surrogate seeks to create the motion picture that will further remove the individual from him- or herself. As discussed in Chapter 5, and earlier in this chapter with regard to Deleuze, Warhol's contribution to the cinema was the removal of vitality from the frame. *The Blair Witch Project* is the perfect example of *underground* having become *indie*, as it is the commodification of the progressive evolution of cinema wherein the audience is left literally in the dark for minutes on end and the soundtrack (the voice of the *mOther*) rules. A reading of *Psycho* as Marion's dream leads to a reading of *The Blair Witch Project* as its protagonist's, Heather's, dream — a dream which expounds on *Psycho's* dichotomy of gender and cinema. In "Spelling It Out," published in the *Village Voice* in August 1999, Amy Taubin perceptively does just that:

> *The Blair Witch Project* blends the timeless terror about the evil that lurks in the woods at night with current fantasies about instant indie success and current confusions about cinematic fact and fiction.... *Blair Witch* is a cautionary tale about

Heather Donahue as "Heather Donahue" in *The Blair Witch Project* (Daniel Myrick, Eduardo Sánchez, 1999). The movie is the perfect example of the underground having become "indie" as it is the commodification of the progressive evolution of cinema wherein the audience is left literally in the dark for minutes on end and the soundtrack (the voice of the mOther) rules. (Courtesy Andrew's Video Vault at the Rotunda.)

what happens when a woman directs a movie. That the film is set in rugged terrain and involves much fiddling with compasses and maps suggests a parallel between moviemaking and war and calls up the commonplace analogy between directors and generals. Heather, the director of the aborted "Blair Witch project," fails in her primary responsibility — to bring her boys home safely. An overreacher who gets her comeuppance, Heather spends the last third of the film crying and apologizing for having fucked up. To add insult to injury, it is not Heather's film that is currently breaking box office records at the Angelika. The fame and glory belong to Daniel Myrick and Eduardo Sánchez, the filmmakers who packaged her raw footage into a commercial product. No matter that Heather is a fictional character and Myrick and Sánchez are indisputably the real deal. The blurring of boundaries is the essence of the *Blair Witch* experience ... an allegory for the indie boys club: if a woman dares to enter, she dies.[13]

Marion has entered the boys club of sexual promiscuity in *Psycho*, and in her dream, the viewer is titillated and revolted at the same time in equal measure. *Psycho* 1960 was released into a culture *ashamed* of movies such as *Psycho*, whereas *Psycho* 1998 is created by a culture who thinks nothing of *Psycho* 1960's near pornography and thus celebrates it, remaking it in living color.

Mark Lewis might have liked *Psycho* 1960. Perhaps the illustration of his fantasy might have freed him of the compulsion to murder. Or — who knows? — it might have just exacerbated his lust for blood. *Psycho* is an Oedipal myth like *The Magnificent Ambersons*, and the inside of the Bates house recalls the eerie Amberson mansion. Welles himself remakes Norman Bates, as that remake of Bartleby, Joseph K in *The Trial* (1962), by casting Anthony Perkins in the role. The Welles reading of *Psycho* is indicative of Norman/Joseph experiencing a type of Hamletian paralysis; that is — like Walker in *Point Blank*— he is Oedipus remade wherein the offstage Sophoclesian carnage becomes the drama. Just as in the Middle Ages becoming the Renaissance, and like sound cinema becoming media, the reality of *The Zapruder Film*— that is, penetration — is the reality that would have been reported in Classical Greek theater by a messenger.

Marion smirks at Norman's retreat into the parlor of the motel's office after he has been humiliated out of his mother's house. "Eating in an office is just too officious," Norman says, and here, his turn of phrase is similar to Joseph's use of the word "ovalular" in *The Trial*, which makes him further suspect to the persecuting detectives. Marion's self-hatred is such that she will never find herself less than suspect, and so her phantastic undoing in the shower is a sort of self-deliverance. *Psycho* is a road movie, one that prefigures *Crash* in spirit and perverse tone. *Psycho* ends with the image of the car and the swamp, and the abrupt finish is like being suddenly woken from an engaging dream. Perhaps *Psycho*'s linking of sexuality and death is too much, but there is deliverance there too. In *Psycho*, body and object have been made one by murder couched in technological advance. The fact that it may all be just a dream suggests death as being the only escape from the modern age.

Janet Leigh in the shower scene in the 1960 Alfred Hitchcock version of *Psycho*. (Courtesy the Chestnut Hill Film Group.)

Psycho (1998)

Psycho 1998 is an odd movie — that it was made seems not so much improbable as inevitable — but that it was executed as a (somewhat) shot-by-shot remake is uncanny. Usually with remakes, there is the drive to literally remake, and recreate, whereas this remaking is largely transcription, which denies the action that is part of the pattern of twentieth-century cinematic redaction.

Van Sant liberates the second unit director with his work on *Psycho* 1998. The second unit director orchestrates what are usually establishing shots but can also include stunts or action. It is an important gesture on Van Sant's part, as removing the director visually illustrates how many people it takes to make a movie and points to those peripheral credits beneath the top five or ten, which are often overlooked by the casual viewer. At its best, Van Sant's *Psycho* 1998 proposes a socialistic cinema ensemble, where each individual does his and/or her part, and the true authority is the community of artisans — or the unseen yet oppressive father — a sort of modern-day Shakespearean original practice.

Van Sant is also like photographer Cindy Sherman, whose "Untitled Film Stills" represented an individual actually physically remaking herself into movie myths. Like a novelist who types out extended passages from great books in order to get his or her hands familiar with connecting words skillfully, a filmmaker may apply the same technique and reshoot a preexisting shot list. However in Van Sant's case, the evidence suggests that his methods are closer to Warhol's appropriating a black-and-white photograph for the basis of a silk screen. As with Warhol, the sensation of the canvas is not just its images, but

Anne Heche in the shower scene in the 1998 Gus Van Sant version of *Psycho*. (Photofest.)

the textures, and often the way color is added. Hitchcock's black and white is hypnotic; Van Sant's color is garish. In 1960, cinematographer Russell was *Psycho*'s star; in 1998 the movie belongs to costume designer Beatrix Aruna Pasztor.

Marion's much-seen slip is green in 1998 — what was once voyeuristic is now performative and visually coded. The point of *Psycho* 1960 was that it looked so normal and unremarkable at first, and this effect was achieved with Russell's journalist-like camera work. Much has been made of Hitchcock working with a "TV crew" to capture the 1960 movie, and this reflects back to the thesis of media assuming the sound era of cinema by means of television and televised reality. In 1998, the movie is a spectacle of Christopher Doyle's post-pop photography. At the start of *Psycho*, the Imagine Entertainment logo is remade in blood red. Tellingly to his importance, Herrmann's music is the same. Shocking green opens the movie in 1998 rather than the gray of 1960. The green is literally money, as money, not blood, drives the *Psycho* movies. Green is also the color of envy, and it is Marion's desire for things outside her current reach that fosters her guilt, which manifests as something her subconscious needs to dominate as a cultural survival technique.

In 1998, or as the inter-title informs, Friday, December 14, 1998, the lover's tiff is far less serious. Marion is in the same type of underwear as she was in

1960, but Sam is remade nude. Anne Heche's performance as Marion is Edie Sedgwick–like; she is more herself than the role, yet the naturalism at her being "her kooky self" compensates. Heche is not acting. Her performance is ironic, mugging, winking — so 1990s — ditzy where Leigh is cagey. Unlike Jamie Leigh Curtis' mother, Heche is skeletal like Norman's mom. Heche's presence in the 1998 movie derails almost everything else that is going on, just like when Warhol threw Sedgwick into *Vinyl*'s boy club at the last minute. As a thespian, Heche leaves no room for anything other than her action. Tonally, her added parasol completes her remake as a type of parodic Tennessee Williams character — not a 1950s good girl turned bad by desire for sex and lack of money.

As Caroline, Marion's fellow office assistant, Rita Wilson is cunty, whereas Pat Hitchcock interpreted the role as something close to a Shakespearean fool. Obviously this cinematic remaking is not cultural progress — as when Daisy became Chris in *One More Tomorrow*— but an indication of a sicker society where ignorance has become disgruntled in addition to unwise. Vince Vaughn's portrayal of Norman diminishes the character's universal, frightening nature. Confessing his anxiety about his mother to Marion in 1998, Vaughn's Norman fantasizes about the desire to "curse her out," whereas in 1960, Perkins sought to "curse her forever." Because of her distanced performance, there is a lack of empathy for Heche's Marion. Her intention to return to Phoenix with the stolen money is meaningless, and she is prey from the moment she meets Vaughn's Norman, if not before. Van Sant's new shower curtain, unlike the one in 1960, refracts prisms of light and cuts Heche's Marion before "Mother's knife." To illustrate how unimportant the performances are, Van Sant brings in music underneath Norman's "madhouse" freak-out in the motel office parlor with Marion, as Warhol often put the radio on in the background of his sync-sound movies.

William H. Macy's Arbogast still comes bearing the bait of family — telling Norman that the "family wants to forgive her" when he's looking for Marion — but as in 1960, this only serves to escalate Norman's patterns. Norman starts to remake himself faster and faster, dressing up as Mother in greater and greater haste. He seeks to recreate the castrating influence he needs for meaning because he is so dissimilar to the world. Van Sant remakes the murder inserts of *Cruising* (1980) in the 1998 shower scene with a storm, and at Arbogast's death with sheep and nude model interjected — even more oblique than the white horse in *Twin Peaks: Fire Walk with Me*. Yet at the end of the 1998 movie, Van Sant deletes the suggestion of the other missing young women being at the bottom of the Bates swamp. The last shot of *Psycho* 1998 starts the same, with the car being tugged out of the mire, but the shot continues when Hitchcock's would have ended, and, Warhol-like, Van Sant's camera rolls on, disinterestedly surveying a landscape of workers dredging the swamp behind the Bates Motel. *Psycho* 1998 redoubles 1983's *Psycho II*'s dedication to Hitchcock at the end credits, but a more honest nod to the "Master of Suspense" is when Van Sant cameos outside Tom's office in the act of being chewed out by a Hitchcock double.

The Parent Trap (1961)

The Parent Trap 1961 opens on a stage, representative of the synonymous nature of theater and cinema in the twentieth century. As the orchestra plays and the curtain rises, there is thunder and lightning and a cross-stitch inscribed with "Bless Our Broken Home." Tears drip off of "Walt Disney presents," and the movie delivers its message of "kids knowing better" by presenting a world that parents have ruined. In a link to Marx as being Disney's antithesis — one that Godard often references — "Uncle" Walt understands from years in the movie business that postwar, post–Depression children have the power to drive the economics of a family's buying, as children consuming enables manic reparations on the part of the parent, and that the child — thanks to himself and others — increasingly feels justified in his or her sense of entitlement.

Disney's masterful genius, apart from branding, was largely the contributions of other highly talented individuals. For example in *The Parent Trap* 1961, the cinematographer was Lucien Ballard of *Blind Alley*, *Murder by Contract* (1958), *The Wild Bunch* (1969), *Mikey and Nicky* (1976), etc., and the special photographic effects (i.e., the twinning of Hayley Mills) were by Ub Iwerks. Together L. Ballard and Iwerks present a fantasy of wish fulfillment realistically, still credible with the ensuing media era's CGI. Collaboration, the *as if* of "together we could solve anything," radiates from the Disney studio's movies, and largely this message has been the secret of their success and popularity — a myth anyone could buy into.

The other first-reel tip-off for children that *The Parent Trap* 1961 represents "for them" is established very early in the Camp Inch sequence, when the film lobbies for candy, as candy is cool. The thirteen-year-old twins Sharon and Susan, who have no idea of the other's existence, meet at camp and are dead ringers. Like many Americans, rather than examining their differences, their respective friends immediately goad them to violence toward each other. Trading insults, Susan says Sharon's profile is the "spitting image of Frankenstein." It is interesting that her allusion is to *Frankenstein* rather than *Psycho* because it is something more than an indication of the movie being directed to children too young to have seen Norman Bates in 1960. It is also *The Parent Trap* attaching itself to mythic greatness, citing Frankenstein and his monster, so as to inform even the youngest viewers of the archetypical-iconic nature of the drama unfolding before them. Sharon later embellishes Susan's *Frankenstein* references — that of the (solo) parent and child — with her interpretation of their parent's split in terms of the equally iconic *Pelléas and Mélisande* and *Daphnis and Chloe*. It is, as she says, "how true love creates its myth of agony." Sharon, the better schooled of the twins, understands the commodification of relationships and that relationships need an imposed arc to better lay the foundations for a sturdy false reality like marriage or "happily ever after." Also being an avid consumer, due to her mother's family's money, Sharon sees how to remake her parents' breakup and present it in a way that is a product and desired commodity to her twin and their parents. After all, Sharon knows her mother can afford summer camp; therefore she knows her agency as an economic decider.

Camp dances shape the girls' idea of romance and reconciliation. The cheap sentiments expressed and invoked by these rituals — virtually remade shot by shot by Kubrick in *Lolita* (1962) — awaken the children to the value of symbolic actions. Cinema has already made them aware of the symbolic meanings of action — for instance, Susan "feels naked without lipstick" — but pop culture has cemented these events as having greater cultural meaning, that of personal identity and a deserved rite of passage; the *fetishism of the commodity* that Debord writes on as quoted earlier in this chapter. Susan-posing-as-Sharon gives her Grandmother the metaphoric popsicle-stick birdcage, wryly alluding to her impression of what a stay at her Grandmother's house will be like. Susan is a bad criminal like Marion, but her mother, Margaret (Maureen O'Hara), is too busy to talk to her daughter until Susan invents the narrative of a boy. This lie illustrates

Una Merkel as Verbena and Hayley Mills as Susan Evers, pretending to be Sharon McKendrick, in *The Parent Trap* (David Swift, 1961). Verbena is part of the family not out of affection but duty and vocation, joining a long line of servants more clever than their masters, but also illustrating a disturbing portrait of latchkey kids and children raised by surrogates. (Courtesy the Chestnut Hill Film Group.)

Margaret as malleable to her daughter when myth is evoked, and symbolizes to the viewer that parents can easily be manipulated by kids, as they are made oblivious to their children by their own scheming. As early as the 1960s, it was apparent that the post-war American climate resulted in a domination of adults who were emotionally still arrested adolescents themselves. True adulthood is not represented in *The Parent Trap*, as it has largely been removed from cinema by 1961. The parents that viewers meet are easily subverted, and perhaps a confirmation to adults of their own parental fears, anxieties and guilt.

The best adult in *The Parent Trap* 1961, if the viewer discounts Margaret's mother and father (who despite stability do seem to be locked in some Strindbergian tempest), is Verbena (Una Merkel), the housekeeper of the twins' father, Mitch (Brian Keith). Verbena comes from a long line of servants more clever than their masters, but also illustrates a disturbing portrait of latchkey kids and children raised by surrogates. Parents are aware that this abandonment of their children is counterintuitive to raising a balanced child and therefore engage in manic reparations to compensate for what they cannot deny themselves. This is compounded with the faulty ideology of servants selling their affections in addition to their service — a cultural myth that further rationalizes the twentieth century's separation of parent and child among other things.

To the truly adult viewer, Mitch and Margaret's romance seemed worth abandoning before they split up, as they both admit a history of domestic violence. Margaret apparently hit Mitch several times, and within hours of their reunion, he again has a black eye at her hands. Comparatively, Mitch's new girlfriend, Vicky (Joanna Barnes), seems like an improvement. She speaks to Sharon of that "wonderful, delicate mystery that happens between a man and a woman sometimes," and yet the twins do not really consider her potential, as they do not like her simply because she is not their biological mother. Vicky's other great crime in *The Parent Trap* 1961 is not being rich, and therefore that makes her motives inherently suspect. Vicky, like Marion, is a message if not warning to children, especially to young girls, not to be poor. It is unfair because Sharon, Susan or Margaret do not have to sell themselves because of their inherited family wealth, so they can afford to remain virginal, whereas Vicky must apparently use her physical assets, having no other. Sharon and Susan's rich grandfather echoes George's rich grandfather in *The Magnificent Ambersons*. Margaret's willingness to play along with the girls, and Mitch's drinking, betray their generation as more interested in consuming than conserving, illustrating the removal in thinking that the post-literate demands.

Demonstrating how much the twins believe that myth can shape destiny, they sing "Let's Get Together" to their parents, hoping the song will send a subliminal message. Myth is encoded in performance and here "entertainment" has been reshaped to mirror cinema's Pirandello-like subversion of the individual. *The Parent Trap* is myth, and so it removes children from the reality of adult relationships, telling them what not to expect, and instilling a faulty logic of enactment and entitlement.

Like Paul Cartwright in *Strange Illusion*, the success of the twins' plan manifests in a euphoric dream at the movie's end. In California, the twins are in bed together, and one wakes the other, saying, "I've had the craziest dream." Whereas Paul is too unusual and does not fit in, the twins seek conformity with society and therefore can wake up from the dream. The twin's dream is the wedding remarriage of her and her sister's parents, and viewers know it is a fantasy because their Grandmother looks so happy — something she has not been anywhere else in the movie, especially when concerned with her daughter and Mitch. That it is the middle of the night makes the twin's awakening perhaps simultaneous to Margaret and Mitch's lovemaking in the next room. Margaret's potential orgasm — like Virginie's actual orgasm in *The Immortal Story*— is a triumphant psychic rupture outward into the psychic universe. To the careful viewer, however, this dream undermines the fantasy and points to the unreality at work.

The Parent Trap (1998)

The Parent Trap 1998 opens aboard the *QE2* in the very past which the twins in the 1961 film devote great effort to climactically recreate. It is now 1986, and Margaret has been remade as Elizabeth James (Natasha Richardson) and Mitch as Nick Parker (Dennis Quaid). The silky images in *The Parent Trap* 1998 are from Dean Cundey, who shot that other spiritual remake-child of *Psycho*, *Halloween*, and in *The Parent Trap* 1998 uses his knowledge of the horror genre to inform the comedy. Fireworks and wine sell the romance to the viewer in shorthand aboard the *QE2* without providing any true reality. "The Way You Look Tonight" plays, replacing "Let's Get Together," for here — as in the *Psycho* remake — action (1960s) has been reduced to sensation (1990s).

Eleven years, nine months later, viewers meet the twins. Camp Walden in 1998 is as frantic as Camp Inch — the retinue of the campers is piled up like the Nazi-confiscated luggage in *Schindler's List* (1993). However, in 1998, authority is ineffectual and naïve illustrating more evidence of stunted adults. The children are all clearly copies of adults, a sort of preformed mini-consumer poised at the point — synonymous with puberty — of getting a first credit card.

Father Mitch's ranch gives way to Nick's Napa vines as Sharon is renamed Hallie Parker and Susan is rechristened Annie, her new London home finally accounting for Hayley Mills' English accent. Verbena is echoed in Chessy (Lisa Ann Walter), but initially in the more alarming new character of Martin (Simon Kunz). He is Elizabeth's butler, of questionable sexual orientation, and because he hugs Annie and shares a somewhat surreal secret handshake with her, it is okay for him to be at work twenty-four hours a day, seven days a week. Taking

Lisa Ann Walter as Chessy (Verbena's remake) with Lindsay Lohan as Annie James pretending to be her twin, Hallie Parker, in the 1998 Nancy Meyers remake of *The Parent Trap*. (Jerry Ohlinger's Movie Material Store.)

Thamal in *The Black Cat* past *The Maids* by Genet to the next level of outrageousness, Elizabeth tells her servant, Martin, that he is really her dear (and sexually emasculated) friend — "Martin, you know that you're more than a butler. You're more like a lovable brother who just happens to wait on us." Paid relations are now more certain than unpaid ones, and Martin is indicative of how freelance workers begin to predominate the late 1990s workforce. Martin's dropping Annie off at camp is not unlike Tom and Regan's goodbye in *One More Tomorrow* dipped in the murky pool that hosts *Reflections in a Golden Eye*

(1967). If *The Parent Trap* 1961 is wish fulfillment, the 1998 remake is about fantasy—as in the 1990s, things are far more surreal, like the twins' fencing duel, and the near constant music on the soundtrack that makes the picture nearly (soap) operatic.

The Oedipal rewriting of *The Parent Trap* 1998 is certainly grander than most Hollywood movies. Hallie comments of her father, "He's like my best friend, we do everything together," and later adds, "Dad always says I'm the only girl in his life." The knowingness in Lindsay Lohan's eyes in the delivery of this line is beyond chilling. *The Parent Trap* remake underlines some English-U.S. tensions, while the night raid of Annie's cabin by Hallie is a sort of *Carrie* (1976) redux, doubled into masochism like that other great De Palma sibling movie, *Sisters* (1973)—which is of course a pastiche of *Psycho* and *The Parent Trap* along the lines of *Whatever Happened to Baby Jane?* (1962). The ripped family picture in *The Parent Trap* 1998 invokes De Palma's sisters, as does Hallie uttering, "I'm not an only child, I'm a twin," and citing her doubled agency. Moments like Hallie's haircut of Annie, or the truly shocking ear-piercing scene—resulting in the twins' duel scream at penetration—are as pornographic as anything in *Psycho* 1960. Just as Hollywood sex rarely carries with it the risk of venereal desire, so this ear piecing is without infection.

Like Dr. Frankenstein, children seem close to controlling their parents' breeding habits because they have so much buying power. Further evidence is given to Hallie regarding the malleability of all things by her mother designing wedding gowns—helping to create and sell the wedding dream which *The Parent Trap*s are so clearly about. Elizabeth both constructs and lives the fantasy. In the photo shoot sequence, which replaces 1961's trip to Boston Park, Elizabeth has to jump in and direct, causing Hallie to remark, "My mom is too cool." As Elizabeth, Natasha Richardson remakes her mother Vanessa Redgrave in *Blow-Up*, and the generational difference is as pronounced as Edina and Saffy on *Absolutely Fabulous* (1992–on). However, none of Redgrave's carnal exuberance is traced in Richardson's sophisticated blandness.

The photo shoot makes *The Parent Trap* 1998 a movie-movie (and in Deleuze's stance a film about money), wherein the process is revealed, but the message—now self-conscious as the sound era turns to media—remains the same. It is the Hollywood-perpetuated dream of knowing exactly where you are in relation to the world via objects that confirm status. Little girls must also see here in the photo shoot sequence the covenant offered them—that on their wedding day they will be confirmed as star. At the climax of the photo shoot, Hallie herself tries on a veil, and rather than boy talk with her mother as in 1961, Hallie's F-word is "father."

Certainly, however, Elizabeth must be a better mother than Margaret with her stuffy "Red Cross meetings" and own dragon mother played like a witch from Disney's *Snow White* (1937). Nick seems improved too, for in 1998 there is no clear reason for the breakup, and when reunited the whole event is quite civilized. Gone is the domestic violence, and the couple's alcoholism has receded under the veneer of Nick's winery — his profit-producing business.

Better schooled — as Sharon was in 1961— Annie gives her father a speech in the car upon her arrival, saying, "A dad is an irreplaceable person in a girl's life." For a moment, *The Parent Trap* 1998 explores the fantasy of the missing father wherein the absent parent is hyper-exoticized, and like so much good filmmaking prototyped by Warhol, it explores what is absent from the frame. Annie is Norman-like in her fascination with Nick, and she herself says, "A baby's first words are 'Dad,' aren't they?"

Cinema is so ingrained into the lives of *The Parent Trap* 1998 that Annie gets a first look at the new Vicky, Meredith Blake, from a camera resting portentously on a bed. Twin Annie remarks, "Twenty-six, only fifteen years older than me." Meredith is a publicist for Nick's vineyard, better at "selling herself, rather than the grapes." The character's mother now makes an appearance and is played by Joanna Barnes from the 1961 movie, recreating her role as Vicky — appearing, as a character, to have done well for herself after Mitch. Here in 1998, Meyer's direction achieves a defanged Sirkian grace — one that is regretfully mostly subverted in her incarnation of the story.

In 1998, Meredith is more clearly a villain than Vicky was, as the social forces which drove the former prospective Wife No. 2 to Wharton-like exploits are absent, and in its place Meredith is somewhat malicious by nature. Echoing Vicky 1961, she says, "First change I make is to send that two-faced little brat off to boarding school in Timbuktu," and it is ironic because the indication in 1998 is that the twins may be closer to turning into Vicky/Meredith than they would like to think. Class and wealth kept the twins and Vicky from any confusion in 1961, but in 1998, Meredith is a far less ambivalent figure than Vicky was. *One More Tomorrow*'s remaking of *The Animal Kingdom*'s Cecelia holds an affinity with Vicky's reconception in *The Parent Trap* 1998 — when she is called an "Ice Woman," Meredith snaps back, like Cecelia, "Proud of it." The twins even have a shorthand nickname for Meredith, "Cruella," regurgitated from the Disney canon.

At the inspired height of Meyer's directorial wit, she has Meredith desire an Elizabeth James wedding gown, not knowing that the object of her admiration is also her romantic rival. When Meredith meets a drunk Elizabeth in the hotel bar steeling her nerves for a reunion with Nick, it invokes Ionesco's sense of absurd farce by way of Sartre's *No Exit*.

On the night of the twins' remaking the "that night" of their parents' first meeting, it is revealed that the servants Chessy and Martin were on the *QE2* in 1986 as well and may have the embers of romance smoldering between them. The camera so captures the fantasy of wealth — the one the twins' Grandfather chipped in to underwrite — that *The Parent Trap* 1998, in its final reel, has the old-time cinematic illusion of the city as existing only for the protagonist and viewer. *The Parent Trap* here remakes its own myth and further offers its message of recreating one's identity and family via consumerism best directed by children.

In 1998, Nick and Elizabeth talk about what went wrong and seem far more communicative than their 1961 counterparts. However, the fact of the initial separation remains. As with Vicky in 1961, Meredith pulls a "me or them" moment with Nick, and he sends her packing. Though Nick may be angry with the twins for their "parent trap," he must "remember to thank them one day." Again climactically, it is confirmed to viewers (i.e., children) that it is the twins — the children — who hold the power.

At the finale, the twins see their parents as lovers and, free from any sexual longing, announce, "We actually did it." It is the inverse of *Easy Rider* and that generation's announcement of "We blew it." However, in *Easy Rider*, the late 1960s sought to break free of the family but lost the chance at social evolution in a flurry of hard drugs and rock music. This leaves only the representation of the actual in *The Parent Trap* 1998 with no greater society possible — and so for Nick and Liz, born in 1960, "their song" is their mindset: "This Will Be (An Everlasting Love)" — when really they stand on the precipice of the huge social changes of the media era and the "everlasting" corroding and undone by the sound era's own destructive fantasies.

CHAPTER 7

Chapter Six, Part 2!

Remaking Hollywood with Forced Entry *(1973 and 1981),* Despair *(1978) and* Raiders of the Lost Ark: The Adaptation *(1989)*

Advances in technology in the service of warfare created smaller cameras for newsreel footage. It resulted in the coverage of the U.S. conflict with Vietnam bringing a startling new level of violence into people's collective consciousness through both cinema and media, specifically television. The studio system withered in the mid–1960s, and the production code was successfully challenged because Hollywood product seemed increasingly coy in its imitation of life. A high point in the drive toward progressive modernism, the force of this mod movement was ultimately and unfortunately dismantled by the use of nostalgia from within the culture industry. It once again made the counterculture Other — first by commodification and then by absorption. Yet by the late twentieth century, Hollywood's models again became more accepted than the reality it imitated, and so behavior in the United States returned to being primarily learned from and dictated by American movies. The phenomenon of movies-about-movies increased, as did those movies that directly mimicked cinema itself, rather than the individual, or drama from the stage.

The 1973 triple "X" hard-core horror porn movie *Forced Entry*, written and directed by Shaun Costello under the pseudonym of "Helmuth Richler," and remade as an even more transgressive "R-rated" movie in 1981 by Jim Sotos, is a product of this transitioning culture and an example of its fears. Costello's movie is a chronicle of latent and actualized violence, depicted in a cinéma vérité style that is the opposite of classic Hollywood product and yet links the facade of Sirk to the gloss of Steven Spielberg. The first of its kind, *Forced Entry* 1973 creates an audience — just as Spielberg largely creates the "blockbuster" genre — being both realistically sexual and realistically violent, and by daring to present people only defined in terms of violence. *Forced Entry* 1973 literally remakes old cinema with its use of newsreel, taking the conditioning of Alex in *A Clockwork Orange* one step further. The 1978 film *Despair* directed by Rainer Werner Fassbinder and *Raiders of the Lost Ark* directed by Spielberg in 1981 both remake themselves out of Hollywood iconography of the 1930s and 1940s, eschewing the reality of documentary-style filmmaking in favor of deliberate artificial realities. In *Despair*, protagonist Herman Herman's desire to change who he is, is self-remaking informed by what he has seen at the movies and can imitate. Cinema production subsequently becomes the medium through which he is able to understand his schizophrenia. Spielberg's motion picture takes the formula of serial cliffhangers and the logic of comic books and remakes them into a two-hour thrill ride — all set pieces and climaxes with little introspection — one of his early triumphs of sensation over substance before deeply maturing as a film director.

What links *Despair* and *Raiders of the Lost Ark* 1981 is their cynicism and bitter sarcasm — a holdover from the Vietnam experience and the resonating sourness from Nixon's betrayal of his office. *Raiders of the Lost Ark* 1981 represents the last publically profitable outing of this knowing irony with its final shots of the Ark of the Covenant being warehoused. By the arrival of *Indiana Jones and The Temple of Doom* in 1984, cynicism has been replaced with callousness and attention to surface detail wherein the individual is removed from the equation for the advancement and perpetuation of sales.

By the time of *Raiders of the Lost Ark: The Adaptation*, a near-scene-for-scene remake of the 1981 movie performed and shot by young teenagers over seven years, directed by Eric Zala and completed in 1989, Spielberg's glossiness is removed, and the children illustrate their desire to enter into the movie world which they feel actually represents adulthood. *Raiders of the Lost Ark: The Adaptation* is therefore the totally successful version of *Psycho* 1998, wherein fetishized remaking liberates its participants in a fulfillment of Warhol's underground cinema, which is conversely finally brought into the mainstream with Zala's remaking. *Raiders of the Lost Ark: The Adaptation* is the actualization of individuals imitating what they see on screen, whereas the Van Sant movie is a hermetic harbinger of the individual's removal. *Raiders of the Lost Ark: The Adaptation* returns joy to something cynical, whereas *Psycho* 1998, like *Forced Entry* 1981, removes raw emotion and replaces it with something contrived for the audience and for consumption.

Forced Entry (1973 and 1981)

The two versions of *Forced Entry*— the "triple-X" original and the "R-rated" remake from 1981— are not pornological literature in the Deleuzian sense, as explored vis-à-vis *Vinyl* and *A Clockwork Orange*, because they can only be reduced into elementary functions, whereas Warhol and Kubrick's movies cannot. As with the two movies discussed in Chapter 5, there is the cultural value of pornography that is asserted and attached to the two versions of *Forced Entry*. This allows a Shakespearean remaking of the individual in relation to themselves, but here, unlike the Burgess adaptations, it does not remove the individual while representing the individual, but offers a direct and perverse surrogacy.

Forced Entry 1973 opens with a July 22, 1972, newspaper article accompanied by the sounds of guns and combat. The text — appearing on screen in a newspaper — reads,

> VIETNAM VET: Some, who had once been under heavy fire in Vietnam are still looking around trying to find "hostiles," the enemy. It is part of what has been called the post–Vietnam syndrome. And, one can understand their problems and the complexity of their confusion.
> Then there are those who have been affected by narcotics, The...

The 1973 movie takes the real situation of damaged soldiers returning home from Vietnam and immediately links it with journalism and the sensation of newsreel. The chanting of natives overwhelms the soundtrack of warfare, and another super-imposition is presented, reading,

> This is the legacy that veterans bring back, a combination of fear, confusion, rage and frustration, and this leads to a desperate need for an enemy....— Dr. Robert Liffon, Air Force Psychiatrist, Winner Nat. Book Award

The two clips of text are as sympathetic as the movie gets and present the information which allows viewers to assume that the gas station attendant who rapes and murders in *Forced Entry* 1973 is one of the vets seeking "hostiles" on the home front and that the intercut newsreel footage of Vietnam represents his flashbacks and sense memories. Sirens and flashing lights bring the viewer to a crime scene, where the visual clues are presented in engaging fragments. As in the movies of Chapter 1, the body and cameras are linked, and unlike the crime movies of Chapter 2 there is no direct link to the financial, other than the (unexplored) impetus for the Vietnam conflict itself. The opening's original (i.e., created, not found) images reveal more information — a man, later understood to be a veteran, lies dead on the floor with unseeing eyes and is being photographed by a man whose eyes are obscured by his camera. The main title card appears over the Vet's gaping brain wound caused by a bullet to the head. Pornography's desire to see inside the body is here given another orifice to explore and suggests *Forced Entry* 1973 as a death dream, like *Citizen Kane* or

Strange Illusion, and links it to the pornography of *Crash* (1996) which sought new orifices.

One of the first images after the opening credits of *Forced Entry* 1973 is another form of penetration — where a Woman (Jutta David) inserts a key into her car door lock — linking to automobiles and urban paranoia. Remaking Divine in *Mondo Trasho* (1969), the unnamed Woman drives into Manhattan — post–Vietnam, pre–9/11. Her hand is shown shifting gears, and the link to performing a hand job is as explicit as the oft-written-about joystick sequence in *Georges Bataille's Story of the Eye* (2003). The Woman stops at "Joe's Friendly Service" in West Greenwich Village where she meets the War Veteran / gas station attendant (first glimpsed by the audience in the opening credit sequence) who will rape and murder her later that day. Explaining that he doesn't like to have too much cash on hand, the Vet asks for payment via the Woman's credit card. The modern-day fear of identity theft and lack of privacy is here illustrated to have evolved out of the automotive oil industries, where early twentieth-century changes in technology altered patterns of movement and thus made credit cards more desirable. The Woman shows the gas station attendant her ID — perhaps the actor's actual ID card — as she does not speak her character's personal information out loud, and so penetrates, if not breaks, the movie's fourth wall with her apparent inability to ad-lib dialogue or act "in character." The fact that her discretion in answering the Vet's personal questions of address seem more for the camera than anything else tangibly dramatic makes the viewer of the movie that much more implicit in what next occurs, as the viewer is here treated as the feared object and thereby linked to the psychotic Vet. The exchange creates the reality of *Forced Entry* 1973 both by lending "truth" to the vérité (she won't say) and making that truth ultimately about the movie-audience connection rather than the character-audience nexus.

The copying down of the Woman's address by the gas station attendant leads to what can be presumed to be his flashbacks of war atrocities, created with the use of newsreel footage. Recalling Benjamin and Duhamel, here in *Forced Entry* 1973, thinking happens in terms of cinema — as pictures connote thought. The war footage is intercut with New York City streets brimming with people, intriguingly confusing the Big Apple with Southeast Asia. The gas station attendant, whom viewers now firmly identify as the Vet because of *Forced Entry* 1973's use of the Kuleshov effect, pulls his knife in his Western urban jungle, seeking the enemy cited by the credits' Dr. Liffon. Finding the Woman's apartment, the Vet scales the fire escape to spy on her and her lover, David (played by the director, "Helmuth Richler"). They are having "sort of erotic, nicely lazy" sexual intercourse, with the Woman telling David, "I want to make love to you." Yet David aggressively probes her with his tongue and keeps pushing her down. This foreplay is mirrored outside by the Vet, who loads his gun, which is the erecting of his penis surrogate. Here Costello masterfully builds the Hitchcockian suspense with the killer outside and the sex within — when the Woman performs fellatio on David, the Vet pulls out his knife as if the sheath is a foreskin that needs to be pulled back for actual intercourse with the erect penis-knife.

Street crime grants the copulating couple a short reprieve as the Vet flees from the commotion below to the roof and his Vietnam flashbacks — made of stock footage — intensify. Time passes, darkness falls, and when the Woman is alone in the apartment, the Vet attacks. She is in his power because of the knife — his penis surrogate — which is also what has allowed him to force the lock and enter into the apartment. *Forced Entry* 1973 links sexual violence (nominally about power) to sex, and in this regard the movie is not untruthful about sexual violence's confused emotional states. The question of the movie being erotic in addition to being pornographic is answered by the eroticization of the stock footage — that is, of the violence — which is revealed as the movie's true subject. As the Vet forces the Woman to suck his member, the mouth rape is intercut with bombs and him telling her, "You do it real nice and good and I'm gonna make your death nice and painless. Or I'm going to cut our eyes out," underlining the movie's exploration of violence through sex, rather than illustrating violent sex. The 1973 movie is only possible because of the then new hard-core market: without the ability to show genital penetration — piston shots — the sexual violence would be obfuscated and therefore eroticized as it is in *Forced Entry* 1981.

Forced Entry 1973 shares much in common with Pier Paolo Pasolini's *Salò, or the 120 Days of Sodom* (1975), which is a grander film, more spectacular at capturing a historical era and has the boon of a great literary source pedigree. However, *Salò* lacks the purity of *Forced Entry* 1973, which blurs the notion of documentary with an assault on the fourth wall, while following the serial killer genre formula and placing Pasolini's movie closer to filmed ballet than cinema. Both movies are about the visceral power of watching — being in on it — active, yet passive. *Forced Entry* 1973 links *Peeping Tom* to *Halloween* (1978), helping to define the slasher film genre, as well as laying the groundwork for Freddy Kruger's defeat in the original *A Nightmare on Elm Street* (1984) with its finale where the power of white magic overcomes all.

A groundbreaking movie, *Forced Entry* 1973 creates continual collusion with the viewer and increases it so that the depiction of sexualized violence born of war trauma is linked to the act of creating/filming pornography. This is underlined when the Vet rants at the Woman while ravishing her, "You like that, don't you? ... That's better. You make me enjoy this, and I'm not going to hurt you too bad. You prima donnas with your great big cars and your great big houses. You think you're something good, don't you? You're no better than the gooks from 'Nam, you know that, lady? You better make that good. I didn't tell you to stop." In this dialogue, the violence within the church toward women is alluded too with the reference to the Virgin Mary, as is the consumer society that places objects like cars and houses as the defining factors of individuality. *Forced Entry* 1973 suggests a level of class warfare and is suggestive of soldiers being made out of improvised, uneducated or undesirable recruits. The equation of the rape victim and the "gooks from 'Nam" is telling because it places the Vet's victim in a greater context and suggests the racism between white and Asian skins inherent in the Vietnam conflict. Stock footage of Asian female faces interrupt the oral rape suggesting these larger implications of the violence on display in the apartment. As the assault continues, the Vet repeatedly tells the Woman that she is making him do this, and viewers see the worst-case scenario of personal responsibility removed by society and then further removed by the military. The Vet pushes the Woman's head down to lick his scrotum, telling her, "You need a little break." Here the camera pushes in, and during "her break," the audience hears the motion picture photography mechanism. While obviously an unintentional or unavoidable production flaw, the presence of the camera noise adds an immediacy and reality that, when coupled with the penis-vagina piston shot, reduces the proceeding to elementary functions. Close to "war-gasm," the Vet grabs his own member and begins to masturbate adjacent to the Woman's head, intercut with aircraft and images of fire and burning. He ejaculates onto her and then immediately denies the pleasure he has taken in his violence, remarking, "That's better. What are you so afraid of? Did you enjoy that? You want to know something, I didn't enjoy it either. I didn't enjoy that one bit." In the background of this scene the astute viewer may spy the overmantel of a cross-stitch sampler reading, "Today is the last time tonight will happen." It is a grim joke, as the existence of the movie itself ensures repetition, as does the serial actions of the fictitious central character.

Later that afternoon, using the same modus operandi, the Vet breaks into another apartment and yanks a Woman (Laura Cannon) from the shower. Dragging her to the bed, he tells her, "You're going to like this." Again conflating the weapon/phallus, the Vet shows her his gun and tells her, "Suck my prick." He traces his knife over the Woman. Next, he fucks her missionary style as the camera operator's shadow appears like the fallout from a newsreel. The Vet forces himself on her doggy-style, then anally penetrates her, as the rape is intercut with newsreel of hooded prisoners being executed. As the Vet asks the Second Victim, "It's starting to bleed a little in there, hun?" the sound boom enters the shot, and the camera zooms in to exclude it as the walls of the cinema tear, like the victim's rectum, when confronted with a movie that is equally a total fiction and a total reality. The Vet climaxes a second time inter-spliced with target practice and guns. He cums on his Second Victim's face, and the ejaculation is paralleled with newsreel of dead children in trenches. The Vet grabs his knife, saying, "I didn't like that. That wasn't so good. Got my prick all full of shit, you know that?" Then very, very realistically, he stabs and rips the woman open, as if to expose her undefecated excrement inside. As she dies, the Vet kisses his Second Victim, and the soundtrack is overwhelmed with the doleful sound of wind.

Outside and later, a minivan picks up a female Hitchhiker on her way to New York City. She's fleeing the conservatism of the suburbs and tells the driver, who is also a young Hippie woman, "Everybody's so straight around here. I can't take my parents anymore." The two Hippie Girls are very high on mescaline and cocaine. Soon the driver suggests they get jobs performing in live sex shows on Forty-Second Street with her boyfriend. The girls then come to the fateful Greenwich Village gas station, and with this structural repetition, *Forced Entry* 1973 reaffirms *Easy Rider*'s oil-sex-cocaine link. The purchase of gasoline by the Hippie Girls is intercut with rioting bodies—metaphoric for the creation of fossil fuel.

The Vet targets the Hippie Girls once they have arrived back at the van driver's suburban home. After having sex, the girls are too stoned to sense danger when the Vet appears inside the house brandishing a knife and threatening to molest and kill them. They believe the Vet to be part of their "trip" and laugh at him. This sets off audio hallucinations as the Vet has a reckoning, remembering what he has

The advertisement for this movie illustrates the horrific moment when the Vet (Tim Long, aka Harry Reems) drags his second female victim (Laura Cannon) to her bed and dubiously tells her, "You're going to like this," while again conflating his weapon/phallus in *Forced Entry* (Helmuth Richler, aka Shaun Costello, 1973). (Courtesy Critical Condition Collection).

forced his victims to do — both here and abroad. Evil is proposed by *Forced Entry* 1973 as feeding on fear that can only be vanquished by positive energy and the "final girls" turning their back, so to speak, on the monster who as a result loses all power. Ironically confronted with the Hippie Girls' oblivious joy and "peace and love" rhetoric, the Vet shoots himself, perhaps here trying to save some goodness within, as in the cases of Herman Herman and Laura Palmer. Like *Salò*, which ends with the two soldiers dancing together finding the joy of life amid atrocity, *Forced Entry* 1973 concludes with the proposition that violence is ultimately meaningless and an expression of self-hatred. The Vet's death reconfirms the moral order and brings closure to the trauma. Like the opening credits, the end titles of *Forced Entry* 1973 are superimposed over the freeze frame of the Vet's head wound revealing the pulpy bloody brain within. At this point, many prints of the movie end; however an alternate version of the film has a final shot of a police squad car pulling off into midtown traffic, suggesting the decedents of *Forced Entry* 1973 — like *Taxi Driver* (1976) and *Cruising* (1980) — as well as proposing to viewers about to go out into the streets the potential for another lurking deranged veteran ready to continue killing.

True to that linage, *Forced Entry* 1981 starts like *Taxi Driver*. The Robert De Niro–like voiceover takes the listener into his confidence and confesses, "The city stinks. Garbage and whores. Garbage, pollution and whores." Departing from the 1973 movie, *Forced Entry* 1981 adds first-person narration and removes any connotation of the killer — here named and called Carl — being a veteran. Both the Vet and Carl work at gas stations, but the Vet does not try to relate to his victims, whereas Carl does. Coupled with the voiceover is the use of subjective camera, which places the viewer firmly on the side of the stalker while removing the personal attributes of a face. In this way, the masks that are so important in *Halloween* and its decedents are represented, but in an original way that links the individual to the violence rather than removing him or her from it. The rapes depicted in *Forced Entry* 1981 do not contain hard-core penis-vagina piston shots as the 1973 edition does. This removal of actual penetration serves to further erotize what is obscured, making the difference between the eroticized and the erotic clear. Movies like *A Clockwork Orange*, *Straw Dogs* (1971) and *The Last House on the Left* (1972) opened the door to explore sexual violence, and are paid homage in the slow-motion second rape sequence in *Forced Entry* 1981. The fragmentation of visual details during Carl's attacks recall the technique of Bresson removed from his profound morality. Director Jim Sotos' movie folds in on itself when it repeats the first rape as extended flashback. The final atrocity of *Forced Entry* 1981 happens inside a Mother's suburban house, and the scene is inter-cut with placid exteriors like the waiting spaces of *Halloween*. The film climaxes much like the 1973 version, except Carl is stabbed by his last victim right before her children come home to witness the scene. The final sequence of *Forced Entry* 1981 is of exterior shots with voiceover gossiping on the soundtrack. Finally, a voice inquires, "I wonder how many other maniacs are right under my nose looking like normal people," again pointing to violence's self-perpetuating cycle of tragedy.

Despair (1978)

In *The Tragic Fallacy* (1929), Joseph Wood Krutch remarks, "Thus for the great ages tragedy is not an expression of despair but the means by which they saved themselves from it." Fassbinder's apparently tragic presentation is like Sirk's in that the suffering on screen is magnified so as to take the audience further into the beyond, as implicated by Eustache, wherein moments reach camp absurdity, but the premise is nearly always treated seriously. For Eustache, this is an authentic representation, but for Fassbinder it is the opportunity for a menagerie of multiplicities and Sirk-like ironic satire. The film *Despair* is an expression of that titular emotion, but one that is conscious of its ridiculous premise. It is an artifact that clearly hopes to provide surrogacy for the audience, for in distancing the viewer from the characters, the film's strong sadism becomes even more pleasurable, and the motion picture can be "enjoyed" as comedy. In this way "despair" saves the audience from tragedy directly. However, the movie is also presented in a fragmented whirl of parts, so that one "side" of the story is never solely visible. The characters of *Despair* all feel superior to each other, but are, in fact, not-totally-smart grotesques. That the movie's action is mirrored by the rise of the Third Reich suggests both the self-absorption that leads to the election of nationalized socialism, as well as sympathetically presenting people behaving as best they can (which, admittedly, is not very good) in a world gone mad with Nazis. It is this that gives the movie its caustic, acrid quality which has often kept it from being better embraced by critics and the public at large.

Based on a Vladimir Nabokov work said to be of the 1930s, *Despair* was reworked by its author several times, in several different languages, until finding its final form in English in 1966. The 1978 film is dedicated to Antonin Artaud, Vincent Van Gogh and Unica Zurn and is the collaboration of several distinct forces — Fassbinder, decor designers Herbert Strabel and Jochen Schumacher, producer Edward R. Pressman, and playwright Tom Stoppard. These equally great but dissimilar collaborators add to the sensation of schizophrenia depicted in the source novel by master gamesman Nabokov. Fassbinder and his designers are theatrical and mordant; Pressman is epic, clearly interested in being thought provoking and yet invested in cinematic fun; whereas Stoppard (of this period) is dry, droll and intellectual — like souls but very different minds, and as a result, the movie of *Despair* is never less than totally challenging. The cynicism of *Despair* is so dark — like Sirk, as well as his and Fassbinder's spiritual successor, Paul Verhoeven — that for the audience to enter into the movie's world is an almost impossible task regardless of the fact that once submerged, *Despair* plays as the wittiest of farces.

Dirk Bogarde stars as Herman Herman ("Hermann" in Nabokov's novel), a chocolatier and "connoisseur of soft centers." Herman is defined by objects, and early on, as they are also in the novel, "love, poetry, philosophy, religion" are cited as being "inventions of the rich" by Herman's false double, Felix, who in his disenfranchisement already sees the commodification of arts and letters caused by mechanical reproduction and the world wars. Facing bankruptcy amid the chaos of the Nazis' ascension, Herman meets the somewhat slow-witted tramp Felix, whom Hermann believes to be his doppelganger, while Fassbinder's camera immediately reveals Felix as looking nothing like Herman. The latter, supplying implausible and unlikely reasons, hires Felix to obey his wishes — to be his "stunt double" — while he plans to murder Felix, fake his own death, assume Felix's identity, and substitute the tramp's body as his own. From their first meeting through Felix's murder, Herman develops an "honest"

Dirk Bogarde as Herman and Klaus Löwitsch as his "double," Felix the tramp, here having "switched" visual identities just before Herman's murder of Felix/himself in the movie *Despair* (Rainer Werner Fassbinder, 1978). (Courtesy the collections of the Margaret Herrick Library, Academy of Motion Pictures Arts and Sciences.)

resentment of the tramp based in their class differences, and so Felix's poverty is understood to also motivate Herman. The chocolatier is equally monetarily motivated in his actions, however, and it becomes threatening to Herman's illusions that the men have one true thing in common — honest hatred — and that this shared class anger provokes active disgust. Rejecting what he calls Herman's "decadence," Felix seems to be equally put off by Herman for the same reasons, albeit at the other end of the economic spectrum. Carl Schmitt writes in *The Concept of the Political* that "the phenomenon of the political can be understood only in the context of the ever present possibility of the friend-and-enemy grouping, regardless of the aspects which this possibility implies for morality, aesthetics, and economics."[1] And so, Fassbinder's film links human behavior to a state of constant warfare that both hosts as well as creates the political. As Schmitt himself prefaced the quote above,

> A world in which the possibility of war is utterly eliminated, a completely pacified globe, would be a world without the distinction of friend and enemy and hence a world without politics. It is conceivable that such a world might contain many very interesting antitheses and contrasts, competitions and intrigues of every kind, but there would not be a meaningful antithesis whereby men could be required to sacrifice life, authorized to shed blood, and kill other human beings. For the definition of the political, it is here even irrelevant whether such a world without politics is desirable as an ideal situation.[2]

Fassbinder-Stoppard place the political within the family in *Despair* and doing so present the Herman-Felix "friendship" as indicative of the warring factions which have shaped both men. While the taboo against murdering family remains, the murder of self and selves becomes the primary agenda of the political, as here most horrifically personified by the Nazi death machine. The basic emotion that survives the slaughter is greed and the thought of reclaiming the self with the destruction of the self as well as the compulsive desire for more and more reclaiming, which links fascism to capitalism as on display currently in the media era.

As discussed earlier with regard to the gangster films in Chapter 2, in *Our Adult World and Its Roots in Infancy*, Klein explores the power of greed for the individual and its links to exasperation as well as causing anxiety in a fashion clearly refracted in *Despair* with regard to Herman's motives. In the child, the desire for the mother's breast creates greed; greed creates anxiety, and therefore insecurity for the individual about his or her own capacity to love, which results in destructive urges. In her text, Klein directly applies her theory of childhood to adults, remarking on the fundamentally unchanging role of greed. Herman is incapable of love, and so his greed is reinforced as an attempt to fill a primal (perhaps cultural) void. Yet Herman is not successfully greedy, as his greed does not comfort him or abate anxiety. Herman's imminent business failure at the movie's opening increases his paranoia, sense of persecution and predisposition for self-sabotage. Herman has unconsciously chosen suicide as his best option, but cloaked it in an elaborately conscious plan of faking his own death inspired by pulp movies and paperbacks, which have assumed a large reality of surrogacy for him. Herman says, "The perfect murder is the one that never happened but was committed." He then listens to himself and recants: "No, no, no, the perfect murder would be the one in which the victim did it"—in other words, a suicide. Hermann does not have the agency of self to actively undo himself, but because of his relationship with the cinema, he has the ability to construct a comedy of suicide not unlike Mr. Clay's morose "comedy" in *The Immortal Story*. Like Mark Lewis in *Peeping Tom*, Herman has the ability to escape into cinema and see his anxiety given shape as plot, which he may then "plot" against. That everyone but himself sees the absurdity isolates Herman and further fans the flames of his paranoid drive to escape his situation and himself. However, and challengingly to the viewer of *Despair*, Herman is not unaware of his dualities. He asks, "What do you know about this subject? Disassociation: the split person, the man who stands outside himself. I'm thinking about writing a book about such a person. Maybe two books." Herman is still a Shakespearean character in that he is able to listen and change in relation to himself, but reason is removed. This trait of reason is increasingly removed from cinema in the late–1970s and especially the 1980s because introspection is usurped by the actuality of the media era where everything is already digested and cannot be remade—only assembled—because it lacks complex form.

In *Despair* it is blatantly obvious what is going on, both personally with Herman's meltdown, as well as with his deteriorating relationship with his wife, Lydia (Andrea Ferreol). Herman tells her, "Intelligence would take the bloom off your carnality," while being literally (and somewhat hysterically) blind to the affair she is carrying on with "her cousin" Ardalion (Volker Spengler). Again, the national is juxtaposed with the individual, and the avoidance of taking the Nazi Party seriously is reflected in Herman's own inability to acknowledge what is actually taking place in his home. The incest taboo is explored vis-à-vis the old adage that "blood is thicker than water," but in *Despair* it also points to a primal scene that Nabokov suggests as perhaps being Herman's initial undoing.

In *On the Sense of Loneliness* (1963), Klein writes that "the schizophrenic feels that he is hopelessly in bits and that he will never be in possession of his self. The very fact that he is so fragmented results in his being unable to internalize his primal object (the mother) sufficiently as a good object and therefore in his lacking the foundation of stability; he cannot rely on an external and internal good object, nor can he rely on his own self."[3] Applicable to Herman's confused state—as well as Germany's national state—the audience sees the roots in bad parenting, where the mother is eclipsed by other desires, stronger and from outside the home, which then take her place. That cultural is repressed and increasingly narcissistic and primitive illustrates its regression. It connects

Despair's thesis of the rise of the Third Reich and this text's thesis of the rise of the media era.

With his "friendship" with Felix, Herman is clearly trying to remake something other than himself. Typical of his late–1970s working methods, Fassbinder obfuscates this point in his direction of the film version of *Despair* so that the tension reads as an omeleting of homosexual desire and masturbatory narcissism. However, the Nabokov source novel is quite clear that it was incestuous desire between Herman and his twin (!) that roots his despair. Nabokov writes his Herman as a completely unreliable narrator, so that it is quite possible that Herman's twin never existed, and Herman's primal scene truly rests in a moment with his parent never touched upon — perhaps also of an incestuous nature. When Herman finds his double — which is not — he remarks, "I stand before me." The fact that the tramp Felix looks nothing like Herman connotes Herman's complete removal from himself via cinema and the forces of the political. On doppelgangers Freud writes

> The "double" was originally an insurance against destruction to the ego, an "energetic denial of the power of death," as Rank says; and probably the "immortal" soul was the first "double" of the body. This invention of doubling as a preservation against extinction has its counterpart in the language of dreams, which is fond of representing castration by a double or multiplication of the genital symbol; the same desire spurred on the ancient Egyptians to the art of making images of the dead in some lasting material. Such ideas, however, have sprung from the soil of unbounded self-love, from the primary narcissism which holds sway in the mind of the child as in that of primitive man; and when this stage has been left behind the double takes on a different aspect. From having been an assurance of immortality, he becomes the ghastly harbinger of death.[4]

The absence of Herman's brother becomes what has been suggested as his primal scene, and the supposed death of the brother represents the loss of his "insurance against destruction to the ego." From that point on, Herman is thus continually castrated by the various factors in his life. His homosexual-incestual desires are repressed and so (as often is the case with unexplored sexual impulses) cause a greater anxiety, which, when coupled with the political, lead to suicidal urges and bring about the created double (Felix) who is the "harbinger of death." However, with their lack of resemblance, and according to his schizophrenic position, Herman's actual physical appearance safeguards the very life Herman tries to immolate. The tragic irony of *Despair* is that it is only in this self-destruction that Herman is realized.

In the source novel, Nabokov writes, "An author's fondest dream is to turn the reader into a spectator: is this ever attained?"[5] Herman's fondest dream is to become the spectator of his own constructed reality, which serves to further remove him into the process, thus gratifying his suicidal urges. Returning to E.T.A. Hoffmann's *Sandman*, which is so important to Freud's theory of the uncanny, the expression of creativity bifurcating the individual at the expense of a total reality is presented as linked into pre-cinematic society through language and its limits. However, by the time of Freud's interpretation, the transference between Hoffmann, his character and his readers is conflated, largely because of cinema, "so that the one possesses knowledge, feeling and experience in common with the other, identifies himself with another person, so that his self becomes confounded, or the foreign self is substituted for his own — in other words, by doubling, dividing and interchanging the self."[6] Herman seeks to remake himself with Felix in the hope that it will make him a whole person healed of schizophrenia. That Herman perhaps had a "true" double — an identical twin brother who was killed during World War I — contributes to his anxiety and proposes itself as the lost object that Herman seeks to reclaim and remake with Felix.

Nabokov writes of the brothers' last parting in the novel:

> People on the platform looked at us, looked at those two identical youths who stood with interlocked hands and peered into each other's eyes with a kind of sorrowful ecstasy....
>
> Then came the war. Whilst languishing in remote captivity I never had any news of my brother, but was somehow sure that he had been killed. Sultry years, black-shrouded years. I taught myself not to think of him; and even later, when I was married, not a word thereof did I breathe to Lydia — it was all too sad.[7]

The incest-love that suggests itself with the boys' shared "sorrowful ecstasy" is that which Herman cannot duplicate or recreate, and so it drives him to self-destruction. "Common" survivor's guilt is added to Herman and — coupled with the agency of cinema — allows Herman to construct false realities as a way of undoing himself. When in the 1978 movie Herman performs a body inspection on Felix, it is implied that masturbation (not, it should be noted, orgasm) is the fulfillment of the relationship. Herman remakes the tramp with "bourgeoisie capitalism from head to toe," and again Herman's identity as a financial entity is reflected. When the gun ejaculates its fire, it is because the men cannot, and so Herman "thanks" the tramp as he murders him.

Despair attacks capital and roots its grotesquerie in skewering bourgeoisie comforts. At the movie's start, Herman's new line of chocolates is a flop because it does not have enough sugar, and Fassbinder suggests this as the metaphoric problem of the American (and perhaps German) public which desires sweet dross rather than substance and thinks its desires are needs. Herman further perverts any alleged nobility of his moneyed class by linking crime and criminality to creativity, so that it is clearly understood that Herman's best chance of self-expression is in his dishonest and/or homicidal impulses. A movie about movies, and therefore as Deleuze espouses, a film about money, the forces of capital overwhelm the individual in *Despair*. The surrogacy offered by early cinema is replaced with the increasing disparity between the actual and the represented, which widens the gulf and contributes to the removal of the individual from him- or herself. In *Despair*, the 1929 New York Wall Street crash is presented as the impetus that leads to the Nazis being elected in Germany, as the failure of the United States' economic system reverberates out, sending further trauma in the direction of World War I–scarred Germany. Wall Street's implied responsibility for the rise of the Nazi regime also again links fascism's propaganda with the product of Hollywood — Wall Street's West Coast doppelganger. In Karsten Witte's *The Indivisible Legacy of Nazi Cinema* (1994), she remarks, "One of the Nazi regime's most glaring contradictions was the removal of modernity from public life and its simultaneous reintroduction by means of film and other mass media,"[8] which returns to the mutation that began with the world wars wherein imaginary cinema was remade as the truer reality. Witte's question of "When the percentage of the total production represented by comedies drops and that of propaganda rises, do propaganda films take on the role of comedies?"[9] may be used to underline what has been identified in this chapter as the satirical bent of *Despair*.

Herman's confusion is increasingly mirrored in the nation's political confusion as the German government collapses around him. Herman's reaction is typical: "I didn't start the war. Why should I pay for it?" Why should Herman take any responsibility for anything? Likewise, when Herman watches Nazi-perpetuated violence, it is not clear if it is (his) fantasy being projected, or if he is seeing another manifestation of violence like his own imitation of a pulp-fiction murder. *Despair* reconstructs the Nazis as enacting the fantasies of the German people — a reading that is controversial because, regardless of the great matter of truth, it is hardly a query that leads to catharsis or healing. It is this anti-catharsis which is Fassbinder's link back to Brecht. *Despair* remakes the violence on display in Kubrick's *A Clockwork Orange*, removing all intelligence in the exchange just as the trait of reason is increasingly removed from post–World War II cinema because introspection is usurped by "digested actuality" incapable of complex form.

During Fassbinder's remaking of Kubrick's interrogation scene of Alex, Herman's conversation with the cops turns to babble. That the police officers see through Herman immediately again points to Herman's active self-destruction vis-à-vis his inability to let himself succeed. Herman is closer to Al Roberts of *Detour* (1939 source novel, 1945 and 1992 movie adaptations) than the cunning Alex of *A Clockwork Orange*. Movies are uncanniness themselves, and *Despair* bares an uncanny resemblance to *Detour* — the *film noir* wherein tramp Al Roberts meets his near-double, a rich bookie named Charles Haskell, Jr., and switches lives with him after the latter's "accidental" demise, only to find himself accused of "Al's" murder. Finally unable to be himself — or Haskell — after his crime is committed, Al wanders the country waiting for punishment. The trajectory of *Detour*, *Despair*, and post–*Twin Peaks: Fire Walk with Me* David Lynch movies — like *Lost Highway* (1997) or *Mulholland Dr.* —

present how the individual is increasingly harmed and removed from him- or herself by cinema's false promises. Freud's premise of the uncanny, gleaned from Schelling, is "something which ought to have been kept concealed but which has nevertheless come to light"[10] and that becomes the working definition for the method of Hollywood cinema. For as cinema becomes more lifelike with color and widescreen, that is, a more gratuitous imitation of life with sex, violence and profanity, it also reveals more and more of a culture where the individual is displaced from him- or herself by object.

In *Some Theoretical Conclusions Regarding the Emotional Life of the Infant* (1952), Klein writes, "Since the phantasied attacks on the object are fundamentally influenced by greed, the fear of the object's greed, owing to projection, is an essential element in persecutory anxiety: the bad breast will devour him in the same greedy way as he desires to devour it."[11] With this, the audience can again understand greed to be Herman's undoing, and the cultural trend — that in his individual remaking — only accelerates his schizophrenic position. Like *The Magnificent Ambersons* and *One More Tomorrow*, *Despair* is a film of false marriage rooted in greed, where the state of matrimony is linked to the corrupting forces of capital. Fassbinder presents viewers with the theory that wedlock is another role forced onto the individual that robs him or her of autonomy outside of the culture industry, which it protects at all costs. Herman remarks that he and Lydia are "the perfect couple. She likes literature, I like trash." He is unable to consider her as more than object, whereas she is able to sense his breakdown, even if she does not realize its serious nature until it is too late. Lydia tells Herman that she'd "like to know what is going on in your head," but Herman himself barely really knows what is going on his head, and, as when he bursts in on Lydia and Ardalion in a sexual situation, he is too engulfed in paranoid fantasy to respond to what is obvious and apparent right in front of his eyes. Stoppard and Fassbinder comment on the selectivity of memory in the twentieth century, and how untruth acts as a survival method placing walls around the absent primal object(s), thereby protecting something, even if that something is not actual.

The ultimate untruth survival mechanism is of course the cinema, which in *Despair* represents the conjoining of the spectacles of sentimentality and death. Herman watches himself in *Despair* as if he is an actor in a movie. In the novel, Nabokov illustrates how Herman's gaze is not his own but the co-opted gaze of the cinema itself. Upon meeting Felix, Herman writes, "Still, it was not at once that I glanced at his face; I started working from his feet upward, as one sees on the screen when the cameraman is trying to be tantalizing."[12] Not only is Herman's vision understood as cinematic, but pleasure becomes in the receiving rather than in the actual, and this mirrors the movement of catharsis from experiencing the climax to the act of ticket purchase. To receive or perceive cinematically, Herman eschews his individuality, initially trying to fit his situation into the mythos of cinema that will serve to remove his essence from the process. For the prolific Fassbinder, the process often appeared more important than the result, and the common legend goes that he was afraid to not be working — similar to how Dan O'Herlihy as director David Edwards is in Sirk's *Imitation of Life* 1959.

Processes' greater success — propaganda assuming the dream state in cinema — is what allows Herman to first watch his life like he is at a movie, and then allows him to begin to watch his own (projected) fantasies the same way. Movies' nature as dream, illusion and untruth is again celebrated in Fassbinder's comedy of *Despair*. Herman's relation to the cinema later becomes the individual's relation to media, delineating that era as featuring a profound cultural schizophrenia and the full-on imitation of life that it suggests. At the end of *Despair*, having reached a new level of detachment, Herman becomes part of the cinema like Norma Desmond at the climax of *Sunset Blvd.* (1950). "Ready for his close-up," Herman says, "We're making a film here. In a minute, I'll be coming out, but you keep the policemen back so I can get away. I'm a film actor. I'm coming out. Don't look at the camera. I'm coming out." Fassbinder's image freezes as Herman exits and so enters a total delusion, where his crime, his greed, is the only "true" thing that informs his character as it will be for many victims of the twentieth and twenty-first centuries.

In the final moments of *Despair*, it is revealed that since crime and greed provide the stage for easy, unthinking cultural judgment, Fassbinder has constructed his movie to lampoon all this. Fassbinder's cruel satire of 1978 remaking 1932 presents the deluded Herman as an emblem of the German people — if not a timeless Everyman of humanity itself. At the least, it is a Germanic remake of Tom Powers from *The Public Enemy*, and the differences between Powers and Herman illustrate the cultural differences between the two great nations. Yet, because *Despair* is a late–1970s movie set in the 1930s, its immediate source value must be questioned. No doubt this unreality effect is an appeal of a period setting for Fassbinder, as well as the fact that in depicting the 1930s in Germany, he is allowed to look back at a defining moment in which he proposes his nation as being still in the grips of. This is unlike other post–World War II German New Wave directors who seem to sever the link between the Nazis and the (then current) era of the 1970s. The pull between the psychological and the anti-psychological political forces of capital is the central undecided tension of *Despair*. They are voiced when Lydia — who, as part of Herman's ruse, goes to accept Herman's insurance settlement after his "death" and is told by a clerk, "I realize money can be no compensation to his loss," and she replies, "I don't think so, there are too many memories." With *Despair* in 1978, memory and money have finally combined into the unreality of cinema that inspires only greed and crime.

Raiders of the Lost Ark: The Adaptation (1989)

   Raiders of the Lost Ark, directed by Steven Spielberg and released in 1981, begins as a smirking pastiche of adventure cliff-hangers. The mountaintops of the Paramount Studios logo glibly dissolves into a jungled hill, as faux–Wagnerian music, care of composer John Williams, stitches the images together. From these first frames, it is apparent that *Raiders of the Lost Ark* is a movie-movie — rich in the mythology of filmmaking filled with both the constructed histories of the sound era, and various class impossibilities that are made to seem wholly possible. Yet, the English-language sound cinema of the 1930s was never so flip or ironic as *Raiders of the Lost Ark* is. What is on display in the movie is the transformation of Nixon-era cynicism into the "Morning in America" attitude that typified the 1980s and rebukes cynicism because it is based in something other than — or contrary to — appearance. Conversely, *Raiders of the Lost Ark's* "retro" style allowed the movie to become "classic" sooner than many of its 1981 contemporaries. Its simulation — preying on nostalgia and absent primal object(s) of baby boomers — took on the perceived value of a 1930s artifact precisely because it removed various "dated" elements of the 1930s that interfere with direct transference between the modern viewers and 1930s cinema.

Director Steven Spielberg and actor Harrison Ford as "Indiana Jones" on the set of *Raiders of the Lost Ark* (Steven Spielberg, 1981). (Courtesy the Chestnut Hill Film Group.)

In the time between *Raiders of the Lost Ark* and *Indiana Jones and the Kingdom of the Crystal Skull* three twelve-year olds in Mississippi — Eric Zala directing, Jayson Lamb shooting, and Chris Strompolos playing Jones — began capturing their own scene-by-scene remake of Spielberg's 1981 movie on Sony Betamax and VHS tape in *Raiders of the Lost Ark: The Adaptation* (Eric Zala, 1989). (Courtesy Rolling Boulder Films.)

Raiders of the Lost Ark signifies the commodification of genre in the late sound era with the solidification of the "blockbuster" as its own specific Hollywood genre. The first release of Spielberg's movie was titled *Raiders of the Lost Ark*, making all the characters "raiders," which is a pleasing irony. However, subsequent prints retitle the movie *Indiana Jones and the Raiders of the Lost Ark*, abolishing the complete relativism of the adventure's first positioning. This is replaced with an expression of the dominance of the symbol of the mythic individual most familiar from Joseph Campbell's and Bill Moyers' *The Power of Myth* (1988). *Raiders of the Lost Ark* 1981 is again remade by *Indiana Jones and the Kingdom of the Crystal Skull* in 2008, which reframes the original to support a more embellished legacy of the characters. Yet lost in all this construction is the Nixon era coda of the original, wherein the Holy Ark is warehoused by the government and the ultimate futility of the quest is made manifest and thereby becomes the supreme meaning of the picture's first edition.

In the time between *Raiders of the Lost Ark* and *Indiana Jones and the Kingdom of the Crystal Skull* three twelve-year-olds in Mississippi — Chris Strompolos playing Jones, Eric Zala directing, and Jayson Lamb shooting — began capturing their own scene-by-scene remake of Spielberg's 1981 movie on Sony Betamax and VHS tape. Finished seven years later in 1989, *Raiders of the Lost Ark: The Adaptation* finally premiered in 2003 at the Alamo Drafthouse, Texas, and became a huge underground cult phenomenon. As of this writing, Zala's great movie remake has yet to see a commercial release due to copyright issues.

The Adaptation begins with the following text crawl:

> This film is a tribute to Steven Spielberg, George Lucas and Lawrence Kasdan for their giving birth to what we consider to be the ultimate adventure film. It is because of their genius that a film exists with such an enduring, nostalgic and adventurous spirit. For eight long years we have been driven by an almost obsessive inspiration. This inspiration was fueled by the collective brilliance of these three men. It is to them we give our thanks for the work they have wrought which has left a permanent impression upon the direction of our lives. It is through them that we have discovered our love for film.

Raiders of the Lost Ark: The Adaptation represents cinema as religion, for Strompolos/Zala/Lamb find and mimic their identity in the fantasy on display. Their desire for cinema, and to be part of it, rivals Professor Ravenwood's on-screen obsession with the ancient, lost city of Tanis, which is the premise for much of the Spielberg film. The actual mise-en-scène of *Raiders of the Lost Ark: The Adaptation* reflects this affinity of identity, as when Zala pushes his camera in during Marcus' monologue to Jones about the profundity of the quest for the sacred Ark. "For nearly three thousand years man has been searching for the lost Ark — it's not something to be taken lightly, no one knows its secrets — it's like nothing you've gone after before." The Herculean quest of creating *Raiders of the Lost Ark: The Adaptation* is visibly profound for its players, and it is clear that the movie is its participants' identity. In this way, *Raiders of the Lost Ark: The Adaptation* holds great allegiance to Andy Warhol's cinema. The camera and performances have the same nonprofessional artifice, often unfortunately reduced into "camp" by theoreticians like Susan Sontag. Zala's visual effects are close to the white-out flares of Warhol's late–1960s underground films, and the soundtrack of *Raiders of the Lost Ark: The Adaptation* is a collage of muddy production audio and "found" cues assembled like an experimental movie or a Dennis Potter television serial. Audio for *Raiders of the Lost Ark: The Adaptation* employs the ultimate Kuleshov effect — where the juxtaposition of the sound samples provides the relation between shots, rather than the viewer, and this is indicative of how the individual is removed from actively being a part of the drama with products like *Raiders of the Lost Ark* 1981. The yellow-green video of the *Raiders of the Lost Ark: The Adaptation* remakes Spielberg's Hollywood product in a way that is proto–Lars von Trier and proto–Dogme 95. In *Raiders of the Lost Ark: The Adaptation*, "Indy" is so remade as "Indie," saint of "independent film." Thus the *Raiders of the Lost Ark* story is given its previously missing genuine emotional and intellectual excitement by its remake and its imitation.

Raiders of the Lost Ark: The Adaptation opens on Indiana Jones' back. The Paramount Pictures logo joke does not exist, and it signals that this remake is not an ironic movie but a satiric one, more complex than its source. Strompolos' impression of Harrison Ford's often wooden acting as Indiana Jones gives *The Adaptation* true charm. He does not do an imitation of Ford's performance but offers a sincerely acted burlesque of a performer out of his depth — which, when coupled with the hero's uncanny on-screen success — gives the audience a sense of giddy pleasure. In *The Visible Human* (1924), Béla Balázs writes that bad acting "is not an incorrect interpretation of an existing character, but rather an incorrect treatment that utterly fails to create a character. It is a case of bad artistic creation. The mistakes are not contradictions with an underlying text, but rather contradictions of the acting with itself."[13] What Strompolos achieves in his remaking is a repair to his own fantasy that both removes anxiety and inflates his own agency within the film's world. The primitive reality of the kid's recreation makes *Raiders of the Lost Ark: The Adaptation* fresh, even though the mise-en-scène is still clearly the work of the deeply talented Spielberg. This links *Raiders of the Lost Ark: The Adaptation* to *Psycho* 1998 in the relation of the elevation and predominance of the second unit director and helps to break down what an auteurist feature film is. In the media era, this breakdown continues with the post-production colorist replacing the cinematographer.

While *Raiders of the Lost Ark: The Adaptation* plays like a school play directed by the Kuchar Brothers, the pyrotechnics on screen are truly impressive. It is true that *Raiders of the Lost Ark: The Adaptation*'s effects owe more to *Ghostbusters* (1984) than the original 1981 Spielberg production, but nonetheless they are such a dazzling representation of actual stunts that they recapture the textual pleasure of early uses of the Schüfftan process or Claymation — increasingly absent toward the end of the sound era. When Strompolos' Indy fights with Angela Rodriguez's Marion, Rodriguez gives Karen Allen a run for her money. The youthfulness of the players gives the scene a real electric, erotic tension, remaking *Raiders of the Lost Ark: The Adaptation* as something close to a teen sex farce. The children play "Raiders" as one would play "doctor" — the Spielberg movie being both an introduction to the adult world as well as a primer on how to behave in it.

Interesting for the great feat of its execution, *Raiders of the Lost Ark: The Adaptation* is also a fascinating time capsule of a time, place and participants. Marion's ill-fated pet monkey is played by a dog named Snickers (1983–1988), and the substitution of a family pet for Marion's monkey supplies further real emotional resonance to *Raiders of the Lost Ark*'s callow and cynical script. That the actors age several years during the course of the shoot gives the movie a breadth of scope like the best of Andrei Tarkovsky or Michael Cimino, while, Warhol-like, also illustrating the childish psychology at work in *Raiders of the Lost Ark* 1981. The fact that Strompolos/Zala/Lamb had the financial where-withal to create their adaptation illustrates the escalation in the 1980s of the (buying) power of the child within the American family unit as explored in Chapter 6. *Raiders of the Lost Ark* 1981 can only appeal to children, or those individuals who wish to avoid a meaningful adult exchange, as the movie brims with a fear of true maturity and is unthinkingly pro-religion — the most of any studio picture since *The Exorcist* (1973), which Spielberg references in his movie's climax. In *Despair*, Fassbinder considered his Nazi legacy, whereas Spielberg avoids his Jewish roots in *Raiders of the Lost Ark*, other than to compartmentalize Nazis as the "ultimate bad guys" in black, and accept religion as something elemental and eternal rather than constructed and evolving. Both *Raiders of the Lost Ark* and *Raiders of the Lost Ark: The Adaptation* are nationalist propaganda. Like its period setting, *Raiders of the Lost Ark*'s religious tone undoubtedly added to its box office success. When viewed in conjunction with the film's rabid nationalism, Spielberg's 1981 motion picture emerges as the successor to such American epics as *The Birth of a Nation* (1915) and *Ben-Hur* (1959). Country and God are linked, but actions have no repercussions other than their symbolic gesture. *The Birth of a Nation* and *Ben-Hur* are parables that are difficult to project oneself into, but, by comparison, *Raiders of the Lost Ark* offers an accessible and empowered fantasy. That *Raiders of the Lost Ark* is irreligious is apparent even to the twelve-year-olds, as two pint-sized G-men satirically break character to look at Zala's camera with a double take after Jones describes the Ark being stolen from Jerusalem and being hidden in the city of Tanis, which was then engulfed by a sandstorm and "wiped clean by the wrath of God." The G-men roll their eyes at the source movie's earnestness and heavy-handedness, letting the viewer concretely know — even to tweens — that religion in America is only a signifier for other things, namely money and jingoism.

The market sequence where Jones dispatches the threatening Arab is recreated in *Raiders of the Lost Ark: The Adaptation* in a single take brimming with an ingenuity of staging not seen since the heyday of Producers Releasing Corporation in the early 1940s. In this way, *Raiders of the Lost Ark: The Adaptation* returns the story to its era and sources, and plays like what *Raiders of the Lost Ark* would have been as a two-reel Monogram programmer. This "reduction" illustrates how much John Williams' score helps the movie's momentum and emotional viscera. It also illuminates how the best parts of Spielberg's majestical direction of action is rooted in the examples of silent comedy, and his remaking of what has come before. The product of a colony that has become an economically (and otherwise) colonialist society, in *Raiders of the Lost Ark* resolving the long-standing tensions between the Arab and Western world is as quick as shooting a gun — as when Jones executes the sword-wielding Arab in the marketplace set piece. The World War II era setting allows for a harnessing of moral superiority by the audience in emulation of politicians, which, when culturally adopted, ultimately unroots post–World War II America by being an agent of the removal of critical thinking and introspection in favor of nationalism and action. *Raiders of the Lost Ark: The Adaptation*'s greatest prop is the Nazi flag, and its display illustrates the mainstreaming of the fetishism of fascism and the disavowal of actual content in the late sound era. The "bad guys" in *Raiders of the Lost Ark* remark that they are "uncomfortable with Jewish ritual," and it reflects modern Americans' fear of ethnicity, intriguingly (and subversively) linking it to the Nazis' fear of Jews. This reactionary bent to *Raiders of the Lost Ark* is again what has added to its popular appeal and "modern classic" status. With Hollywood product thusly so rancid, it is no surprise that the sound era enters its *fin de siècle* in the 1990s.

CHAPTER 8

I Know Who Killed Me

Remaking the Artist in
The Immortal Story *(1968)* and
Twin Peaks:
Fire Walk with Me *(1992)*

The modern individual has been remade by cinema in the way that people use to remake themselves prior to the invention of the medium. During the sound era of cinema, 1931–1998, the forces of technology, capital, the pornological, and Hollywood itself fused with the dynamic of parental influences in the development of personality — both culturally and personally — while at the same time refashioning cinema into a new form with new properties called media. In this study, Melanie Klein's psychoanalytic play technique has been treated as the method of the sound era and used to analyze children's increasing control of the American family unit — which has been illustrated to be perpetuated by cinema in its transition into media. Cinema has been narrowed down to feature-length films and approached from the perspective of genre, largely eschewing the auteur theory because of the reality of movies being the product of many collaborators and cultural influences and not just one director. However, the importance of director-authors cannot be denied, especially when creators achieve a level of true artistry — as already examined along the lines of Warhol and/or Kubrick.

In "What Is Cinema?" Jean-Luc Godard remarks that "art attracts us only by what it reveals of our most secret self,"[1] and the best auteurs are the ones who bring something uniquely personal to their presentation of story. Throughout the oeuvre of these special directors, a development via self-remaking can be traced. Sexual awakening and sexual taboo often double as perfect mirror images with artistic awakening and artistic taboo, and in cinema they are presented in a dream state wherein it is impossible to quantify which factor — awakening or taboo — comes first, or ultimately dominates. Creating a movie becomes a primal scene surrogate, while sex acts return actors (or "models" in Bresson's definition) to their most primal state of symbolic meaning. In *Some Reflections on "The Oresteia"* (1963), Klein notes,

> The drive to create symbols is so strong because even the most loving mother cannot satisfy the infant's powerful emotional needs. In fact no reality situation can fulfill the often contradictory urges and wishes of the child's phantasy life. It is only if in childhood, symbol formation is able to develop in full strength and variety and is not impeded by inhibitions, that the artist later can make use of the emotional forces which underlie symbolism. In an early paper [*Early Stages of the Oedipus Conflict* (1923)] I have discussed the pervading importance of symbol formation in infantile mental life and implied that if symbol formation is particularly rich, it contributes to the development of talent or even of genius.[2]

Trauma is the formation of self and artistic expression, yet when the body of work of a director is sufficient, there sometimes comes a point wherein the auteur ceases to remake him- or herself and doubles back into earlier themes without adding to them. Regurgitation is the deepest and truest artistic taboo and the one hardest for nonartists to recognize. For director Orson Welles, *The Immortal Story* (1968) represents a hugely impressive summation of his personal cinema, whereas his last commercially released film, *F for Fake* (1974), wallows in a "junk drawer" of found footage and intriguing but disjointed and minor ideas. Whereas for David Lynch, *Twin Peaks: Fire Walk with Me* (1992) represents a great moment of self-remaking before two movies, *Mulholland Dr.* (2001) and *Inland Empire* (2007), which increasingly self-cannibalize earlier ideas without transforming them — so sadly suggesting an artistic stylistic impasse as undesirable as a speech impediment.

Unless the legendary unfinished movies of Welles finally surface — like *The Deep* or *The Other Side of the Wind*— scholars are able to see and judge Welles' output as a totality. However, Lynch is — as of this writing — alive and sixty-five years of age, and so it is premature to not imagine that he has several more, great, original feature films still to create. Yet, global economic problems, the break from art cinema, and the move away from sound cinema may conspire otherwise. However, with work like his website, DavidLynch.com, and the short *Lady Blue Shanghai* (2010) for LadyDior.com, Lynch is at the forefront of artists working with media. Regardless, there can be little doubt that he is among the most important and influential of his generation of American moviemakers no matter what he does or does not do next.

Directors remaking themselves do so not only in relationship to themselves but to or against the reception of — or lack thereof — their work. From electricity, to war, to cyberspace, twentieth-century artists are shaped by the world and times they exist in. By examining how two great directors refashion themselves, this analysis can be linked with the cultural changes explored in previous chapters illuminating two unique perspectives on cinema's mutation into media.

The Immortal Story (1968)

In the filmography of Orson Welles, *The Immortal Story* immediately reflects both *Citizen Kane* (1941) and *The Trial* (1962)—the former remade in many obvious ways by the latter. Yet *Citizen Kane* and *The Trial* represent only one side of their creator's nature—the other side, the sentimental romantic of *The Magnificent Ambersons* (1942) or *Chimes at Midnight* (1965), is also present in *The Immortal Story*, and therefore the unity of what audiences can understand to be Welles makes the movie one of the—if not *the*—finest films of his vivid career as a director of motion pictures. On first viewing, *The Immortal Story* reads as a deceptively light allegory that ponders wealth, legacy and narrative. With a running time of just over one hour, it is dream-like and feverish, self-reflective to itself and Welles, whom it features all of the cinematic trademarks of, such as deep focus, low angels, complex sound design, rapid shifts in perspective and multiple narrators. Much of the movie's effect is also gleaned from Erik Satie's music, which Welles uses (and reuses) so as to haunt the soundscape of *The Immortal Story*. Playing Mr. Clay—a powerful, largely off-screen force who conspires an allegory as a final action, almost an extended death throe—Welles finds another cinematic expression of himself as a director.

Based on an "anecdote of destiny" by Karen Blixen (written under the pseudonym Isak Dinesen), *The Immortal Story* is "essentially a true story" in the way that *The Public Enemy*'s opening credit insists it is too—that is as an allegory of archetypes. *The Immortal Story* is set in nineteenth-century China, in Welles' Brechtian creation of the exotic, which is not-actual and metaphoric. Mr. Clay is a wealthy old miser, and the world he inhabits is an earlier economic system where the U.S. treasury only had so much actual money and was bailed out on occasion by loans from private individuals like Stephen Girard of Philadelphia. Mr. Clay is very much like late-period Charles Kane. Kane's betrayal of himself and of Jedediah Leland is mirrored in Mr. Clay's betrayal and financial ruining of his business partner, Louis Ducrot, who wished to start out on his own years before. Rather than build his own Xanadu, Mr. Clay assumes Decrot's house. It is left in shambles for him by Decrot, who, before his suicide, burns and destroys all objects of beauty and art within, save for the mirrors to reflect Mr. Clay so that, "it would be his murderer's punishment ... to meet wherever he went, the portrait of a hangman."

Years later, after endless nights of ledger readings and rereadings, old Mr. Clay and his clerk Elishama (Roger Coggio) are haunted by a past personally and professionally in their need and drive to review and account—seeking

Director and star Orson Welles as "Mr. Clay" with Roger Coggio as his son/servant/double "Elishama" in *The Immortal Story* (1968). (Jerry Ohlinger's Movie Material Store.)

something beyond the net of capital instinctually, yet unable to imagine, or directly confront, anything else. Blixen's prose expresses the solidarity between the two in a way that Welles' mise-en-scène makes explicit: "In this way the master and the servant seemed to be standing back to back, facing the rest of the world, and did indeed, unknowingly, behave exactly as they would have behaved had they been father and son."[3] Yet, for all his cunning, Mr. Clay only understands Elishama as a tool of his will, and here *The Immortal Story* comments on a very iconic interpretation of fatherhood rooted in *Hamlet* as explored in Chapter 4.

"Father and son" are like the Lewis' in *Peeping Tom*. Mr. Clay's plot — to cause to happen the "immortal story" of legend — is conceived of as a "comedy," or theater, or *commedia dell'arte*, because, as Blixen informs readers, "Elishama began to realize the value of what is named a comedy, in which a man may at last speak the truth." Mr. Clay's final act is a combining of fact and truth, with which he seeks to restore what is absent within himself. Clay elaborates to Elishama, thinking outloud:

I myself ... am hard. I am dry. I have always been so, and I would not have it otherwise. I have a distaste for the juices of the body. I do not like the sight of blood,
I cannot drink milk, sweat is offensive to me, tears disgust me. In such things a
man's bones are dissolved. And in those relationships between people which they
name fellowship, friendship or love, a man's bones themselves are likewise
dissolved.[4]

There is a sexual impulse sterile or missing from both Mr. Clay and Elishama,
and it is the legacy of father to son that the voyeurism of their constructed
"comedy" stimulates them both. Elishama, unlike Mr. Clay, does not fear his
mortality, but rather the emotional trauma that isolation hibernates: "Elishama
did not want friends any more than Mr. Clay did. They were, to him, people
who suffered and perished — the world itself meant separation and loss, tears
and blood dripped from it."[5] Elishama is a direct link to Joseph K of *The Trial*,
whose individuality is threatened by the process around him, as well as Gregor
Samsa in *The Metamorphosis*, whose best expression comes (in English translation
anyway) as insect — intelligent but not "human." The existential absurdity
around Elishama is as rich as in Kafka's writings. Blixen and Welles here seem
to be exploring a Jewish morality and moral seriousness, which they — like Susan
Sontag — see as one of the "pioneering forces of modern [i.e. twentieth-century]
sensibility."[6] It is Elishama who chooses to employ Virginie Ducrot (Jeanne
Moreau) for Mr. Clay, and therefore it is Elishama who allows Virginie's cathartic, Shakespearean "revenge" to happen. Virginie remakes Elishama as Judas for
his pains when she cites "thirty pieces of silver" after he volleys Mr. Clay's first
offer to her. Without Elishama's "aestheticism and irony," Mr. Clay's comedy
would serve no true restorative purpose. It is only because of Elishama's clev-
erness that he is able to instinctively inject healing and balance. Elishama is different than his master/father in that he understands that account books are
"worth nothing when added in reverse," and, like the narrator of E.T.A. Hoffmann's *Sandman* or David Lynch, he senses the danger which can be unleashed
from within.

It is this danger from within that manifests with crescendoing intensity
during the sound era and is indicative of a greater and greater internal absence
in the individual brought about by media. For Welles this is always in the
periphery of his movies as in George's last walk home in *The Magnificent Ambersons* or Charles Rankin's true identity in *The Stranger* (1946). For Lynch, it will
become a time-space that is actually manifest — for instance much of *Eraserhead*
and the Black Lodge in *Twin Peaks*. Hoffmann — so important to Freud — orates
it as follows:

Perhaps there does exist a dark power which fastens on to us and leads us off along
a dangerous and ruinous path which we would otherwise not have trodden: but
if so, this power must have assumed within us the form of ourself, indeed have
become ourself, for otherwise we would not listen to it, otherwise there would be

no space within us in which it could perform its secret work. But if we possess a firm mind, a mind strengthened through living cheerfully, we shall always be able to recognize an inimical influence for what it is; and then that uncanny power must surely go under in the struggle we must suppose takes place before it can achieve that form which is, as I have said, a mirror-image of ourself.[7]

The reader immediately sees Hoffmann's appeal for Freud as his tonic, for the darkness within is the self-confrontation and self-recognition of a remaking. In *The Immortal Story*, the only character not living already as one of Hoffmann's "mirror images" is Paul the sailor, who is remade by the film's end by Mr. Clay, Elishama and Virginie.

Elishama states Mr. Clay's (and Welles') goal — "to demonstrate his omnipotence, to do what cannot be done," that is, translate myth into fact. As a lad, Mr. Clay had heard the story of a random sailor chosen to impregnate a woman at a rich man's house only to be forever banished from the scene the next morning. Mr. Clay is distressed to find out from Elishama that the tale is a legend told by all sailors over the centuries and that it had — in fact — probably never actually happened. In the movie, Mr. Clay vows, "I don't like pretense. I don't like prophecies. I like facts. If this story has never happened, I am going to make it happen now." In the Blixen novella, he adds, "It is insane and immoral to occupy oneself with unreal things. I like facts. I shall turn this piece of make believe into solid fact."[8] It is interesting, but understandable, that Welles deleted these lines as they would have separated the Mr. Clay/Welles dichotomy that the movie highlights at its center because it is the portrait of the artist — Welles — as an old man. The transformation Mr. Clay wishes to orchestrate in the film is not unlike creating a movie, which is a physicality of turning make-believe into fact. This is Welles' affinity with the material — not just as a film director — but as a part-time magician who seeks to conjure out of the air. Based on this and what is publically available from Welles' unfinished movie *The Other Side of the Wind* at the time of this writing, it is possible to believe that Welles was headed in the direction of psychedelic psychoanalytic phantasmagoria hinted at here in *The Immortal Story*, and best realized by Alejandro Jodorowsky in his cinema of the 1970s. In any case, *The Immortal Story* thus becomes the central movie about Welles as a creative artist.

Blixen's source text is followed rather faithfully by Welles, but is ambiguous in the way that Welles, like Mr. Clay, seeks to make things "real" — that is, nonambiguous. For Welles, and finally perhaps the character Mr. Clay, the pursuit of story is more interesting than the pursuit of money — a metaphor for filmmaking itself. Mr. Clay leaves wealth to his unborn "child" just as Kane calls for his sled before he expires. The Kleinian play technique is not only of importance in assuming roles but also to the concept of how narrative is played with and becomes the second half — the double — of performance. "The realization of a story was the thing to set a man at rest" is what Elishama

knows, and which he uses to perform reparation for Mr. Clay's original transgression. Here, Welles underlines the power and value of story and of play and
is, in this regard, totally dissimilar to the role he plays — as Mr. Clay only values
facts and assets. *The Immortal Story* is thusly a movie-movie as it investigates
story and play as well as builds its narrative around the forces of capital, making
the motion picture something Deleuze would quantify as being a film about
money.

Mr. Clay can only understand his desire for "make-believe" in terms of
the philosophy of capital. The extent to which those forces have remade him
are so extreme that he understands wealth to be "half" of himself— if not also
his double which serves to remove him from the danger of death. For Welles,
the double of capital leads to the fragmentation of his efforts. Blixen writes of
Mr. Clay speaking of this phenomenon,

> "I have comprehended that I myself shall not last as long as my fortune. The
> moment will come, it is approaching, when we two shall have to part, when one
> half of me must go and the other half live on. Am I to let it fall into the hands
> which till now I have managed to keep off it, to be fingered and meddled with by
> those greedy and offensive hands? I would as soon let my body be fingered and
> meddled with by them. When at night I think of it I cannot sleep."
> "I have not troubled," he said, "to look for a hand into which I might like to
> deliver my possessions, for I know that no such hand exists in the world. But it
> has, in the end, occurred to me that it might give me pleasure to leave them in a
> hand which I myself had caused to exist."
> "Had caused to exist," he repeated slowly. "Caused to exist, and called forth.
> As I have begotten my fortune, my million pounds.'"[9]

Mr. Clay so links creation to capital. Virginie states that "rich traders and mer-
chants are all mad" and compares Clay to Nero. Here the unadministered forces
of capital have transformed the miser into a historic caricature with no agency
in the tangible present as a result. Even Virginie's choice to participate in the
"comedy" is based on her own motives and not Mr. Clay's money. With Mr.
Clay's madness, Welles remakes his early aborted film of Joseph Conrad's *Heart
of Darkness*, where the camera was to be framed only from Marlow's first-person
point of view, and Welles would play Kurtz. Apart from driving him mad,
money for Mr. Clay involves penetration, and here capital is substituted for his
own physical sexuality. Conversely, Mr. Clay has "begotten" a fortune and thus
confirmed the surrogacy that wealth offered him. Mr. Clay's desires are suggested
as being that of a virgin's — "the immortal story" for him is the (adolescent)
dream of a one-night stand that becomes a lifetime of experience. Virginie is
no virgin, and as a result, this worldly experience — more than that of the three
men immediately around her — makes her the Hamlet figure of Welles' movie,
thrust into avenging the father she feels ambivalent toward. Like the Danish
prince, Virginie flirts with suicide and thus aligns with other protagonists
examined in this study like Mark Lewis, Paul Cartwright, Herman Herman

and even Alex/Victor—if their aggression is understood as Kleinian destructive impulses.

Virginie, however, is closest to Laura Palmer of *Twin Peaks*, as she is forced into adult sexuality too soon by the actions of the father. Blixen writes of this that "this night would bring about the final judgment of their old deadly enemy; the disgrace and humiliation of their daughter provided the conclusive evidence against him. The daughter, according to her vow long ago, would not see his face at the verdict, but the dead father and mother were there to watch it."[10] Virginie is like Norman Bates of *Psycho* or Tom Collier of *One More Tomorrow*, each largely doomed by their parents. As a result, Virginie's (and Laura's) living is a type of active dying. Returning to Klein and *A Contribution to the Psychogenesis of Manic-Depressive States* (1935), suicide is put into active perspective:

> According to the findings of Abraham and James Glover, a suicide is directed against the introjected object. But, while in committing suicide the ego intends to murder its bad objects, in my view at the same time it also always aims at saving its loved objects, internal or external. To put it shortly: in some cases the phantasies underlying suicide aim at preserving the internalized good objects and that part of the ego which is identified with good objects, and also at destroying the other part of the ego which is identified with the bad objects and the id. Thus the ego is enabled to become united with its love objects.[11]

In both *The Immortal Story* and *Twin Peaks: Fire Walk with Me*, murder/saving is present. For Welles, there is no threat of violence because the characters are nearly ghosts already. In *Twin Peaks: Fire Walk with Me*, the characters are very physically active and infused with the type of anxious spirits that *The Immortal Story* lulls to rest. From viewing *Citizen Kane* as Charles' possible death dream, to Dorothy Vallens' eroticizing of abusive violence in *Blue Velvet* (1986), what is important to the work of both Welles and Lynch are the phantasies underlying suicide that inspire them—what Klein calls "the emotional forces which underlie symbolism." Virginie only appears finally removed from the threat of suicide when Mr. Clay dies because she has gained an actual internalized good object as the result of Paul's fertilization of her egg and, because of Mr. Clay's destruction, she is also left mother to his heir.

Like Laura Palmer, Virginie finds her reality in sex and, also like Laura, Virginie is intimated to be a prostitute. The sailor confesses his virginity to Virginie, and in this way he becomes (probable virgin) Mr. Clay's full surrogate. Elishama's metaphysical "father and son" relationship to Mr. Clay is confirmed by the doubling of Clay and the sailor—for in his agency of sexually initiating Clay, Elishama has made Clay's paternity both possible and actual, finally uniting the metaphoric and the specific. Having no sexual experience to unmake, Paul's coitus with Virginie becomes the youth's primal scene. Welles' first on-screen intercourse depiction—between Virginie and Paul the sailor—has a heated, erotic discretion which presents Blixen's declaration that "[Virginie] felt

[Paul's] mighty grip round her as a hitherto-unknown kind of reality, which made everything else seem hollow and falsified."[12] As in Wilhelm Reich and Philip Barry, the powerful truth of the orgasm is again confirmed as the human energy force that is as powerful, if not superior to, any of its opposites — including technology or capital.

Mr. Clay and the sailor have an erotic bond, just as Herman and the Felix share in *Despair*, and the link between repressed homosexuality and capitalism is again affirmed. Here, to avoid the actual, the sailor is explicitly paid to leave and renounce love (with Virginie) as Mr. Clay had renounced love — like Wagner's Alberich — for financial success and the power it brings. Again, the manifestation of evil, as cited in Hoffmann, arises, but this time it is transformed into the subtlety of commerce and inhumanity which set the stage for the twenty-first century and the media era. As the sailor remarks, "Yes, he has paid me. And I took his money. But at that time, I did not know!"

Twin Peaks: Fire Walk with Me (1992)

David Lynch described his debut feature film *Eraserhead* (1977) as "a dream of dark and troubling things,"[13] and all his movies since then have had pronounced elements of slumber logic. Of course, nothing as conscious as cinema can be a dream in and of itself, yet it can present a dream state wherein the viewer's subconscious may engage in transference with surrogates. With *Twin Peaks: Fire Walk with Me*, Lynch adds to this a boogie-man figure — BOB — who can manifest inside people during waking hours, as well as prey on them, perhaps Freddy Kruger–like in their subconscious terrain. Some *Twin Peaks* mythology further suggests that this evil — and evil in a larger context — may be extraterrestrial, and this notion places evil outside the individual, when traditionally Sandman figures are within. The uncanniness of Hoffmann's mirror image is updated by Lynch for the twentieth century, so that now the individual is helpless and the "mind strengthened through living cheerfully"[14] is an impossible reality, as the sad fate of the "good" Dale Cooper trapped in the Black Lodge proves in *Twin Peaks: Fire Walk with Me*.

BOB is a direct descendant of the figure that bedevils and takes many uncanny forms in *The Sandman* and, of which Hoffmann's narrator writes, "pursued me everywhere, and I am almost ashamed to confess that he was able even to disturb my sleep, which is usually so sound, with all kinds of strange dreams."[15] In her dreams and hallucinations, Laura Palmer (Sheryl Lee) begins to understand herself as a cubist multiplicity — first through the way her vision folds into itself, then in her twinning with Teresa Banks, Donna Hayward, Ronette Pulaski and finally with the two angels — one of whom is, most suggestively, faceless. In *On the Sense of Loneliness* (1963), Klein, inspired by Bion, remarks that the twin figure "represents those un-understood and split off parts which the individual is longing to regain in the hope of achieving wholeness and complete understanding; they are sometimes felt to be the ideal parts. At other times the twin also represents an entirely reliable, in fact, idealized internal object."[16] Laura needs doubles because of all the "bad objects" inside her, and/or her self-hatred. She is an icon in her own house (and at her own school) — where pictures of her are displayed like holy relics even before her demise — and this has tragically removed Laura from herself, making her uncanny in life.

Laura is only one-half of herself — so she is both tormented and tormentor — largely as the result of an incestuous relationship with her father, Leland (Ray Wise). Laura imagines Leland to be the evil entity "BOB" when he repeatedly rapes her; as she tells her agoraphobic confidant, Harold Smith (Lenny Von Dohlen), "BOB is real — he's been having me since I was twelve." Laura has BOB inside her *literally* during the rapes, and also differently — metaphysically — as when she acts out and so feels his spirit within her. The trauma of abuse is not only within, but without as well, and predicates a cycle of tragedy.

As in Hoffmann, Leland is the father remade as Sandman, and he becomes the clear villain in the cosmology of *Twin Peaks: Fire Walk with Me*. When Laura conclusively learns that her father is BOB, she denies it, insisting, "It's

As in Hoffmann, Leland (Ray Wise) is the father remade as Sandman, and he becomes the clear villain to Laura (Sheryl Lee) in the cosmology of *Twin Peaks: Fire Walk with Me* (David Lynch, 1992). (Courtesy Andrew's Video Vault at the Rotunda.)

not him." It is Leland's denial of his own actions that necessitates Laura's murder in *Twin Peaks: Fire Walk with Me*. When Leland sees Teresa, Ronette and Laura waiting for him at the motel, he is confronted with his daughter's "infidelity" and the realization that his "princess" is engaged in the sex industry, which he himself feels ashamed to participate in, because — unlike the ritualized rapes of his daughter — it is both public and a choice. The boundaries between home and public are blurred, and so Leland's rationalization of what Sade would too-sympathetically term his "crimes of love" are challenged. Thus Leland must restore the Kleinian "good breast" within by destroying it without. Seeing his daughter remade as a whore, Leland needs to kill all three women at the motel in an attempt to regain the loss he now feels and to so keep his sexual impulses and shame a secret.

Yet, despite these impulses and deeds, Leland is treated with empathy by Lynch — if not outright sympathy. In the TV show, Leland alludes to being a victim of sexual abuse at Pearl Lakes. Sexual abuse, like evil in *Twin Peaks*, is again removed from the individual and placed as beholden to some greater, external force — as is also true in Lynch's *Blue Velvet* (1986) and *Wild at Heart* (1990). *Twin Peaks: Fire Walk with Me* grants Leland a very weird absolution in the scene where he comes to kiss Laura good night, and what Lynch adds to psychosis — perhaps dangerously — is a self-pity that creates a shocking moral relativism. This erotic trauma is the powerful but not subversive core of the work and is paralleled in the United States' national identity after the end of the Vietnam conflict as a nation that is "powerful but not subversive" and therefore the slave — not the master — of the forces of capital. Leland recalls Humbert Humbert in *Lolita* as the dejected lover — his consummate grief at the end of his affair overwhelming its pedophilic nature to flirt with true tragedy. In the train car right before he murders Laura, Leland says to his daughter, "I always thought you knew it was me," and he seems remorseful that she is aghast to know her father is her ph/fantastic rapist, BOB. Again, responsibility is removed from the individual by cinema, as Leland tells her, "Don't make me do this," and then kills her.

The train car in which Laura Palmer is murdered remakes Sirk's privileged cabins in the woods, as both are extra to society. Lynch's *neo-noir* mocks Sirk's melodrama but does not break the link between satire and surrealism, as the level of social commentary remains constant. Suggested by the TV show that lasted a season and a half in 1990 and 1991, Lynch's *Twin Peaks* movie, *Fire Walk with Me*, refilters the program's titillation into sexual grotesque and its homespun humor into violent absurdism. A television is literally smashed to bits in the opening scene of *Fire Walk with Me*, and — unlike the show — the *Twin Peaks* characters are now totally archetypes, "adapted" into the movie. This makes them the same characters they were on TV, but in a different context — a different *Twin Peaks*. Too schizophrenically for many viewers, characters are at once themselves and not. *Twin Peaks: Fire Walk with Me* is a nightmarish "bad trip" brimming with depravity and unresolved climaxes. Laura tells James, her remake of Bobby, who is her remake of BOB, to "quit trying to hold on so tight," and it is good advice for the viewer as well.

In an intimate moment in the school shower, Laura makes the emotional encounter with James sexual by placing his hand on her breasts. Reading Lynch's fantastic depiction of small-town America and incest, a primal social need is presented to make sex emotional rather than physical, which is a line of thinking that can only remove the individual from him- or herself. *Twin Peaks: Fire Walk with Me* is the "good" (moral) double of the (amoral) TV show.

Fire Walk with Me is filled with romantic pathos, and the movie's most lyrical moments reflect on the tragedy of youth. The film is bittersweet with the knowledge that it is sad to die before your maturity — yet aware of the poetry in dying young when everything is new and feels more — even the pleasure-pain of death. Donna Hayward, originally played by Lara Flynn Boyle, is recast with Moira Kelly, and the fissure between the two actresses and their portrayal of the character are reflected in the way Laura tries to unmake Donna, while Donna tries to become like Laura. *Twin Peaks: Fire Walk with Me* is not Laura's tragedy, but Donna's, and it is her innocence that is lost in the seven days before Laura's death. Donna's initiation in the film at the Roadhouse — lit brilliantly by Ron García like a late-period Warhol silk screen — is indicative of one-night binges typical of youth where individuals *almost* go "too far." Laura-Leland do go "too far" for the viewer, and it results in the movie's catharsis and reflections.

Rather than address many of the issues left hanging at the end of the second season of the TV show, *Twin Peaks: Fire Walk with Me* prequels the series' pilot episode, and after a somewhat unrelated initial half hour presents a narrative of Laura's death that is largely familiar to viewers of the show — save for the fact that Laura has never been characterized as herself because she was already dead at the start of the pilot. These factors give Lynch's movie a chance to focus on mood and sensation rather than plot, using eroticism as its primary tool of exploration. In *Coldness and Cruelty*, Deleuze remarks that "eroticism is able to act as a mirror to the world by reflecting its excesses, drawing out its violence and even conferring a 'spiritual' quality on these phenomena by the very fact that it puts them at the service of the senses."[17] With *Twin Peaks: Fire Walk with Me*, eroticism reflects the most excess when Lynch couples it with death, which is frequent given the trajectory of Laura's "passion." Laura sexualizes everything, and it is both her allure and tragedy. The movie achieves the spiritual quality postulated by Deleuze, and in this way the Lynch film is a female companion piece to *Bad Lieutenant*, coincidentally released the same year. However, it must be noted that the *Twin Peaks* universe is a Western White/Asian fantasy wherein money seems to have little importance — especially when not linked to crime. Like the Lieutenant, Herman, and Virginie, Laura is trying to kill herself to relieve and "top" her torment, thus preserving her Kleinian "internalized good objects,"[18] which her small town has removed with its objectifications and underbelly. As the Log Lady tells the viewer in *Twin Peaks: Fire Walk with Me*, "all goodness is in jeopardy," and thus Laura's immolation is imminent.

As with Otto Preminger's Laura Hunt, culled in his 1944 movie from the 1943 novel by Vera Caspary, Laura Palmer is a female Hamlet. However, depiction of gender can be problematic in Lynch as there is rarely equality. In *Twin Peaks: Fire Walk with Me*, Special Agent Chester Desmond (Chris Isaak) is introduced busting two buxom vixens outside a yellow school bus. He is interrupted to investigate Teresa Banks' death — as if all the FBI does is hunt down underage femme fatales. But it is also as if the FBI protects "purity," as gender seems unable to advance in Lynch's worldview past pure and impure, female and male. In *Eraserhead* and *Twin Peaks: Fire Walk with Me*, gender gives way to marital discord, and one of the roots of the incest in the Palmer house may be what is

The uncanny picture of female Hamlet and ur–Laura Palmer, Laura Hunt (Gene Tierney) gazed at by Detective Lt. Mark McPherson (Dana Andrews) in the film *Laura* (Otto Preminger, 1944). (Courtesy the Chestnut Hill Film Group.)

absent from Leland and his wife Sarah's union. With a nod to Hitchcock's *Suspicion* (1941), on the nights he rapes Laura, Leland drugs the milk he gives Sarah (Grace Zabriskie) and ever so gently forces her to finish the glass.

Lynch feeds on other movies as well as himself, and perhaps this explains why his films have begun to feed on themselves in the twenty-first century. There are many links to *Eraserhead* in *Twin Peaks: Fire Walk with Me*— the floor of the Black Lodge resembles the floor in Henry's apartment, Leland evolves the Man in the Planet, and when Leland shuts the train car door after Laura's murder, the sound effect is an *Eraserhead* quotation from the levers and gears that start the 1977 feature. Early crime drama like *The Public Enemy* becomes a point of reference with the social context removed, making *Twin Peaks: Fire Walk with Me* a movie-movie. This depicts the individual — but the individual as removed from capital by capital — perhaps because of "damn fine" coffee and pie, which might as well be a stand-in for beer and television. Laura is a female Tom Powers, and Paddy Ryan mutates into Jacques Renault (Walter Olkewicz). The needle running out of record on the Victrola phonograph while playing "I'm Forever Blowing Bubbles" in *The Public Enemy* is restaged in the *Twin Peaks* series with the murder of Laura's twin cousin, Maddy Ferguson, in Episode 15 (first broadcast November 10, 1990), and in the film with the prominence of the phonograph in the Palmer home. As well as hosting many classic crime drama tropes, there are many elements of neo-*noir* in *Twin Peaks: Fire Walk with Me*. The Roadhouse is a different Movie House — the club in *Point Blank*. The cinema of Roman Polanski is specifically referenced in *Twin Peaks: Fire Walk with Me* with the recalling of the apartments of *Repulsion* (1965) and *The Tenant* (1976) and, most obviously, the *noir* incest of *Chinatown* (1974). Unlike Pressman, Stoppard and Fassbinder's *Despair*, which uses nostalgia pastiche to drive home witty satire, *Twin Peaks: Fire Walk with Me* references just as many cinematic events, but never in a way to distance the audience or flirt with actual self-satire. This removes the political, and *Twin Peaks: Fire Walk with Me* uses quotations from other cinema to avoid being about anything political. It is reflective of the era of George H.W. Bush's presidency (1988–1992) and serves to thus draw patient viewers deeper into the mystery — a movie-movie — with no solution because it has no context.

However, while *Twin Peaks: Fire Walk with Me* eschews the political as a reference to the decade it was created in, the movie does have a relationship with the technological. In *Twin Peaks: Fire Walk with Me*'s first movement, Kiefer Sutherland is FBI agent Sam Stanley, who can be considered the actor's dry run for *24*'s Jack Bauer. The link between *Twin Peaks* and *24* (2001–2010) — other than object lesson — is the queasy subtext of what intelligence agencies, fueled by technology, endeavor to do and are willing to do. *Twin Peaks* embraces uncanniness whereas *24* denies it, though both are rooted in the soap opera genre that thrives on it. The *Twin Peaks* movie-movie universe reflects the pop

Director and star David Lynch (left) as FBI Regional Bureau Chief Gordon Cole who speaks in code to his agents with Chris Isaak as the ur-Dale Cooper, Special Agent Chester Desmond. Lynch and *Twin Peaks: Fire Walk with Me*'s (1992) use of private language allow the visuals to be removed from speech taking cinema to its highest plane. (Jerry Ohlinger's Movie Material Store.)

culture which is used to create narrative tropes setting up unrealistic surrogacies for American viewers. This is how Lynch began to devour his own work in the 1990s leading to projects like *Mulholland Dr.* and *Inland Empire* in the naughts that flirted only with self-reference, if not self-cannibalism. This reductive period of Lynch's work begins with the "haunted" elevator at the Philadelphia FBI office in *Twin Peaks: Fire Walk with Me* that invokes *The Shining*, just as Kubrick's 1980 motion picture invoked *Eraserhead*. Kubrick can quote Lynch, but when Lynch quotes Lynch, it is a manifestation of artistic incest.

At the FBI office, Phillip Jeffries (David Bowie) dissolves into TV grain and a burned-out Black Lodge — two key visuals in terms of *Twin Peaks: Fire Walk with Me*'s relationship to its television predecessor. In addition, the character of Jeffries shows the astute series viewer how the "good" Dale might have been lost in the Black Lodge and suggests how the "good" Dale may one day return. It is never clear what the Black Lodge is, just as it is never clear why Gordon Cole (David Lynch) speaks in code to his agents. Yet Lynch and *Twin Peaks'* use of private language and the language of code allows the visuals to be removed from speech as in the turn-of-the-last-century plays of Alfred Jarry which destroyed classical theater. *Twin Peaks: Fire Walk with Me* creates with visuals, while it destroys with dialogue, taking cinema to its final plane just before its endpoint. Lynch recycles himself because there is nowhere else for sound cinema to evolve. Thus, *Twin Peaks: Fire Walk with Me* is true, great and important modernist art in its impenetrability. The film's incoherency gives it a frantic and raw power and places the viewer in Laura's mind-set. Lynch is not a filmmaker to interpret but reflect upon, and with *Twin Peaks: Fire Walk with Me* he takes studio moviemaking as far as it can go in terms of art and object.

Conclusion

For a Remaking

It has been a goal of this project to consider cinema apart from auteur theory. While the prism of a director's vision and oeuvre is a seductive lens through which to view the medium, it also falls, as Leo Braudy points out in *The World in a Frame* (1976), into "the Romantic trap of searching for only what is obviously original and personal in a work."[1] To seek the personal is to deny the cultural and that motion pictures are always the product of multiple hands. Cinematographers, editors and composers play just as crucial a role as the producer and/or director of a movie and are too often slighted because it is more comfortable for an individual to place the responsibility for the work on one being. Today, colorists have taken on roles as paramount as cinematographers, and this shift from creation in production to post-production is indicative of the medium of cinema's evolution into media and how media has changed the very method of moving pictures.

Of the twenty-three movies examined in depth in this work, it is interesting to examine the current stature of the directors represented. Several of these individuals like Edgar G. Ulmer, Michael Powell, David Cronenberg, Andy Warhol, Douglas Sirk, Alfred Hitchcock, Gus Van Sant, Nancy Meyers, Rainer Werner Fassbinder, and David Lynch remain vital to cinema, whereas directors like William A. Wellman, John Boorman, Abel Ferrera, Peter Godfrey, Orson Welles, Stanley Kubrick, John Stahl, David Swift, Shaun Costello, Jim Sotos, Eric Zala, and David Lynch have been ushered to the periphery of the canon because the movies they are associated with have either become far more iconic than their careers, or because their cinema offers vantage points unable to be easily digested in this current media era focused on sound bites and advertising. This segregation reflects in no way on the individual's life and/or work and its quality, just as it is no mistake that David Lynch appears on both lists of directors.

198

Film Cans Behind the Stage — The Art Holiday Theater, 4204 Kensington Avenue at Frankford Avenue, December 2007. With the help of Jay Schwartz of the Secret Cinema, I was able to rescue only a few of over 1,000 poorly labeled cans of 35mm film stored and forgotten behind the screen of the Art Holiday theater — the rest were destroyed by an ashamed and malicious owner. What movies were in those cans that are now forever lost? (Photograph by the author.)

Lynch's cinema is hugely imitated; however his methods are sadly almost never adopted, and so his importance as a filmmaker is one of the most controversial issues facing cinema studies today. What does it mean when style has been separated from idea?

The established directors of importance still working in English-language cinema in the second decade of the twenty-first century — like Woody Allen, James Cameron, John Carpenter, Francis Ford Coppola, Wes Craven, David Cronenberg, Joe Dante, Jonathan Demme, Brian De Palma, Stephen Frears, William Friedkin, Buddy Giovinazzo, Peter Greenaway, Richard Linklater, David Lynch, Terrence Malick, Sally Potter, George A. Romero, Paul Schrader, Martin Scorsese, Steven Soderbergh, Paul Verhoeven, John Waters and Steven Spielberg — continue to make movies of interest, well versed in the grammar of cinema, politics and media. Directors of the future — or those at the start of their (potentially) great careers — like Paul Thomas Anderson, Darren Aronofsky, Drew Barrymore, Vernon Chatman, Louis C.K., Sofia Coppola, Vincent Gallo, Todd Haynes, Harmony Korine, John Cameron Mitchell, Trey Parker, J.T. Petty, Mathew Porterfield, Todd Solondz and Whit Stillman — challenge marketing expectations with moving pictures which provoke thought without pushing any clear analysis onto viewers. If there is hope for a remaking of visual culture within the United States of America it may well begin with the aforementioned directors' work or their collaborations with crew — this may be the rubric, that cinema persons not listed above (*sorry!*) may work off of, or against.

Apart from directors, the greatest hope for motion pictures is the embrace of genre, which repositions content, relegating it to the sidelines while enabling style, which — so long as the predetermined expectations are heeded or ignored — presents a viable platform and/or structure for feature-length cinema. With genre, directors happily evaporate into style and the culling of archetypes and motifs. The horror genre now remains the best expression for emerging stylists, while also allowing some true subversion to still exist within the culture industry. For Jacques Lacan, the real *is* trauma, and therefore horror movies should be viewed as the last vestige of dealing with reality in American cinema because they represent actual (if sometimes too cautionary) trauma. Currently, Hollywood is remaking the "classic" *film rouges* of the 1970s and 1980s (such as *The Last House on the Left, The Crazies, The Texas Chain Saw Massacre, Halloween, The House on Sorority Row, Halloween II, A Nightmare on Elm Street, The Stepfather,* etc.) in a way that supports the examination of remakes in this project. The most interesting of these theoretically is Marcus Nispel's "reboot," *Friday the 13th* from 2009. In this, story- and screenwriters Damian Shannon, Mark Swift and Mark Wheaton condense *Friday the 13th* parts 1 (1980), 2 (1981) and 3-D (1982) into one story line. This acceleration of public mythology catapults the movie to the forefront of excitement because the format of the established plot is respected — thus eliciting viewer transference all around — while the pace is sped up to provide ingenuity to the momentum. Unfortunately, *Friday the 13th* 2009 does not provide ingenuity for the actual plot, which remains reactionary and largely without surprise or true shock.

It will take a great cultural shift, a true event — like the assassination of President John F. Kennedy or of John Lennon — to break the United States out of its current patterns. It is no mistake that the event must be violent — as capital has an unbreakable link to violence, and violence is the universal language of twenty-first century media culture. The greatest fight today lies within the issues of copyright and creative commons as juxtaposed between the individual and the corporate. For example, the works of playwright Samuel Beckett have been staunchly guarded by his estate so that his performance texts are unable to be reinterpreted or enacted by emerging visionaries. When that material is finally in the public domain — and *if* it is allowed to enter the public domain — it will allow an illustration of the value of freedom so clearly missing from the United States since September 12, 2001.

The History of War
Or, "Aren't You the Little Play Actor?"

The reasons for the demise of the appreciation and respect of culture in the United States of America at the start of the twenty-first century — as represented in this text by cinematic culture — are the result of the decrease in literacy, the antisocial effect of media, and the rise of infotainment over the course of the twentieth century. Intellectualism — the ultimate human achievement to overcome the animal/biological parameters of birth and survival — has been, since the American colonies' eighteenth-century revolution against the English, conceptualized as the antithesis of religious devotion, the unmooring of character, and therefore symbolic of decadence. Yet this belief is in direct contradiction with the human — as what is chosen when survival is not an anxiety must be considered as one of the purest forms of humanity. This is especially true when thinking — as it is now — is positioned as the domain of the divine and so intellectual curiosity becomes heresy. The United States' sense of "moral superiority," gleaned by its involvement in World War II, along with the cancerous growth of the military-industrial complex, has led to this active embrace of ignorance and stupidity in the name of social egalitarianism by the citizenry fed by products and taught to consume. At the same time, twentieth-century technology, and especially personal computers in its later years, accelerated modernity and its cycles so that intellect can only be split into a deceptive binary of "simplicity" or "fragment." Thinking requires thought not only regarding the subject, but of itself, so that thought becomes (the) action. It is only through assemblages and symbolic logic that thinking can be attempted. The resistance to creativity suggests that the United States has reached a plateau of moribundity and no doubt explains the analogies to the end of the Roman Empire afloat in the zeitgeist.

In *The Dehumanization of Art* (1925), José Ortega y Gasset points to the emotions at play that rationalize anti-intellectualism: "When a man dislikes a work of art, but understands it, he feels superior to it; and there is no reason for indignation. But when his dislike is due to his failure to understand, he feels vaguely humiliated and this rankling sense of inferiority must be counterbalanced by indignant self-assertion."[2] It is this need to compensate and to find a footing in the largely contradictory and illusory web of capital that *plays* into the system itself by presenting an enemy and which results in anti-intellectualism. That man or woman seeks "self-assertion" is a healthy drive as illustrated by Melanie Klein; however capital only allows the expression in terms of negation, which is not progressive but reactionary and core to problems currently undermining the nation.

William Earle, writing in *Revolt against Realism in the Films* (1968), argues,
"The satisfactions of realist art almost seem to be created precisely in order to
extinguish the lurking anxiety that the real world is nothing in the first place
but a delusive fiction."[3] Cinema has perpetuated the problems it has provoked
and doing so has deluded itself and, ironically, its power. Now media has
replaced and reformed cinema — but the psychology of late twentieth-century
viewership remains, wherein Fassbinder comments, "The most friendly reception
[is] reserved for the kind of film that very skillfully avoided the risk that the
viewer might be reminded of his own reality."[4] True reality can only be attempted
to be perceived without electricity or technology, for these modern comforts
distort just as much as they illuminate and ignite. True darkness, or the
unknown, is culturally repressed, informing cinema's dreams and allegories
while also allowing the forces of capital to operate without an impetus to con-
ceal their actions, which are increasingly monopolistic. As stated by Max
Horkheimer and Theodor W. Adorno in *The Culture Industry: Enlightenment
as Mass Deception* (1944), "Under monopoly all mass culture is identical, and
the lines of its artificial framework begin to show through. The people at the
top are no longer so interested in concealing monopoly: as its violence becomes
more open, so its power grows. Movies and radio need no longer pretend to be
art. The truth that they are just business is made into an ideology in order to
justify the rubbish they deliberately produce."[5] Media is violence, and ideology

In *Telephone* (Jonas Åkerlund, 2010), this music video cum short film starring
Lady Gaga (left) and Beyoncé displays a kaleidoscoping of cinema by media,
alluding again to a medium where content has been entirely replaced by form.

has replaced justice, and the only "truths" that remain are fictions more poetic than actual.

The Judgment of Fidelity and Compression

Cinema is the *Gesamtkunstwerk* of the twentieth century, and with cinema's end circa 1998, the possibilities of a total work of art return to the (well-funded) opera house and advance into the realm of video games and audio/visual installation. More than ever, media is viewer controlled and viewer remixed. Creativity has changed from the redaction of (literary) convention (for instance Shakespeare's use of Ovid, Wagner's use of the *Nibelungenlied*, or Chaplin's use of Charles Perrault, etc) to the mash-up, where idea is not manifested with visuals but where preexisting visuals are juxtaposed, and the core ideology and purpose of assemblage is thus obscured even while sensation is communicated. It is something more symbolic but with less content. In this regard, media might excel into a great art form, but only if it can be removed from the product of technology, which could be impossible.

Certainly, the most exciting vestiges of cinema are currently outside the frame and, true to this concern, the most inspiration is now displayed by advertising departments. While of highly questionable artistic and entertainment value, it is no surprise that *Mad Men* is one of the most popular shows of this era. 2009's hit summer movie, *The Proposal*, directed by Anne Fletcher, is a lackluster affair; however its faux-backstage spoof of its own production, which appeared as a sketch on the website funnyordie.com as a marketing promotion, has more merit (and laughs) in its four minutes than in the feature's often uninspired one hundred eight. *Middle Men* (2010), directed by George Gallo, is another unexceptional movie, yet the distributor's choice to market the motion picture via a "deleted orgy sequence" on pornhub.com presents a nexus of ideas more challenging than anything explored with the central product, while also displaying the double standard which has removed the "adult"—and adult sexuality—from the screen except as unequivocal pornography.

YouTube's current two-gigabyte and eight-minute space and time limits have shaped production and the thinking about production. Retroactively as a result, movies in the media era have increasingly become sequences of sequences rather than cohesive wholes. It is not a matter of what computers can do for the individual, but how computers can digest media. Sadly, what is easiest to digest is that which has been devoured and regurgitated. At the time of this writing, Lady Gaga remakes early Madonna, just as Madonna remade Chaplin for the "Me Generation." Chaplin, like Mickey Mouse, is iconic because of timing as much as talent. That Chaplin's career coincided with the birth of cinema, which exponentially increased his audience and made him reproducible, is similar to Madonna who reaped the same benefits from the inception of MTV in the early 1980s. As a result, both Chaplin and Madonna gained an iconic stature that might have otherwise passed them by. As artists they branded themselves, made and remade themselves, and had the luck to be created as well as facilitated by technology. Lady Gaga's *Telephone* music video cum short film (directed by Jonas Åkerlund) from 2010 displays this kaleidoscoping of cinema by media. Its fetishized references to the movies of Quentin Tarantino alludes again to a medium where content has been entirely replaced by form. This mainstreaming or normalization of subversion removes any trace of the political from motion pictures themselves and makes the media product only, which, of course, is wholly political but, of course, now without debate or consciousness. This leads the individual to create oneself as the work, and the work becomes merely an accoutrement of that performance. It can be argued that Wagner saw this internalization of *Gesamtkunstwerk* when in *The Art-Work of the Future* (1849) he remarked,

> Who, then, will be the Artist of the Future?
> Without a doubt, the Poet.
> But who will be the Poet?
> Indisputably the *Performer*.[6]

What is essential to Wagner's later, great work is its cyclical nature. This text's final challenge to the reader is to reboot the cycle of our era which is at ebb tide. A pure cinema must be remade from scratch wherein the individual is nourished rather than refashioned. Imitation must give way to analysis. This attempted rebirth must begin with the individual — the performer — but resonate out to re-encompass literacy and critical thinking, privileging responsible intellectual curiosity above everything else.

Chapter Notes

Introduction

1. Harold Bloom. *Shakespeare: The Invention of the Human* (New York: Riverhead Books, 1998), 714.

2. Bloom, *Shakespeare: The Invention of the Human*, 9.

3. Helmut Käutner, "Gratitude toward the Theater," in *German Essays on Film*, ed. Richard W. McCormick and Alison Guenther-Pal (New York: Continuum, 2004), 168.

4. Friedrich Hebbel, "Preface to *Maria Magdalena*" (1844), in *Masterpieces of the Modern German Theatre*, ed. Robert W. Corrigan (New York: Collier, 1967), 74–75.

5. Hebbel, "Preface to *Maria Magdalena*," 74.

6. Hugo von Hofmannsthal, "The Substitute for Dreams" (1921), in *German Essays on Film*, ed. Richard W. McCormick and Alison Guenther-Pal (New York: Continuum, 2004), 53.

7. Walter Benjamin, "The Work of Art in the Age of Mechanical Reproduction" (1935), in *Illuminations: Essays and Reflections*, edited and with an introduction by Hannah Arendt (New York: Schocken, 1969), 224.

8. Benjamin, "The Work of Art in the Age of Mechanical Reproduction" (1935), 224.

9. Béla Balázs, "The Visible Human" (1924), in *German Essays on Film*, ed. Richard W. McCormick and Alison Guenther-Pal (New York: Continuum, 2004), 74.

10. Melanie Klein, "On the Theory of Anxiety and Guilt" (1948), in *The Writings of Melanie Klein*, vol. 3, *Envy and Gratitude and Other Works 1946–1963* (New York: Free Press, 1975), 26.

11. Melanie Klein, "Love, Guilt and Reparation" (1937), in *The Writings of Melanie Klein*, vol. 1, *Love, Guilt and Reparation and Other Works 1921–1945* (New York: Free Press, 1975), 311.

12. Klein, *Love, Guilt and Reparation* (1937), 311.

13. Klein, *Love, Guilt and Reparation* (1937), 311–313.

14. Gilles Deleuze, *Cinema 2: The Time-Image* (1985), trans. Hugh Tomlinson and Robert Galeta (Minneapolis: University of Minnesota Press, 1989), 37.

15. Melanie Klein, "Notes on Some Schizoid Mechanisms" (1946), in *The Selected Melanie Klein*, ed. Juliet Mitchell (New York: Macmillan), 238.

16. Benjamin, "The Work of Art in the Age of Mechanical Reproduction," 230–231.

17. Balázs, "The Visible Human," 86.

18. Susan Sontag, *Against Interpretation and Other Essays* (New York: Farrar, Straus and Giroux, 1966), 227.

19. V. F. Perkins, "Film as Film" (1972), in *Film Theory and Criticism: Introductory Readings*, eds. Gerald Mast and Marshall Cohen (New York: Oxford University Press, 1979), 53.

20. Klein, "The Psycho-analytic Play Technique: Its History and Significance," 46.

21. Melanie Klein, "The Psychological Principles of Infant Analysis" (1926), in *The Selected Melanie Klein*, ed. Juliet Mitchell (New York: Macmillan), 64.

22. Siegfried Kracauer, "The Little Shopgirls Go to the Movies" (1927), in *German Essays on Film*, ed. Richard W. McCormick and Alison Guenther-Pal (New York: Continuum, 2004), 100.

23. Sigmund Freud, "The Uncanny" (1919), in *Collected Papers*, vol. 4, *Papers on Metapsychology: Papers on Applied Psycho-Analysis*, trans. Joan Riviere (New York: Basic Books, 1961), 394.

24. Siegfried Kracauer, "From Caligari to Hitler: A Psychological History of the

German Film" (1947), in *German Essays on Film*, ed. Richard W. McCormick and Alison Guenther-Pal (New York: Continuum, 2004), 182–183.

25. Theodor Adorno, *Transparencies on Film*, in *German Essays on Film*, ed. Richard W. McCormick and Alison Guenther-Pal (New York: Continuum, 2004), 274.

26. Guy Debord, *Society of the Spectacle* (1967), trans. Ken Knabb (London: Rebel Press), 13.

Chapter 1

1. Bertolt Brecht, "The Three-Penny Trial: A Sociological Experiment" (1931), in *German Essays on Film*, ed. Richard W. McCormick and Alison Guenther-Pal (New York: Continuum, 2004), 127.

2. Susan Sontag, *Against Interpretation and Other Essays* (New York: Farrar, Straus and Giroux, 1966), 215.

3. Melanie Klein, "Mourning and Its Relation to Manic-Depressive States" (1940), in *The Selected Melanie Klein*, ed. Juliet Mitchell (New York: Macmillan), 237.

4. Klein, "Mourning and Its Relation to Manic-Depressive States," 172.

5. Klein, "Mourning and Its Relation to Manic-Depressive States," 237.

6. Walter Benjamin, "The Work of Art in the Age of Mechanical Reproduction" (1935), in *Illuminations: Essays and Reflections*, edited and with an introduction by Hannah Arendt (New York: Schocken, 1969), 242.

7. Friedrich Dürrenmatt, "Problems of the Theatre" (1954), in *Dramatic Theory and Criticism: Greeks to Grotowski*, ed. Bernard F. Dukore (New York: Holt, Reinhart and Winston, 1974), 855.

8. Guy Debord, *Society of the Spectacle* (1967), trans. Ken Knabb (London: Rebel Press), 15.

9. Melanie Klein, "Early Stages of the Oedipus Conflict" (1928), in *The Selected Melanie Klein*, ed. Juliet Mitchell (New York: Macmillan), 72.

10. Octavio Paz, "An Erotic Beyond" (1961), in *An Erotic Beyond: Sade* (1993), trans. Eliot Weinberger (New York: Harcourt, Brace, 1998), 45.

11. Bertolt Brecht, *The Rise and Fall of the City of Mahagonny* (1930), Metropolitan Opera: 16 November 1979.

12. Paz, "An Erotic Beyond," 49.

13. Paz, "An Erotic Beyond," 9.

14. Melanie Klein, "Weaning" (1936), in *The Writings of Melanie Klein*, vol. 1, *Love, Guilt and Reparation and Other Works 1921–*

1945 (New York: Free Press, 1975), 293.

15. Paz, "An Erotic Beyond," 10.

16. Paz, "An Erotic Beyond," 11–12.

17. Paz, "An Erotic Beyond," 14.

18. Béla Balázs, "The Visible Human" (1924), in *German Essays on Film*, ed. Richard W. McCormick and Alison Guenther-Pal (New York: Continuum, 2004), 81.

19. Paz, "An Erotic Beyond," 13.

20. Gilles Deleuze, "Coldness and Cruelty" (1967), in *Masochism*, by Gilles Deleuze and Leopold van Sacher-Masoch (New York: Zone Books, 1991), 116.

21. Paz, "An Erotic Beyond," 23.

22. Paz, "An Erotic Beyond," 20.

23. Gertrud Koch, "Ex-Changing the Gaze: Re-Visioning Feminist Film Theory" (1985), in *German Essays on Film*, ed. Richard W. McCormick and Alison Guenther-Pal (New York: Continuum, 2004), 279.

24. Melanie Klein, "The Psycho-analytic Play Technique: Its History and Significance" (1940), in *The Selected Melanie Klein*, ed. Juliet Mitchell (New York: Macmillan), 50.

25. Klein, "Early Stages of the Oedipus Conflict," 72.

26. Jurij Lotman, "Semiotics of Cinema" (1973), in *Film Theory and Criticism: Introductory Readings*, ed. Gerald Mast and Marshall Cohen (New York: Oxford University Press, 1979), 58.

27. Robert Bloch, *Three Complete Novels: Psycho, Psycho II, Psycho House* (New York: Wing Books, 1993), 230.

28. Sontag, *Against Interpretation and Other Essays*, 61.

29. Sergei Eisenstein, "Film Form: The Cinematographic Principle and the Ideogram" (1929), in *Film Theory and Criticism: Introductory Readings*, ed. Gerald Mast and Marshall Cohen (New York: Oxford University Press, 1979), 94.

30. Koch, "Ex-Changing the Gaze: Re-Visioning Feminist Film Theory," 283.

31. Jean Baudrillard, "War Porn" (2004), in *The Conspiracy of Art: Manifestos, Interviews, Essays* (2005), ed. Sylvere Lotringer, trans Ames Hodges (New York: Semiotext(e), 2005), 206.

Chapter 2

1. Carl Schmitt, *The Concept of the Political* (1932), trans. George Schwab (Chicago: University of Chicago Press, 1996), 38.

2. Melanie Klein, "Our Adult World and Its Roots in Infancy" (1959), in *The Writings of Melanie Klein*, vol. 3, *Envy and Gratitude and Other Works 1946–1963* (New York: Free Press, 1975), 256.

3. Melanie Klein, "A Study of Envy and Gratitude" (1956), in *The Selected Melanie Klein*, ed. Juliet Mitchell (New York: Macmillan), 213.

4. William Earle, "Revolt against Realism in the Films" (1968), in *Film Theory and Criticism: Introductory Readings*, ed. Gerald Mast and Marshall Cohen (New York: Oxford University Press, 1979), 33–34.

5. Gene Youngblood, "Expanded Cinema" (1970), in *Film Theory and Criticism: Introductory Readings*, ed. Gerald Mast and Marshall Cohen (New York: Oxford University Press, 1979), 755.

6. Siegfried Kracauer, "The Little Shopgirls Go to the Movies" (1927), in *German Essays on Film*, ed. Richard W. McCormick and Alison Guenther-Pal (New York: Continuum, 2004), 111.

7. Søren Kierkegaard, "The Ancient Tragical Motive as Reflected in the Modern" (1943), in *Dramatic Theory and Criticism: Greeks to Grotowski*, ed. Bernard F. Dukore (New York: Holt, Reinhart and Winston, 1974), 554.

8. Guy Debord, *Society of the Spectacle* (1967), trans. Ken Knabb (London: Rebel Press), 58.

9. Melanie Klein, "Love, Guilt and Reparation" (1937), in *The Writings of Melanie Klein*, vol. 1, *Love, Guilt and Reparation and Other Works 1921–1945* (New York: Free Press, 1975), 326–327.

10. Klein, "Love, Guilt and Reparation" (1937), 330.

11. Harold Bloom. *Shakespeare: The Invention of the Human* (New York: Riverhead Books, 1998), 714.

12. Melanie Klein, "Criminal Tendencies in Normal Children" (1927), in *The Writings of Melanie Klein*, vol. 1., *Love, Guilt and Reparation and Other Works 1921–1945* (New York: Free Press, 1975), 170.

13. Gilles Deleuze, *Cinema 2: The Time-Image* (1985), trans. Hugh Tomlinson and Robert Galeta (Minneapolis: University of Minnesota Press, 1989), 78.

14. Guy Debord, *Society of the Spectacle* (1967), 58.

15. Klein, "Love, Guilt and Reparation" (1937), 343.

16. Klein, "Love, Guilt and Reparation" (1937), 333.

17. Klein, "Love, Guilt and Reparation" (1937), 340.

18. Melanie Klein, "Personification in the Play of Children" (1929), in *The Writings of Melanie Klein*, vol. 1., *Love, Guilt and Reparation and Other Works 1921–1945* (New York: Free Press, 1975), 206.

19. Donald E. Westlake, *The Hunter* (New York: Avon Books, 1962) 136.

20. Deleuze, *Cinema 2: The Time-Image* (1985), 77.

21. Debord, *Society of the Spectacle* (1967), 24.

22. William Shakespeare, *Hamlet*, Act 3, scene 2, line 190.

23. Deleuze, *Cinema 2: The Time-Image* (1985), 7.

24. Earle, "Revolt against Realism in the Films" (1968), 44.

25. Gilles Deleuze, "Coldness and Cruelty" (1967), in *Masochism*, by Gilles Deleuze and Leopold van Sacher-Masoch (New York: Zone Books, 1991), 86.

26. Kierkegaard, "The Ancient Tragical Motive as Reflected in the Modern" (1943), 554.

Chapter 3

1. Fanny Hurst, *Imitation of Life* (1933) (New York: Harper and Row, 1990), 97.

2. Susan Sontag, *Against Interpretation and Other Essays* (New York: Farrar, Straus and Giroux, 1966), 13.

3. Parker Tyler, "Magic and Myth of the Movies" (1947), in *Film Theory and Criticism: Introductory Readings*, ed. Gerald Mast and Marshall Cohen (New York: Oxford University Press, 1979), 753.

4. Julius Caesar Scaliger, "Poetics" (1561), in *Dramatic Theory and Criticism: Greeks to Grotowski*, ed. Bernard F. Dukore (New York: Holt, Reinhart and Winston, 1974), 138.

5. Scaliger, "Poetics" (1561), 139.

6. Hurst, *Imitation of Life* (1933), 63.

7. Hurst, *Imitation of Life* (1933), 20.

8. Hurst, *Imitation of Life* (1933), 56.

9. Hurst, *Imitation of Life* (1933), 7.

10. William Shakespeare, *Hamlet*, Act 3, scene 1, line 177.

11. Melanie Klein, "Criminal Tendencies in Normal Children" (1927), in *The Writings of Melanie Klein*, vol. 1, *Love, Guilt and Reparation and Other Works 1921–1945* (New York: Free Press, 1975), 170.

12. Melanie Klein, "Weaning" (1936), in *The Writings of Melanie Klein*, vol. 1, *Love, Guilt and Reparation and Other Works 1921–1945* (New York: Free Press, 1975), 293–294.

13. Melanie Klein, "Love, Guilt and Reparation" (1937), in *The Writings of Melanie Klein*, vol. 1, *Love, Guilt and Reparation and Other Works 1921–1945* (New York: Free Press, 1975), 309.

14. Siegfried Kracauer, "The Little Shopgirls Go to the Movies" (1927), in *German Essays on Film*, ed. Richard W. McCormick and

Alison Guenther-Pal (New York: Continuum, 2004), 109.

15. Hurst, *Imitation of Life* (1933), 149.

16. Hurst, *Imitation of Life* (1933), 2.

17. Hurst, *Imitation of Life* (1933), 35.

18. Hurst, *Imitation of Life* (1933), 47.

19. Hurst, *Imitation of Life* (1933), 100.

20. Melanie Klein, "Some Theoretical Conclusions Regarding the Emotional Life of the Infant" (1952), in *The Writings of Melanie Klein*, vol. 3, *Envy and Gratitude and Other Works 1946–1963* (New York: Free Press, 1975), 74–75.

21. Hurst, *Imitation of Life* (1933), 243.

22. Hurst, *Imitation of Life* (1933), 86.

23. Hurst, *Imitation of Life* (1933), 19.

24. Hurst, *Imitation of Life* (1933), 108.

25. Hurst, *Imitation of Life* (1933), 164.

26. Bertolt Brecht, "The Three-Penny Trial: A Sociological Experiment" (1931), in *German Essays on Film*, ed. Richard W. McCormick and Alison Guenther-Pal (New York: Continuum, 2004), 122.

27. Heide Schlupmann, "Melodrama and Social Drama in the Early German Cinema" (1990), in *German Essays on Film*, ed. Richard W. McCormick and Alison Guenther-Pal (New York: Continuum, 2004), 292–293.

28. Schlupmann, "Melodrama and Social Drama in the Early German Cinema," (1990), 294.

29. Siegfried Kracauer, "The Little Shopgirls Go to the Movies" (1927), 104.

30. Philip Roth, *The Human Stain* (New York: Vintage, 2000), 2.

31. Hurst, *Imitation of Life* (1933), 229.

32. Hurst, *Imitation of Life* (1933), 142.

33. Hurst, *Imitation of Life* (1933), 310.

34. Aelius Donatus, "Comedy and Tragedy" (c. 350), in *Dramatic Theory and Criticism: Greeks to Grotowski*, ed. Bernard F. Dukore (New York: Holt, Reinhart and Winston, 1974), 100.

35. Denis Diderot, "Encyclopedia: Comedy" (1755–1780), in *Dramatic Theory and Criticism: Greeks to Grotowski*, ed. Bernard F. Dukore (New York: Holt, Reinhart and Winston, 1974), 287.

Chapter 4

1. Sigmund Freud, "On Oedipus and Hamlet," in *Dramatic Theory and Criticism*, ed. Bernard F. Dukore (New York: Holt, Reinhart and Winston, 1974), 827.

2. Heiner Müller, quoted in *"Hamletmachine" and Other Texts for the Stage*, ed. Carl Weber (New York: Performing Art Journal Publications, 1984), 50.

3. Susan Sontag, *Against Interpretation and Other Essays* (New York: Farrar, Straus and Giroux, 1966), 55–56.

4. Gilles Deleuze, "Coldness and Cruelty," in *Masochism*, by Gilles Deleuze and Leopold van Sacher-Masoch (New York: Zone Books, 1991), 101.

5. Melanie Klein, "The Psycho-analytic Play Technique: Its History and Significance" (1955), in *The Selected Melanie Klein*, ed. Juliet Mitchell (New York: Macmillan), 46.

6. William Shakespeare, *Hamlet*, Act 4, scene 7, lines 41–46.

7. Melanie Klein, "Mourning and Its Relation to Manic-Depressive States" (1940), in *The Selected Melanie Klein*, ed. Juliet Mitchell (New York: Macmillan), 172.

8. Heiner Müller, "Hamletmachine," in *"Hamletmachine" and Other Texts for the Stage*, ed. Carl Weber (New York: Performing Art Journal Publications, 1984), 58.

Chapter 5

1. Carl Jung, "On the Relation of Analytical Psychology to Poetry" (1922), in *Dramatic Theory and Criticism: Greeks to Grotowski*, ed. Bernard F. Dukore (New York: Holt, Reinhart and Winston, 1974), 844.

2. Béla Balázs, "The Visible Human" (1924), in *German Essays on Film*, ed. Richard W. McCormick and Alison Guenther-Pal (New York: Continuum, 2004), 74.

3. Rudolf Arnheim, "Film" (1932), in *German Essays on Film*, ed. Richard W. McCormick and Alison Guenther-Pal (New York: Continuum, 2004), 142.

4. Theodor W. Adorno, "Transparencies on Film," in *German Essays on Film*, ed. Richard W. McCormick and Alison Guenther-Pal (New York: Continuum, 2004), 271.

5. Gilles Deleuze, "Coldness and Cruelty" (1967), in *Masochism*, by Gilles Deleuze and Leopold van Sacher-Masoch (New York: Zone Books, 1991), 18.

6. Gilles Deleuze, "Coldness and Cruelty" (1967), 23.

7. Walter Benjamin, "The Work of Art in the Age of Mechanical Reproduction" (1935), 238.

Chapter 6

1. Melanie Klein, "Notes on Some Schizoid Mechanisms" (1946), in *The Selected Melanie Klein*, ed. Juliet Mitchell (New York: Macmillan), 187.

2. Philip Roth, *The Human Stain* (New York: Vintage, 2000), 2.

3. Guy Debord, *Society of the Spectacle*

(1967), trans. Ken Knabb (London: Rebel Press), 7.

4. Gene Youngblood, "Expanded Cinema" (1970), in *Film Theory and Criticism: Introductory Readings*, ed. Gerald Mast and Marshall Cohen (New York: Oxford University Press, 1979), 755.

5. Melanie Klein, "Early Stages of the Oedipus Conflict" (1928), in *The Selected Melanie Klein*, ed. Juliet Mitchell (New York: Macmillan), 72.

6. Melanie Klein, "Inhibitions and Difficulties at Puberty" (1922), in *The Writings of Melanie Klein, vol. 1, Love, Guilt and Reparation and Other Works 1921–1945* (New York: Free Press, 1975), 57.

7. Søren Kierkegaard, "The Comical" (1846), in *Dramatic Theory and Criticism: Greeks to Grotowski*, ed. Bernard F. Dukore (New York: Holt, Reinhart and Winston, 1974), 556.

8. Gilles Deleuze, *Cinema 1: The Movement-Image* (1983), trans. Hugh Tomlinson and Barbara Habberjam (Minneapolis, University of Minnesota Press, 1986), 201.

9. Deleuze, *Cinema 1: The Movement-Image*, 200.

10. Deleuze, *Cinema 1: The Movement-Image*, 200.

11. Guy Debord, *Society of the Spectacle*, 19.

12. Melanie Klein, "Notes on Some Schizoid Mechanisms," 187.

13. Amy Taubin, "Spelling It Out," *Village Voice*, August 3, 1999.

Chapter 7

1. Carl Schmitt, *The Concept of the Political* (1932), trans. George Schwab (Chicago: University of Chicago Press, 1996), 35.

2. Schmitt, *The Concept of the Political* (1932), 35.

3. Melanie Klein, "On the Sense of Loneliness" (1963), in *The Writings of Melanie Klein*, vol. 1, *Envy and Gratitude and Other Works 1946–1963* (New York: Free Press, 1975), 303.

4. Sigmund Freud, "The Uncanny" (1919), in *Collected Papers*, vol. 4, *Papers on Metapsychology: Papers on Applied Psycho-Analysis*, trans. Joan Riviere (New York: Basic Books, 1961), 387.

5. Vladimir Nabokov, *Despair* (1965) (New York: Pocket Books, 1968), 13.

6. Freud, "The Uncanny" (1919), 387.

7. Nabokov, *Despair* (1965), 115.

8. Karsten Witte, "The Indivisible Legacy of Nazi Cinema" (1994), in *German Essays on Film*, ed. Richard W. McCormick and Alison Guenther-Pal (New York: Continuum, 2004), 308.

9. Witte, "The Indivisible Legacy of Nazi Cinema" (1994), 312.

10. Freud, "The Uncanny" (1919), 394.

11. Melanie Klein, "Some Theoretical Conclusions Regarding the Emotional Life of the Infant" (1952), in *The Writings of Melanie Klein*, vol. 3, *Envy and Gratitude and Other Works 1946–1963* (New York: Free Press, 1975), 64.

12. Nabokov, *Despair* (1965), 61.

13. Béla Balázs, "The Visible Human" (1924), in *German Essays on Film*, ed. Richard W. McCormick and Alison Guenther-Pal (New York: Continuum, 2004), 83.

Chapter 8

1. Jean-Luc Godard, "*What Is Cinema?*" *Les Amis du Cinéma* (1952).

2. Melanie Klein, "Some Reflections on 'The Oresteia'" (1963), in *The Writings of Melanie Klein*, vol. 3, *Envy and Gratitude and Other Works 1946–1963* (New York: Free Press, 1975), 299.

3. Karen Blixen, "The Immortal Story" (1958), in *Anecdotes of Destiny*, by Isak Dinesen (Great Britain: Penguin, 1958), 163.

4. Blixen, "The Immortal Story" (1958), 203–204.

5. Blixen, "The Immortal Story" (1958), 165.

6. Susan Sontag, *Against Interpretation and Other Essays* (New York: Farrar, Straus and Giroux, 1966), 292.

7. E.T.A. Hoffmann, "The Sandman" (1816), in *Tales of Hoffmann*, ed. and trans. R.J. Hollingdale (Great Britain: Penguin, 1982), 96–97.

8. Blixen, "The Immortal Story" (1958), 173.

9. Blixen, "The Immortal Story" (1958), 202.

10. Blixen, "The Immortal Story" (1958), 210–211.

11. Melanie Klein, "A Contribution to the Psychogenesis of Manic-Depressive States" (1935), in *The Selected Melanie Klein*, ed. Juliet Mitchell (New York: Macmillan), 131.

12. Blixen, "The Immortal Story" (1958), 218–219.

13. Danny Peary, "Eraserhead," in *Cult Movies: The Classics, the Sleepers, the Weird, and the Wonderful* (1981) (New York: Dell, 1989), 86.

14. Hoffmann, "The Sandman" (1816), 96–97.

15. Hoffmann, "The Sandman" (1816), 95.

16. Melanie Klein, "On the Sense of Loneliness" (1963), in *The Writings of Melanie Klein*,

vol. 3, *Envy and Gratitude and Other Works 1946–1963* (New York: Free Press, 1975), 302.

17. Gilles Deleuze, "Coldness and Cruelty" (1967) in *Masochism*, by Gilles Deleuze and Leopold van Sacher-Masoch (New York: Zone Books, 1991), 37.

18. Klein, "A Contribution to the Psychogenesis of Manic-Depressive States" (1935), 131.

Conclusion

1. Leo Braudy, "The World in a Frame" (1976), in *Film Theory and Criticism: Introductory Readings*, ed. Gerald Mast and Marshall Cohen (New York: Oxford University Press, 1979), 447.

2. José Ortega y Gasset, "The Dehumanization of Art" (1925), in *Dramatic Theory and Criticism: Greeks to Grotowski*, ed. Bernard F. Dukore (New York: Holt, Reinhart and Winston, 1974), 757.

3. William Earle, "Revolt against Realism in the Films" (1968), in *Film Theory and Criticism: Introductory Readings*, ed. Gerald Mast and Marshall Cohen (New York: Oxford University Press, 1979), 34.

4. Rainer Werner Fassbinder, "The Third Generation" (1978), in *German Essays on Film*, ed. Richard W. McCormick and Alison Guenther-Pal (New York: Continuum, 2004), 231.

5. Max Horkheimer and Theodor W. Adorno, "The Culture Industry: Enlightenment as Mass Deception" (1944), in *German Essays on Film*, ed. Richard W. McCormick and Alison Guenther-Pal (New York: Continuum, 2004), 170.

6. Richard Wagner, "The Art-Work of the Future" (1849), in *Dramatic Theory and Criticism: Greeks to Grotowski*, ed. Bernard F. Dukore (New York: Holt, Reinhart and Winston, 1974), 791.

Bibliography

Adair, Gilbert. *Flickers: An Illustrated Celebration of 100 Years of Cinema*. London: Faber and Faber, 1995.

Adorno, Theodor W. *Aesthetic Theory*. Minneapolis: University of Minnesota Press, 1997.

_____. *Alban Berg: Master of the Smallest Link*. Cambridge: University of Cambridge Press, 1994.

_____. *Dream Notes*. Malden: Polity Press, 2007.

_____. *In Search of Wagner*. New York: Verso, 2009.

Agamben, Giorgio. *Homo Sacer: Sovereign Power and Bare Life*. Stanford, CA: Stanford University Press, 1998.

_____. *Profanations*. New York: Zone Books, 2007.

_____. *State of Exception*. Chicago: University of Chicago Press, 2005.

Albee, Edward. *The Collected Plays of Edward Albee*. Vol. 1, *1958–65*. New York: Overlook Duckworth, 2004.

_____. *The Collected Plays of Edward Albee*. Vol. 2, *1966–77*. New York: Overlook Duckworth, 2005.

_____. *The Collected Plays of Edward Albee*. Vol. 3, *1978–2003*. New York: Overlook Duckworth, 2005.

_____. *Stretching My Mind*. New York: Carroll and Graf Publishers, 2005.

Andy Warhol, "Giant" Size. Introduction by Dave Hickey. New York: Phaidon, 2006.

Angell, Callie. *Andy Warhol Screen Tests: The Films of Andy Warhol Catalogue Raisonne*. Vol. 1. New York: Harry N. Abrams, 2006.

_____. *The Films of Andy Warhol: Part II*. New York: Whitney Museum of American Art, 1994.

Anger, Kenneth. *Hollywood Babylon*. New York: Dell, 1981.

Arnheim, Rudolf. *Film as Art*. Berkeley: University of California Press, 1957.

Balázs, Béla. *Theory of the Film: Character and Growth of a New Art*. New York: Dover, 1970.

Ballard, J.G. *The Atrocity Exhibition*. San Francisco: V/Search Publications, 1990.

_____. *Crash*. New York: Vintage, 1985.

Banks, Russell. *The Sweet Hereafter*. New York: Harper Perennial, 1991.

Barlow, Judith E. *Plays by American Women 1930–1960*. New York: Applause Books, 1994.

Barry, Philip. *States of Grace: Eight Plays (You and I, White Wings, Holiday, Hotel Universe, The Animal Kingdom, Here Come the Clowns, The Philadelphia Story, Second Threshold)*. New York: Harcourt Brace Jovanovich, 1975.

_____. *Tomorrow and Tomorrow: A Play in Three Acts*. New York: Samuel French, 1931.

Barthes, Roland. *On Racine*. Translated by Richard Howard. New York: Hill and Wang, 1964.

Baskervill, Charles Read, Virgil B. Heltzel, and Arthur H. Nethercot, eds. *Elizabethan and Stuart Plays (Roister Doister, Gammer Gurton's Needle, Gorboduc, Supposes, Cambises, Endymion, The Arraignment of Paris, The Old Wives' Tale, Friar Bacon and Friar Bungay,*

George a Greene, Tamburlaine Part I, Doctor Faustus, Edward II, The Spanish Tragedy, Arden of Feversham, Attowell's Jig [Francis' New Jig], Mucedorus, The Shoemakers' Holiday, The Honest Whore Part I, A Woman Killed with Kindness, The Malcontent, Bussy d'Ambois, The Duchess of Malfi, Every Man in His Humor, Sejanus His Fall, Volpone or The Fox, The Alchemist, The Hue and Cry after Cupid, The Sad Shepherd, The Knight of the Burning Pestle, The Faithful Shepherdess, Philaster, The Maid's Tragedy, A Trick to Catch the Old One, The Changeling, A New Way to Pay Old Debts, The Maid of Honor, The Witch of Edmonton, The Broken Heart, Perkin Warbeck, The Lady of Pleasure, The Cardinal). New York: Holt, Rinehart and Winston, 1963.

Bataille, Georges. *The Accursed Share: An Essay on General Economy.* Vol. 1, *Consumption.* New York: Zone Books, 1991.

_____. *The Accursed Share: An Essay on General Economy.* Vol. 2, *The History of Eroticism.* New York: Zone Books, 1993.

_____. *The Accursed Share: An Essay on General Economy.* Vol. 3, *Sovereignty.* New York: Zone Books, 1993.

_____. *Erotism.* San Francisco: City Lights Books, 1986.

_____. *The Impossible.* San Francisco: City Lights Books, 1991.

_____. *Literature and Evil.* New York: Marion Boyars, 2001.

_____. *Story of the Eye by Lord Auch.* Translated by Joachim Neugroschel. San Francisco: City Lights Books. 1987.

_____. *The Tears of Eros.* San Francisco: City Lights Books, 1989.

_____. *Theory of Religion.* New York: Zone Books, 1992.

_____. *The Trial of Gilles de Rais.* Los Angeles: Amok, 2004.

Baudelaire, Charles. *The Painter of Modern Life and Other Essays.* New York: Phaidon Press, 2005.

Baudrillard, Jean. *The Conspiracy of Art: Manifestos, Interviews, Essays.* Ed. Sylvere Lotringer. New York: Semiotext(e), 2005.

Bayard, Pierre. *Who Killed Roger Ackroyd? The Mystery behind the Agatha Christie Mystery.* New York: New Press, 2000.

Bazin, Andre. *What Is Cinema?* Berkeley: University of California Press, 1967.

Beauvoir, Simone de. *The Second Sex.* New York: Vintage, 1974.

Beckett, Samuel. *Endgame.* New York: Grove Press, 1958.

Benjamin, Walter. *Illuminations: Essays and Reflections.* Edited with an introduction by Hannah Arendt. New York: Schocken, 1968.

_____. *Reflections: Essays, Aphorisms, Autobiographical Writings.* New York: Schocken, 1978.

_____. *Selected Writings.* Vol. 1, *1913–1926.* Cambridge: Belknap Press of Harvard University Press, 2004.

Bentham, Jeremy. *The Panopticon Writings.* London: Verso, 1995.

Berger, William. *Wagner without Fear: Learning to Love — and Even Enjoy — Opera's Most Demanding Genius.* New York: Vintage, 1998.

Blanchot, Maurice. *The Book to Come.* Stanford: Stanford University Press, 2003.

_____. *The Instant of My Death (with Demeure — Fiction and Testimony by Jacques Derrida).* Stanford, CA: Stanford University Press, 2000.

_____. *The Station Hill Blanchot Reader: Fiction & Literary Essays.* Barrytown, NY: Station Hill Press, 1999.

_____. *The Unavowable Community.* Barrytown, NY: Station Hill Press, 1988.

_____. *The Writing of the Disaster.* Lincoln: University of Nebraska Press, 1995.

Bloch, Robert. *Three Complete Novels: Psycho, Psycho II, Psycho House.* New York: Wings Books, 1993.

Block, Haskell M., and Robert G. Shedd, eds. *Masters of Modern Drama (Peer Gynt, Ghosts, Miss Julie, The Ghost Sonata, The Weavers, The Intruder, Death and the Fool, The Sea Gull, The Cherry Orchard, The Lower Depths, La Ronde, The Marquis of Keith, Man and Superman, Major Barbara, Riders to the Sea, The Playboy of the Western World, At the Hawk's Well, Juno and the Paycock, Cock-a-Doodle Dandy, From Morn to Midnight, Henry*

IV, Orphee, Blood Wedding, The Emperor Jones, The Iceman Cometh, Awake and Sing!, The Time of Your Life, Electra, The Madwoman of Chaillot, Thieves' Carnival, Antigone, No Exit, Caligula, Mother Courage and Her Children, The Good Women of Setzuan, The Devil's General, The Matchmaker, The Glass Menagerie, Death of a Salesman, Marty, Look Back in Anger, Endgame, The Bald Soprano, The Visit, Biedermann and the Firebugs). New York: Random House, 1962.

Bloom, Harold. *"Hamlet": Poem Unlimited.* New York: Riverhead Books, 2003.

_____. *How to Read and Why.* New York: Scribner, 2000.

_____. *Shakespeare: The Invention of the Human.* New York: Riverhead Books, 1998.

_____. *The Western Canon: The Books and School of the Ages.* New York: Harcourt, Brace, 1994.

Bogdanovich, Peter. *John Ford.* Berkeley: University of California Press, 1968.

_____. *Who the Devil Made It: Conversations with Legendary Film Directors.* New York: Ballantine, 1998.

Braudy, Leo. *From Chivalry to Terrorism: War and the Changing Nature of Masculinity.* New York: Knopf, 2003.

Brecht, Bertolt. *The Rise and Fall of the City of Mahagonny.* Translated by W.H. Auden and Chester Kallman. Boston: David R. Godine, 1976.

_____. *Threepenny Novel.* London: Penguin, 1962.

Bresson, Robert. *Notes on the Cinematographer.* København: Green Integer, 1997.

Brook, Peter. *The Empty Space.* New York: Avon, 1968.

Buchner, Georg. *Georg Buchner: Complete Plays and Prose.* New York: Hill and Wang, 1963.

Burgess, Anthony. *A Clockwork Orange.* New York: Ballantine, 1988.

_____. *99 Novels.* New York: Summit Books, 1984.

Cagney, James. *Cagney by Cagney.* New York: Pocket Books, 1977.

Callow, Simon. *BFI Film Classics: The Night of the Hunter.* London: BFI Publishing, 2000.

Canham, Kingsley. *The Hollywood Professionals.* Vol. 1, *Michael Curtiz, Raoul Walsh, Henry Hathaway.* New York: A.S. Barnes, 1973.

Carringer, Robert L. *The Magnificent Ambersons: A Reconstruction.* Berkeley: University of California Press, 1993.

_____. *The Making of Citizen Kane.* Berkeley: University of California Press, 1985.

Carter, Angela. *The Sadeian Woman and the Ideology of Pornography.* New York: Pantheon Books, 1978.

Cavell, Stanley. *Cavell on Film.* Albany: State University of New York Press, 2005.

Clover, Carol J. *Men, Women and Chain Saws: Gender in the Modern Horror Film.* Princeton, NJ: University of Princeton Press, 1992.

Colter, Ephen Glenn. *Policing Public Sex: Queer Politics and the Future of AIDS Activism.* Boston: South End Press, 1996.

Cooke, Deryck. *An Introduction to Wagner's "Der Ring des Nibelungen."* London, England: Decca Record Company, 1968.

Cooper, Dennis. *All Ears: Cultural Criticism, Essays and Obituaries.* New York: Soft Skull Press, 1999.

Corrigan, Robert W, ed. *Masterpieces of the Modern Central European Theatre (The Game of Love, La Ronde, Electra, R.U.R., The Play's the Thing).* New York: Collier, 1967.

_____, ed. *Masterpieces of the Modern French Theatre (The Parisian Woman, Christopher Columbus, Electra, Eurydice [Legend for Lovers], The Queen after Death, Improvisation or The Shepherd's Chameleon).* New York: Collier, 1967.

_____, ed. *Masterpieces of the Modern German Theatre (Woyzeck, Maria Magdalena, The Weavers, The Marquis of Keith, The Caucasian Chalk Circle).* New York: Collier, 1969.

_____, ed. *Masterpieces of the Modern Irish Theatre (The Countess Cathleen, The Playboy of the Western World, Riders to the Sea, The Silver Tassie, Cock-a-Doodle Dandy).* New York: Collier, 1979.

_____, ed. *Masterpieces of the Modern Italian Theatre (Six Characters in Search of an Author, The Pleasure of Honesty, Crime on Goat Island, Filumena Marturano, The Academy, The Return).* New York: Collier, 1967.

_____, ed. *Masterpieces of the Modern Russian Theatre (A Month in the Country, Uncle Vanya, The Cherry Orchard, The Lower Depths, The Bedbug)*. New York: Collier, 1967.

_____. *Masterpieces of the Modern Scandinavian Theatre (Hedda Gabler, Miss Julie, The Ghost Sonata, The Difficult Hour, The Defeat, Anna Sophie Hedvig)*. New York: Collier, 1967.

_____. *Masterpieces of the Modern Spanish Theatre (The Witches' Sabbath, The Cradle Song, The Love of Don Perlimplin and Belisa in the Garden, The Dream Weaver, Death Thrust)*. New York: Collier, 1967.

Cowie, Peter. *The Cinema of Orson Welles*. New York: Da Capo, 1989.

Daumal, Rene. *Mount Analogue: A Novel*. New York: Overlook Press, 2004.

Debord, Guy. *Society of the Spectacle*. Translated by Ken Knabb. London: Rebel Press, n.d.

DeLanda, Manuel. *A New Philosophy of Science: Assemblage Theory and Social Complexity*. New York: Continuum, 2006.

_____. *A Thousand Years of Nonlinear History*. New York: Swerve Editions, 2000.

Delany, Samuel R. *Times Square Red, Times Square Blue*. New York: New York University Press, 1999.

Deleuze, Gilles. *Cinema 1: The Movement-Image*. Minneapolis: University of Minnesota Press, 1986.

_____. *Cinema 2: The Time-Image*. Minneapolis: University of Minnesota Press, 1989.

_____. "Coldness and Cruelty" (1967). In *Masochism*, by Gilles Deleuze and Leopold van Sacher-Masoch. New York: Zone Books, 1991.

_____. *Difference and Repetition*. New York: Columbia University Press, 1994.

Derrida, Jacques. *Writing and Difference*. Chicago: University of Chicago Press, 1978.

Dewey, John. *The Influence of Darwin on Philosophy and Other Essays*. New York: Prometheus, 1997.

Dickinson, Thomas H., ed. *Chief Contemporary Dramatists: Third Series (The Emperor Jones, In Abraham's Bosom, The Silver Cord, The Dover Road, Juno and the Paycock, Such Is Life, From Morn to Midnight, Electra, The Steamship Tenacity, Time Is a Dream, Naked, The Love of the Three Kings, Malvaloca, A Lily among Thorns, He Who Gets Slapped, The Theatre of the Soul, Liliom, R.U.R., The Dybbuk, Eyvind of the Hills)*. Boston: Houghton Mifflin, 1930.

Dika, Vera. *Games of Terror: Halloween, Friday the 13th, and the Films of the Stalker Cycle*. Rutherford, NJ: Fairleigh Dickinson University Press, 1990.

Dinesen, Isak. *Anecdotes of Destiny*. Great Britain: Penguin, 1958.

Doyle, Jennifer, Jonathan Flatley, and Jose Esteban Munoz, eds. *Pop Out: Queer Warhol*. Durham, NC: Duke University Press, 1996.

Du Maurier, George. *Peter Ibbetson*. New York: Harper and Brothers, 1892.

Dukore, Bernard F., ed. *Dramatic Theory and Criticism*. New York: Holt, Reinhart and Winston, 1974.

Duras, Marguerite. *Duras by Duras*. San Francisco: City Lights Books. 1987.

_____. *The North China Lover*. Translated by Leigh Hafrey. New York: New Press, 1992.

Eco, Umberto. "'Casablanca': Cult Movies and Intertextual Collage." *SubStance* 14, no. 2 (1985).

Eisner, Lotte. *Fritz Lang*. New York: Da Capo, 1976.

Eliot, T.S. *The Complete Poems and Plays, 1909–1950*. New York: Harcourt, Brace and World, 1962.

Farber, Manny. *Negative Space: Manny Farber on the Movies*. Expanded ed. New York: Da Capo, 1998.

Fassbinder, Rainer Werner. *Plays*. New York: PAJ Publications, 1985.

Fernett, Gene. *Hollywood's Poverty Row 1930–1950*. Satellite Beach, FL: Coral Reef Publications, 1973.

Fitzgerald, Gerald, et al., eds. *The Ring: Metropolitan Opera*. New York: Metropolitan Opera Guild, 1988.

Fornssler, Barbara, and Micha Cardenas. *Trans Desire/Affective Cyborgs*. New York, Atropos Press, 2010.

Freud, Sigmund. *Beyond the Pleasure Principle*. New York: Bantam, 1959.

_____. *Character and Culture.* New York: Collier, 1978.

_____. *Civilization and Its Discontents.* New York: Norton, 1961.

_____. *Collected Papers.* Vol. 1. New York: Basic Books, 1961.

_____. *Collected Papers.* Vol. 2. New York: Basic Books, 1961.

_____. *Collected Papers.* Vol. 3. New York: Basic Books, 1961.

_____. *Collected Papers.* Vol. 4, *Papers on Metapsychology — Papers on Applied Psycho-Analysis.* New York: Basic Books, 1961.

_____. *Collected Papers.* Vol. 5. New York: Basic Books, 1961.

_____. *The Future of an Illusion.* New York: Norton, 1961.

_____. *General Psychological Theory.* New York: Collier, 1978.

_____. *The Interpretation of Dreams.* New York: Avon, 1966.

_____. *Introductory Lectures on Psycho-Analysis.* New York: Norton, 1989.

_____. *Sexuality and the Psychology of Love.* New York: Collier, 1978.

_____. *Three Contributions to the Theory of Sex.* New York: Nervous and Mental Disease Publishing., 1920.

Fujiwara, Chris. *Jacques Tourneur: The Cinema of Nightfall.* Jefferson, NC: McFarland, 1998.

Gaffney, Jace. *Post-Mortem Effects: A Critical, Philosophical Narrative on the Subject of Cinema in the Twentieth Century; or simply, A Personal Dialogue with the Movies.* Unpublished manuscript. Philadelphia, 2009.

Geis, Deborah R., and Steven F. Kruger, eds. *Approaching the Millennium: Essays on "Angels in America."* Ann Arbor: University of Michigan Press, 2001.

Genet, Jean. *Letter to Roger Blin: Reflections on the Theater.* New York: Grove Press, 1969.

Gillespie, Gerald, ed. *German Theater before 1750 (Dulcitius, Fool Surgery, Susanna, Leo Armenius, Sophonisba, The Dumb Beauty).* New York: Continuum, 1992.

Godard, Jean-Luc. *Godard on Godard.* New York: Da Capo, 1972.

_____. "What Is Cinema?" *Les Amis du Cinéma,* 1952.

Goethe, Johann Wolfgang von. *Faust (Parts I and II).* Translated by Walter Arndt. Edited by Cyrus Hamlin. New York: Norton, 1976.

Goldsmith, Kenneth, ed. *I'll Be Your Mirror: The Selected Andy Warhol Interviews — Thirty-Seven Conversations with the Pop Master.* New York: Carroll and Graf, 2004.

Goldsmith, Martin M. *Detour.* Lexington: Disruptive Publishing, Blackmask.com, 2006.

_____. *Double Jeopardy.* Lexington: Disruptive Publishing, Blackmask.com, 2006.

Golson, Barry, ed. *The Playboy Interviews with John Lennon & Yoko Ono (Conducted by David Sheff).* New York: Berkley Books, 1982.

Gorchakov, Nikolai M. *Stanislavsky Directs.* USA: Minerva Press, 1968.

Goux, Jean-Joseph. *Oedipus, Philosopher.* Stanford, CA: Stanford University Press, 1993.

Grant, Barry Keith, ed. *The Dread of Difference: Gender and the Horror Film.* Austin: University of Texas Press, 1996.

Gras, Vernon, and Marguerite Gras, eds. *Peter Greenaway Interviews.* Jackson: University of Mississippi, 2000.

Greenaway, Peter. *The Baby of Macon.* Paris: Dis Voir, 1994.

_____. *The Cook, the Thief, His Wife and Her Lover.* Paris: Dis Voir, 1989.

_____. *The Falls.* Paris: Dis Voir, 1993.

Hagen, Uta, with Haskel Frankel. *Respect for Acting.* New York: Macmillan, 1973.

Hardy, Phil, ed. *The Overlook Film Encyclopedia: The Gangster Film.* Woodstock: Overlook Press, 1998.

_____. *The Overlook Film Encyclopedia: Horror.* Woodstock: Overlook Press, 1995.

_____. *The Overlook Film Encyclopedia: Science Fiction.* Woodstock: Overlook Press, 1991.

_____. *The Overlook Film Encyclopedia: The Western.* Woodstock: Overlook Press, 1991.

Hart, Lynda. *Fatal Women: Lesbian Sexuality and the Mark of Aggression.* Princeton, NJ: Princeton University Press, 1994.

Haskell, Molly. *From Reverence to Rape: The Treatment of Women in the Movies.* Baltimore, MD: Penguin, 1974.

Hawkins, Joan. *Cutting Edge: Art-Horror and the Horrific Avant-Garde*. Minneapolis: University of Minnesota Press, 2000.

Hebbel, Friedrich. *Three Plays by Hebbel (Judith, Herod and Mariamne, Gyges and His Ring)*. New Jersey: Associated University Press, 1974.

Heilbroner, Robert L. *The Worldly Philosophers: The Lives, Times and Ideas of the Greatest Economic Thinkers*. New York: Simon and Schuster, 1989.

Hellman, Lillian. *The Collected Plays*. Boston: Little, Brown, 1971.

Henkin, Bill. *The Rocky Horror Picture Show Book*. New York: Hawthorn/Dutton, 1979.

Heraclitus. *Fragments*. New York: Penguin, 2003.

Herzogenrath, Bernd, ed. *The Films of Edgar G. Ulmer*. Lanham, MD: Scarecrow Press, 2009.

Hoberman, J. *The Dream Life: Movies, Media, and the Mythology of the Sixties*. New York: New Press, 2003.

_____. *The Magic Hour: Film at Fin de Siècle*. Philadelphia: Temple University Press, 2003.

Hoberman, J., and Jonathan Rosenbaum. *Midnight Movies*. New York: Harper and Row, 1983.

Hoffmann, E.T.A. *Tales of Hoffmann*. Edited and translated by R.J. Hollingdale. Great Britain: Penguin, 1982.

Hofmannsthal, Hugo von. *Der Rosenkavalier*. Hayes Middlesex: EMI Records, 1987.

Holderlin, Friedrich. *The Death of Empedocles: A Mourning-Play*. Translated by David Farrell Krell. New York: SUNY Press, 2008.

hooks, bell. *Reel to Real: Race, Class and Sex at the Movies*. New York: Routledge, 1996.

Horowitz, Mark Eden. "Biography of a Song: A Bowler Hat." *Sondheim Review* 12, no. 3 (Spring 2006): 16–23.

Hurst, Fannie. *Imitation of Life*. New York: Harper and Row, 1990.

Ibsen, Henrik. *Ibsen: The Complete Major Prose Plays*. New York: Plume, 1978.

_____. *Ibsen's Plays*. New York: Modern Library, date unknown.

_____. *Peer Gynt*. New York: Oxford University Press, 1970.

Isenberg, Noah. *BFI Film Classics: "Detour."* New York: Palgrave Macmillan, 2008.

James, William. *The Will to Believe and Other Essays in Popular Philosophy*. New York: Dover, 1956.

Jarman, Douglas. "Berg: Wozzeck; an Introduction." *Wozzeck Wiener 1987*. Hamburg: Polydor International GmbH, 1988.

Jeffords, Susan. *Hard Bodies: Hollywood Masculinity in the Reagan Era*. New Brunswick, NJ: Rutgers University Press, 1994.

Jodorowsky, Alejandro. *El Topo: A Book of the Film by Alejandro Jodorowsky*. New York: Douglas Book Corporation, 1971.

_____. *Psychomagic: The Transformative Power of Shamanic Psychotherapy*. Vermont: Inner Traditions, 2010.

Johnson, Charles S. *Middle Passage*. New York: Plume, 1991.

Joseph, Branden W., ed. *Andy Warhol: Artist of the (Next?) Century*. Unpublished course reader. New York: Parsons School of Design, 1998.

Joyce, James. *Ulysses*. New York: Random House, 1990.

Kael, Pauline. *The Citizen Kane Book*. New York: Bantam, 1974.

Kagan, Norman. *The Cinema of Stanley Kubrick*. New expanded ed. New York: Continuum, 1993.

Kane, Sarah. *Complete Plays (Blasted, Phaedra's Love, Cleansed, Crave, 4.48 Psychosis, Skin)*. London: Methuen, 2001.

Kauffman, Linda S. *Bad Girls and Sick Boys: Fantasies in Contemporary Art and Culture*. Berkeley: University of California Press, 1998.

Kaufman, Moises. *Gross Indecency: The Three Trials of Oscar Wilde*. New York: Vintage, 1998.

Kazan, Elia. *Kazan on Directing*. New York: Knopf, 2009.

Kearney, Richard, and David Rasmussen. *Continental Aesthetics: Romanticism to Postmodernism; an Anthology*. Malden, MA: Blackwell Publishers, 2001.

Kempis, Thomas A. *The Imitation of Christ*. New York: Penguin, 1952.

Keyssar, Helene. *Robert Altman's America*. New York: Oxford University Press, 1991.

Kierkegaard, Søren. *The Essential Kierkegaard*. Edited by Howard V. Hong and Edna H. Hong. Princeton, NJ: Princeton University Press, 2000.

King, Stephen. *On Writing: A Memoir of the Craft*. New York: Pocket Books, 2000.

Kittler, Friedrich A. *Gramophone, Film, Typewriter*. Stanford, CA: University of Stanford Press, 2000.

Klein, Melanie. *The Selected Melanie Klein*. Edited by Juliet Mitchell. New York: Macmillan, 1986.

_____. *The Writings of Melanie Klein*. Vol. 1, *Love, Guilt and Reparation and Other Works, 1921–1945*. New York: Free Press, 1975.

_____. *The Writings of Melanie Klein*. Vol. 3, *Envy and Gratitude and Other Works, 1946–1963*. New York: Free Press, 1975.

Kleist, Heinrich von. *The Marquise of O— and Other Stories*. London: Penguin, 2004.

Klinger, Barbara. *Melodrama and Meaning: History, Culture, and the Films of Douglas Sirk*. Bloomington: Indiana University Press, 1994.

Klossowski, Pierre. *Sade My Neighbor*. Evanston, IL: Northwestern University Press, 1991.

Knapp, Laurence F. *Brian De Palma Interviews*. Jackson: University of Mississippi Press, 2003.

Koestenbaum, Wayne. *Andy Warhol: A Penguin Life*. New York: Viking, 2001.

_____. *Hotel Theory*. New York: Soft Skull Press, 2007.

Korine, Harmony. *A Crackup at the Race Riots*. New York: Doubleday, 1998.

Kosinski, Jerzy. *Being There*. New York: Bantam, 1972.

Kott, Jan. *The Eating of the Gods: An Interpretation of Greek Tragedy*. New York: Vintage, 1974.

_____. *Shakespeare, Our Contemporary*. New York: Doubleday, 1964.

Kracauer, Siegfried. *From Caligari to Hitler: A Psychological History of the German Film*. Princeton, NJ: Princeton University Press, 1947.

Kramer, Larry. *The Tragedy of Today's Gays*. New York: Jeremy P. Tarcher/Penguin, 2005.

Kristeva, Julia. *The Portable Kristeva*. New York: Columbia University Press, 1997.

Kubrick, Stanley. *Stanley Kubrick's "Clockwork Orange" Based on the Novel by Anthony Burgess*. New York: Ballantine, 1972.

Kushner, Tony. *Angels in America: A Gay Fantasia on National Themes*. Vol. 1, *Millennium Approaches*. New York: Theatre Communications Group, 1993.

_____. *Angels in America: A Gay Fantasia on National Themes*. Vol. 2, *Perestroika*. New York: Theatre Communications Group, 1993.

Lacan, Jacques. *Ecrits*. New York: Norton, 2006.

_____. *The Seminar of Jacques Lacan*. Vol. 11, *The Four Fundamental Concepts of Psychoanalysis*. Edited by Jacques-Alain Miller. Translated by Alan Sheridan. New York: Norton, 1998.

_____. *Television: A Challenge to the Psychoanalytic Establishment*. New York: Norton, 1990.

Laclos, Choderlos de. *Les Liaisons Dangereuses*. New York: Signet, 1962.

Landis, Bill, and Michelle Clifford. *Sleazoid Express: A Mind Twisting Tour through the Grindhouse Cinema of Times Square!* New York: Simon and Schuster, 2002.

Lavery, David, ed. *Full of Secrets: Critical Approaches to "Twin Peaks."* Detroit, MI: Wayne State University Press, 1995.

Lawrence, D.H. *Studies in Classic American Literature*. Maryland: Penguin, 1971.

Lee, M. Owen. *Wagner: The Terrible Man and His Truthful Art: The 1998 Larkin-Stuart Lectures*. Toronto: University of Toronto Press, 1999.

_____. *Wagner's Ring: Turning the Sky Round; Commentaries on "The Ring of the Nibelung."* Ontario: Summit Books, 1990.

Lescov, Nikolai. *The Enchanted Wanderer: Selected Tales*. New York: Modern Library, 2003.

Lessig, Lawrence. *Code: Version 2.0*. New York: Basic Books, 2006.

Lester, Julius. *Look Out Whitey! Black Power's Gon' Get Your Mama!* New York: Grove, 1969.

Locke, John. *Two Treatises of Government*. New York: Signet Classics, 1965.

Lodge, David. *The Art of Fiction*. New York: Penguin, 1992.

Ludlam, Charles. *Ridiculous Theatre: Scourge of Human Folly; the Essays and Opinions of Charles Ludlam.* New York: Theatre Communications Group, 1992.

Lyotard, Jean-François. *Driftworks.* Cambridge, MA: MIT Press, 1984.

MacKenzie, Norman, and Jeanne MacKenzie. *H.G. Wells: A Biography.* New York: Simon and Schuster, 1973.

Magee, Bryan. *The Tristan Chord: Wagner and Philosophy.* New York: Henry Holt, 2001.

Mamet, David. *On Directing Film.* New York: Penguin, 1992.

_____. *Theatre.* New York: Faber and Faber, 2010.

Mao Tse-tung. *On Guerrilla Warfare.* New York: Dover, 2005.

_____. *Quotations from Chairman Mao Tse-tung.* New York: Bantam, 1967.

Marx, Karl. *Capital: A Critique of Political Economy.* Vol. 1. New York: Penguin, 1990.

Mast, Gerald, and Marshall Cohen William Earle, eds. *Film Theory and Criticism: Introductory Readings.* New York: Oxford University Press, 1979.

McCormick, Richard W., and Alison Guenther-Pal. *German Essays on Film.* New York: Continuum, 2004.

McDonough, Jimmy. *The Ghastly One: The Sex-Gore Netherworld of Filmmaker Andy Milligan.* Chicago: A Cappella Books, 2001.

McLuhan, Marshall, and Quentin Fiore. *The Medium Is the Message: An Inventory of the Effects.* New York: Bantam, 1967.

Mitchell, Juliet. *Psychoanalysis and Feminism: A Radical Reassessment of Freudian Psychoanalysis.* New York: Basic Books, 2000.

Mizejewski, Linda. *Divine Decadence: Fascism, Female Spectacle, and the Makings of Sally Bowles.* Princeton, NJ: Princeton University, 1992.

Morton, Frederic. *A Nervous Splendor: Vienna 1888/1889.* New York: Penguin, 1979.

Müller, Heiner. *Germania.* New York: Semiotext(e), 1980.

_____. *"Hamletmachine" and Other Texts for the Stage.* New York: Performing Art Journal Publications, 1984.

_____. *Titus Anatomy Fall of Rome: A Shakespeare Commentary.* Translated by Julian Hammond. Manchester: Unpublished Manuscript, 1990.

Nabokov, Vladimir. *Despair.* New York: Pocket Books, 1968.

_____. *Novels 1955–1962 (Lolita, Pnin, Pale Fire, Lolita: A Screenplay).* New York: Library of America, 1996.

Nagib, Lucia, and Cecilia Mello. *Realism and the Audiovisual Media.* New York: Palgrave Macmillan, 2009.

Naremore, James. *More Than Night: Film Noir in Its Contexts.* Berkeley: University of California Press, 1998.

Nattiez, Jean-Jacques. *Wagner Androgyne: A Study in Interpretation.* Princeton, NJ: Princeton University Press, 1993.

Nelson, Thomas Allen. *Kubrick: Inside a Film Artist's Maze.* Bloomington: Indiana University Press, 1982.

Newman, Ernest. *The Wagner Operas.* Princeton, NJ: Princeton University Press, 1991.

Newman, Kim. *BFI Classics: "Cat People."* London: BFI Publishing, 1999.

Nielsen, Helen. *Detour.* Berkeley: Black Lizard Books, 1988.

Nietzsche, Friedrich. *Basic Writings of Nietzsche.* New York: Modern Library, 1992.

_____. *The Gay Science with a Prelude in Rhymes and an Appendix of Songs.* New York: Vintage, 1974.

_____. *The Portable Nietzsche.* New York: Viking, 1966.

_____. *The Will to Power.* New York: Vintage, 1968.

Oates, Whitney J., and Eugene O'Neill Jr., eds. *Complete Greek Drama: All the Extant Tragedies of Aeschylus, Sophocles and Euripides, and the Comedies of Aristophanes and Menander, in a Variety of Translations in Two Volumes.* Vol. 1. New York: Random House, 1938.

_____. *Complete Greek Drama: All the Extant Tragedies of Aeschylus, Sophocles and Euripides, and the Comedies of Aristophanes and Menander, in a Variety of Translations in Two Volumes.* Vol. 2. New York: Random House, 1938.

O'Brien, John. *Leaving Las Vegas*. New York: Grove, 1995.

O'Neill, James. *Terror on Tape: A Complete Guide to Over 2,000 Horror Movies on Video*. New York: Billboard Books, 1994.

Ovid. *The Metamorphoses of Ovid*. Translated by Allen Mandelbaum. New York: Harcourt, 1993.

Paglia, Camille. "On the New Age of 'Nervous Splendor.'" *Interview*, February, 2006.

_____. *Sex, Art, and American Culture: Essays*. New York: Vintage, 1992.

_____. *Sexual Personae: Art and Decadence from Nefertiti to Emily Dickinson*. New York: Vintage, 1991.

Paz, Octavio. *An Erotic Beyond: Sade*. New York: Harcourt, Brace, 1998.

Peary, Danny. *Cult Movies: The Classics, the Sleepers, the Weird, and the Wonderful*. New York: Dell, 1981.

_____. *Cult Movies 2: Fifty More of the Classics, the Sleepers, the Weird, and the Wonderful*. New York: Dell, 1983.

_____. *Cult Movies 3: Fifty More of the Classics, the Sleepers, the Weird, and the Wonderful*. New York: Dell, 1988.

Peirce, Charles S. *The Essential Writings*. New York: Prometheus, 1998.

Perkins, V.F. *BFI Film Classics: "The Magnificent Ambersons."* London: BFI Publishing, 1999.

Pessoa, Fernando. *The Book of Disquiet*. New York: Penguin, 2003.

Philips, Baxter. *Cut: The Unseen Cinema*. New York: Bounty Books, 1975.

Philips, Gene D. *Stanley Kubrick Interviews*. Jackson: University of Mississippi Press, 2001.

Pinedo, Isabel Cristina. *Recreational Terror: Women and the Pleasure of Horror Film Viewing*. Albany: State University of New York Press, 1997.

Pirandello, Luigi. *Naked Masks: Five Plays by Luigi Pirandello*. New York: E.P. Dutton, 1952.

Plutarch. *Moralia*. Translated by Edwin L. Minar Jr., F.H. Sandbach, and W.C. Helmbold. Massachusetts: Harvard University Press, 1999.

Poe, Edgar Allan. *The Unabridged Edgar Allan Poe*. Philadelphia: Running Press, 1983.

Ponte, Lorenzo da. *Don Giovanni*. London: Decca Record Company, 1960.

Pratt, Douglas. *The Laser Video Disc Companion: 1995 Edition*. New York: Baseline Books, 1995.

Price, Peter. *Resonance: Sonic Philosophy*. Unpublished dissertation. EGS (The European Graduate School), 2010.

Price, Peter, and Tyler Burba. *On Becoming-Music: Between Boredom and Ecstasy*. New York: Atropos Press, 2010.

Pym, John, ed. *Time Out Film Guide: Eleventh Edition 2003*. London: Penguin, 2002.

Quigley, Martin. *Decency in Motion Pictures*. New York: Macmillan, 1937.

Rand, Ayn. *The Virtue of Selfishness: A New Concept of Egoism*. New York: Signet, 1964.

Reage, Pauline. *Story of O*. New York: Grove, 1965.

Reardon, B.P., ed. *Collected Ancient Greek Novels*. Berkeley: University of California Press, 1989.

Reed, Timothy. *Showing Out*. New York: Thunder's Mouth Press, 2003.

Reich, Wilhelm. *The Discovery of the Orgone*. Vol. 1, *The Function of the Orgasm: Sex-Economic Problems of Biological Energy*. New York: Pocket Books, 1975.

The Revised English Bible with the Apocrypha. Oxford: Oxford University Press and Cambridge University Press, 1989.

Rickels, Laurence A. *The Case of California*. Minneapolis: University of Minnesota Press, 2001.

_____. *Nazi Psychoanalysis*. Vol. 1, *Only Psychoanalysis Won the War*. Minneapolis: University of Minnesota Press, 2002.

_____. *Nazi Psychoanalysis*. Vol. 2, *Crypto-Fetishism*. Minneapolis: University of Minnesota Press, 2002.

_____. *Nazi Psychoanalysis*. Vol. 3, *Psy Fi*. Minneapolis: University of Minnesota Press, 2002.

_____. *The Vampire Lectures*. Minneapolis: University of Minnesota Press, 1999.

Rimbaud, Arthur. *Complete Works, Selected Letters*. Chicago: University of Chicago Press, 1966.

Rimmer, Robert H. *The X-Rated Videotape Guide*. Vol. 1. Revised and updated. Buffalo, NY: Prometheus Books, 1993.

_____. *The X-Rated Videotape Guide*. Vol. 2. Amherst, NY: Prometheus Books, 1991.

Ronell, Avital. *Stupidity*. Chicago: University of Illinois Press, 2003.

_____. *The Test Drive.* Chicago: University of Illinois Press, 2005.

_____. *The UberReader: Selected Works of Avital Ronell.* Edited by Diane Davis. Chicago: University of Illinois Press, 2008.

Roth, Philip. *The Human Stain.* New York: Vintage, 2000.

Roudinesco, Elisabeth. *Why Psychoanalysis?* New York: Columbia University Press, 2001.

Rousseau, Jean-Jacques. *Reveries of the Solitary Walker.* New York: Penguin, 1980.

Russo, Vito. *The Celluloid Closet: Homosexuality in the Movies.* New York: Quality Paperback Book Club, 1995.

Sade, Marquis de. *"The 120 Days of Sodom" and Other Writing.* New York: Grove, 1967.

_____. *The Ghosts of Sodom: The Charenton Journals.* Creation Books, 2003.

_____. *Three Complete Novels: "Justine," "Philosophy in the Bedroom," "Eugenie de Franval" and Other Writing.* New York: Grove, 1966.

Salamon, Julie. *The Devil's Candy: "The Bonfire of the Vanities" Goes to Hollywood.* Boston: Houghton Mifflin, 1991.

Sarris, Andrew. *The American Cinema Directors and Directions 1928–1968.* New York: Da Capo, 1996.

Sartre, Jean-Paul. *Being and Nothingness: An Essay of Phenomenological Ontology.* New York: Philosophical Library, 1956.

Schatz, Thomas. *Hollywood Genres: Formulas, Filmmaking, and the Studio System.* Boston: McGraw-Hill, 1981.

Schickel, Richard, and John Simon. *Film 67/68: An Anthology by the National Society of Film Critics.* New York: Simon and Schuster, 1968.

Schirmacher, Wolfgang. *The End of Metaphysics—What Does This Mean?* Montreal, 1983. EGS.edu, accessed August 17, 2007.

_____. *Homo Generator: Militant Media & Postmodern Technology.* New School, 2002. EGS.edu, accessed August 17, 2007.

_____. *Just Living.* Philosophy in Artificial Life. EGS.edu, accessed August 17, 2007.

_____. *Net Culture: Culture between Conformity and Resistance.* 1985. EGS.edu, accessed August 17, 2007.

Schmitt, Carl. *The Concept of the Political.* Chicago: University of Chicago Press, 1996.

_____. *Hamlet or Hecuba: The Intrusion of the Time into the Play.* New York: Telos Press, 2009.

Schopenhauer, Arthur. *The Essential Schopenhauer: Key Selections from "The World as Will and Representation" and Other Writings.* Edited with a forward by Wolfgang Schirmacher. New York: Harper Perennial, 2010.

Schwarz, Egon, ed. *Nineteenth Century German Plays (King Ottocar's Rise and Fall, The Talisman, Agnes Bernauer).* New York: Continuum, 1990.

Shakespeare, William. *The Arden Shakespeare.* 3rd ed. London: Cengage Learning, 1998.

_____. *The Complete Works of William Shakespeare: Student's Cambridge Edition.* Boston: Houghton Mifflin Company, 1906.

Sinclair, Marianne. *Hollywood Lolitas: The Nymphet Syndrome in the Movies.* New York: Henry Holt, 1988.

Smith, Adam. *An Inquiry into the Nature and Causes of the Wealth of Nations.* Indianapolis: Hackett, 1993.

_____. *The Theory of Moral Sentiments.* New York: Prometheus Books, 2000.

Sondheim, Stephen. *Finishing the Hat: Collected Lyrics (1954–1981) with Attendant Comments, Principles, Heresies, Grudges, Whines and Anecdotes.* New York: Knopf, 2010.

Sontag, Susan. *Against Interpretation and Other Essays.* New York: Farrar, Straus and Giroux, 1966.

_____. *Illness as Metaphor.* New York: Vintage, 1979.

_____. *Regarding the Pain of Others.* New York: Picador, 2003.

_____. *Under the Sign of Saturn.* New York: Picador, 1980.

Sophocles. *The Theban Plays (King Oedipus, Oedipus at Colonus, Antigone).* Translated by E.F. Watling. New York: Penguin, 1947.

Spencer, Hazelton, ed. *Elizabethan Plays (Tamburlaine: Part I, The Tragical History of Doctor Faustus, The Jew of Malta, The Troublesome Reign and Lamentable Death of Edward the Second, Endymion: The Man in the Moon, The Honorable History of Friar Bacon and Friar Bungay, The Spanish Tragedy or Hieronimio Is Mad Again, Every Man in His Humor, Volpone or The Fox, The Alchemist, Bartholomew Fair, Eastward Ho, Bussy D'Ambois, The Malcontent, A Woman Killed with Kindness, The Shoemaker's Holiday, The Honest Whore: Part I, The Honest Whore: Part II, The Knight of the Burning Pestle, Philaster or Love Lies a-Bleeding, The Maid's Tragedy, The Wild-Goose Chase, The White Devil or Vittoria Corombona, A Trick to Catch the Old One, The Changeling, A New Way to Pay Old Debts, The Broken Heart, The Lady of Pleasure).* Boston: D.C. Heath, 1933.

Sternberg, Josef von. *Fun in a Chinese Laundry.* London: Columbus Books, 1987.

Stevens, Brad. *Abel Ferrara: The Moral Vision.* Surrey: FAB Press, 2004.

Stone, Jennifer. *Mind over Media: Essays on Film and Television.* Berkeley: Cayuse Press, 1988.

_____. *Stone's Throw: Selected Essays.* Berkeley: North Atlantic Books, 1988.

Strunk, William, Jr., and E.B. White. *The Elements of Style.* 3rd ed. Boston: Allyn and Bacon, 1979.

Styan, J.L. *Max Reinhardt.* London: Cambridge University Press, 1982.

Susoyev, Steve, and George Birimisa, eds. *Return to the Caffe Cino.* San Francisco: Moving Finger Press, 2007.

Szasz, Thomas S. *The Myth of Mental Illness: Foundations of a Theory of Personal Conduct.* New York: Harper and Row, 1974.

Tannahill, Reay. *Food in History.* New York: Stein and Day, 1973.

_____. *Sex in History.* New York: Stein and Day, 1980.

Tarkington, Booth. *The Magnificent Ambersons.* New York: Tor, 2001.

Taubin, Amy. "Spelling It Out." *Village Voice*, August 3, 1999. http://www.villagevoice.com/1999-08-03/film/spelling-it-out.

"This Could Be Your Last 5 Minutes Alive! (Tract No. 141, R7/94)" Ohio: Fellowship Tract League, 1994.

Thomson, David. *The New Biographical Dictionary of Film.* New York: Knopf, 2002.

Thrower, Stephen. *Beyond Terror: The Films of Lucio Fulci.* Godalming: FAB Press, 2002.

Tolkin, Michael. *The Player, The Rapture, The New Age: Three Screenplays.* New York: Grove, 1995.

Traube, Elizabeth G. *Dreaming Identities: Class, Gender, and Generation in 1980s Hollywood Movies.* Boulder: Westview, 1992.

Truffaut, François, with the Collaboration of Helen G. Scott. *Hitchcock.* New York: Simon and Schuster, 1967.

Tschofen, Monique, and Jennifer Burwell, eds. *Image + Territory: Essays on Atom Egoyan.* Waterloo: Wilfrid Laurier University Press, 2007.

Tucker, Robert C, ed. *Marx-Engels Reader.* New York: Norton, 1978.

Tucker, S. Marion, ed. *Twenty-Five Modern Plays (The Circle, The Cherry Orchard, Comrades, The Coral, Gas Part I, Gas Part II, Cyrano de Bergerac, The Field God, Francesca da Rimini, The Great God Brown, He Who Gets Slapped, The Importance of Being Ernest, In a Garden, John Ferguson, La Malquerida, Light-o'-Love, Liliom, Mary the Third, Pelleas and Melisande, The Rats, R.U.R., The Silver Cord, Sun-Up, S.S. Tenacity, The Thunderbolt, The Truth about Blayds, The Vortex).* New York: Harper and Brothers, 1931.

Valle-Inclan, Ramon Maria del. *Three Plays (Divine Words, Bohemian Lights, Silver Face).* London: Methuen, 1993.

Voltaire. *The Portable Voltaire ("Candide," "Zadig," "Micromegas," plus Letters, Essays, and Selections from Other Works.* New York: Viking, 1971.

Wagner, Richard. *The Authentic Librettos of the Wagner Operas Complete with English and German Parallel Texts and Music of the Principal Airs.* New York: Crown, 1938.

_____. *Jesus of Nazareth and Other Writings.* Lincoln: University of Nebraska Press, 1995.

_____. *Der Ring des Nibelungen.* London, England: Decca Record Company, 1968.

Wakeman, John, ed. *World Film Directors.* Vol. 1, *1890–1945.* New York: H.W. Wilson, 1987.

_____. *World Film Directors*. Vol. 2, *1890–1985*. New York: H.W. Wilson, 1988.

Walker, Gerald. *Cruising*. New York: Bantam, 1980.

Warhol, Andy. *A: A Novel*. New York: Grove, 1998.

_____. *America*. New York: Harper and Row, 1985.

_____. *Blue Movie: A Film by Andy Warhol*. New York: Grove, 1970.

_____. *The Philosophy of Andy Warhol (From A to B and Back Again)*. New York: Harcourt Brace Jovanovich, 1975.

Warhol, Andy, and Pat Hackett. *POPism: The Warhol Sixties*. New York: Harcourt, Brace, 1980.

Waters, John. *Shock Value*. New York: Thunder's Mouth Press, 1995.

Weber, Samuel. *The Legend of Freud*. Expanded ed. Stanford, CA: Stanford University Press, 1982.

_____. *Targets of Opportunity: On the Militarization of Thinking*. New York: Fordham University Press, 2005.

_____. *Theatricality as Medium*. New York: Fordham University Press, 2004.

Wedekind, Frank. *Frank Wedekind's The First Lulu*. Edited by Eric Bentley. New York: Applause Books, 1994.

_____. *Lulu. In a New Version by Nicholas Wright*. London: Nick Hern Books, 2001.

_____. *Princess Russalka and Other Stories*. Boston: John W. Luce, 1919.

_____. *Spring's Awakening: Tragedy of Childhood*. English Version and Ten Notes by Eric Bentley. New York: Applause Books. 1995.

Weininger, Otto. *Sex and Character: An Investigation of Fundamental Principles*. Indianapolis: Indiana University Press, 2005.

Weissberger, L. Arnold. *Famous Faces: A Photographic Album of Personal Reminiscences*. New York: Harry N. Abrams, 1973.

Wells, H.G. *The Croquet Player*. New York: Viking, 1937.

_____. *Mr. Britling Sees It Through*. London: Hogarth, 1985.

_____. *The Passionate Friends*. London: Hogarth, 1986.

_____. *Seven Famous Novels (The Time Machine, The Isle of Doctor Moreau, The Invisible Man, The War of the Worlds, The First Men in the Moon, The Food of the Gods, In the Days of the Comet)*. New York: Garden City Publishing, 1934.

Westlake, Donald E. *The Hunter*. New York: Avon, 1984.

"What Is Cinema?" *Les Amis du Cinéma*, 1952.

White, Armond. *The Resistance: Ten Years of Pop Culture That Shook the World*. Woodstock: Overlook Press, 1995.

Whitehead, Mark. *The Pocket Essential: Slasher Movies*. North Pomfret: Pocket Essentials, 2000.

Wilde, Oscar. *The Complete Works of Oscar Wilde*. New York: Barnes and Nobel Books, 1994.

Williams, Tennessee. *A Streetcar Named Desire*. New York: Signet, 1947.

Wlaschin, Ken. *The Bluffer's Guide to Cinema*. New York: Crown, 1971.

Wood, Robin. *Sexual Politics & Narrative Film: Hollywood and Beyond*. New York: Columbia University Press, 1998.

Wranovics, John. *Chaplin and Agee: The Untold Story of the Tramp, the Writer, and the Lost Screenplay*. New York: Palgrave Macmillan, 2005.

Wyatt, Justin. *Cinetek Series: "Poison."* Wiltshire: Flicks Books, 1998.

Yeats, W.B. *The Collected Plays of W.B. Yeats*. New York: Macmillan, 1953.

Youngblood, Gene. *Expanded Cinema*. New York: E.P. Dutton, 1970.

Žižek, Slavoj. *Enjoy Your Symptom! Jacques Lacan in Hollywood and Out*. New York: Routledge, 1992.

_____. *In Defense of Lost Causes*. New York: Verso, 2008.

_____. *The Parallax View*. Cambridge: The MIT Press, 2006.

_____. *Violence: Six Sideways Reflections*. New York: Picador, 2008.

Žižek, Slavoj, and Mladen Dolar. *Opera's Second Death*. New York: Routledge, 2002.

Index

Page numbers in **_bold italic_** refer to photographs.

223